PRESUMED GUILTY

ALSO BY ERWIN CHEMERINSKY

PRESUMED GUILTY

How the Supreme Court
Empowered the Police
and Subverted Civil Rights

ERWIN CHEMERINSKY

LIVERIGHT PUBLISHING CORPORATION
A Division of W. W. Norton & Company
Independent Publishers Since 1923

———————

Copyright © 2021 by Erwin Chemerinsky

All rights reserved
Printed in the United States of America
First Edition

For information about permission to reproduce selections from this book, write to Permissions, Liveright Publishing Corporation, a division of W. W. Norton & Company, Inc., 500 Fifth Avenue, New York, NY 10110

For information about special discounts for bulk purchases, please contact W. W. Norton Special Sales at specialsales@wwnorton.com or 800-233-4830

Manufacturing by LSC Communications, Harrisonburg
Book design by Lovedog Studio
Production manager: Anna Oler

Library of Congress Cataloging-in-Publication Data

Names: Chemerinsky, Erwin, author.
Title: Presumed guilty : how the Supreme Court empowered the police and
    subverted civil rights / Erwin Chemerinsky.
Description: First edition. | New York : Liveright Publishing Corporation,
    2021. | Includes bibliographical references and index.
Identifiers: LCCN 2021012402 | ISBN 9781631496516 (hardcover) |
    ISBN 9781631496523 (epub)
Subjects: LCSH: Police misconduct—Law and legislation—United States.
    | Police brutality—United States—Prevention. | Police power—United
    States. | Tort liability of police—United States. | United States. Supreme
    Court. | Discrimination in justice administration—United States. | Race
    discrimination—Law and legislation—United States. | Civil rights—
    United States. | African Americans—Civil rights.
Classification: LCC KF5399 .C44 2021 | DDC 344.7305/2—dc23
LC record available at https://lccn.loc.gov/2021012402

Liveright Publishing Corporation, 500 Fifth Avenue, New York, N.Y. 10110
www.wwnorton.com

W. W. Norton & Company Ltd., 15 Carlisle Street, London W1D 3BS

1 2 3 4 5 6 7 8 9 0

For Catherine

CONTENTS

PREFACE

TODAY IN THE UNITED STATES, MUCH ATTENTION is focused on the enormous problems of police violence and racism in law enforcement, but too often that attention fails to place the blame where much of it belongs: on the Supreme Court. The Framers of the Constitution intended many of its provisions to constrain police, to limit what police can do and to protect the rights of us all, including those who are suspected and accused of crimes. Yet throughout American history, the Court has done an ineffective and indeed a poor job of enforcing those provisions. On the contrary, it has consistently empowered police and legitimated the racialized policing that especially harms people of color.

For a very brief time in the 1960s, the Warren Court expanded these constitutional rights and sought to significantly limit certain types of police misconduct. But overall the Warren Court was an aberration in American history. Time and again, both before the 1960s and after, the Court has refused to enforce constitutional limits on police conduct and instead has enabled them to violate citizens' fundamental liberties. Neither the text of the Constitution nor the Framers' intent supports these rulings. Instead, we must regard the Court's decisions as a consistent choice, throughout American history, to favor the interests of law enforcement over the rights of individuals and to ignore the enormous racism that has infected policing since the nation's first days.

My aim in *Presumed Guilty* is to tell this story of the Supreme Court's failure to enforce salient parts of the Constitution and to limit police conduct. The Court develops the law case by case, over the course of its history, and therefore this book focuses on those decisions. The pattern that emerges from the cases is deeply disturbing. It is not hyperbole to say that as a result of these rulings, police today can stop any person at any time and frisk that person, a power that they use disproportionately against Black and Brown people. For suspects undergoing police interrogation, the rulings provide very little protection from coercion, so long as the officers don't use physical force. The Court has all but ignored the problem of false eyewitness identifications that have caused the convictions of many innocent people, especially when a person is identifying someone of a different race. The Court has made it very difficult for victims of police abuse to successfully sue police forces for damages, even when an officer used egregious excessive force that led to a citizen's serious injury or death. In fact, the Court has weakened, or gutted, all remedies that Americans might use to challenge police misconduct.

My goal is to show how we got here and what this has meant for how policing is done on a daily basis and for people's liberty, and especially the rights of people of color. Our society cannot effectively reform police until and unless we recognize its problems and take steps to overcome the Supreme Court's consistent failure.

American policing today shows a chronic pattern of persistent brutalities and flagrant disregard for constitutional rights. I am convinced that it is possible to reform and improve policing, but it requires that we have the will to enforce limits on police conduct. If the Court continues to fail to reform policing—and I fear it will for the foreseeable future given that a majority of the justices have shown no concern or even awareness of the problems—then we must turn to other institutions to control police behavior, check police abuses, and end racist policing. Congress and state legislatures can enact new laws to reform policing. State courts can interpret state constitutions to protect citizens' rights and to impose limits on state and local police departments. The Department of Justice can aggressively enforce existing laws to reform police departments. All these actions could make a big difference in how policing is done. And perhaps someday, the Court will fulfill its duty of enforcing the parts of the Constitution that are meant to control police behavior and thereby ensure that Americans receive equal justice under the law.

Part I

THE SUPREME COURT, RACE, AND POLICING

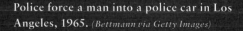

Police force a man into a police car in Los Angeles, 1965. *(Bettmann via Getty Images)*

1

"I Can't Breathe"

Why Courts Can't Stop Police from Using Chokeholds

O
N THE NIGHT OF MAY 25, 2020, A CATASTROPHIC
event was videotaped and soon flashed around the world.
George Floyd, a forty-six-year-old African American
man, was killed by a Minneapolis police officer. Floyd, who was
unarmed, had been suspected of passing a counterfeit bill. He was
arrested by Derek Chauvin, a white police officer who had served on
the Minneapolis police force for nineteen years. Chauvin knelt on
Floyd's neck for almost nine minutes while Floyd was handcuffed
and lying face down, begging for his life and repeatedly saying, "I
can't breathe." Those same haunting words had been uttered by Eric
Garner, another unarmed African American man, who died on July
17, 2014, when a New York City police officer, Daniel Pantaleo, put
a chokehold on him while arresting him for suspicion of selling single
cigarettes from packs without state-mandated tax stamps.

Over the years, dozens of other American citizens, disproportionately men of color, have died from police use of chokeholds.[1]
Shouldn't courts put a stop to this practice as a violation of the Constitution? After all, the law is clear that excessive police force violates
the Fourth Amendment as an unconstitutional "seizure" of a person,
and the evidence is overwhelming that chokeholds are, to say the
least, very dangerous and not necessary to protect officers' safety.[2]
More generally, shouldn't courts be preventing police from practicing

racial profiling, that is, stopping people of color far more often than they stop white individuals? Every time I teach a class on constitutional law or criminal procedure, my Black and Latino students tell of being stopped by the police solely for driving as a person of color; rarely, if ever, do I hear of this from my white students. Police stops always are upsetting and degrading and too often escalate into police violence.

Unfortunately, the kind of chokehold that killed George Floyd remains in use in most of the United States because of the Supreme Court's 1983 ruling in *City of Los Angeles v. Lyons.*[3] That decision dramatically constrains the ability of the federal judiciary to stop police from using unconstitutional and racist practices like the chokehold. It has closed courthouse doors to civil rights litigants who seek to halt them. Because of the Supreme Court's decision, federal courts cannot hear cases that challenge the chokehold and seek to stop it from being used. As a result of *Lyons,* federal courts cannot issue injunctions to stop police misconduct, and they are very limited in what they can do to prevent police from violating citizens' constitutional rights. In countless discussions with civil rights lawyers about how to stop illegal police and other unconstitutional government behavior, we so often come up against the same insurmountable hurdle to litigation: *City of Los Angeles v. Lyons.*

The story behind this case tells a great deal about policing and racism in the United States and about the Supreme Court's attitude toward it. On October 6, 1976, at approximately two a.m., four Los Angeles police officers stopped Adolph Lyons, a twenty-four-year-old African American man, for driving with a burned-out taillight.[4] The officers ordered Lyons out of his car, and as he emerged from it, they greeted him with drawn revolvers.

They told Lyons to face his car and spread his legs. He did so. They then ordered him to clasp his hands and put them on top of his head. He again complied. After one of the officers completed a patdown search, Lyons dropped his hands, but he was ordered to place them back above his head. One of the officers grabbed Lyons's hands and slammed them onto the roof of the car. Lyons complained about the pain caused by the ring of keys he was holding—it was cutting into the skin of his palm. Apparently as a result of that complaint, the officers perceived Lyons as having "mouthed off" to them.[5] Within ten seconds, one officer began to choke Lyons by applying a forearm against his throat. As Lyons struggled for air, the officer handcuffed him but continued to apply the chokehold until Lyons blacked out. When Lyons finally regained consciousness, he was lying face down on the ground, choking, gasping for air, and spitting up blood and dirt. He had urinated and defecated. The officers issued him a traffic citation and allowed him to go. As a result of being choked by the officer, he suffered an injured larynx.

Los Angeles police officers, as well as police departments across the country, commonly used the chokehold to subdue suspects. A survey in 1980, conducted four years after Lyons was choked, found that 90 percent of U.S. police departments authorized the carotid hold and 53.33 percent authorized the similar bar armhold.[6] LAPD policy manuals expressly authorized officers to use chokeholds for that purpose.[7]

The LAPD authorized the use of both the carotid hold and the modified carotid hold,[8] which brings the subject to a sitting position, where the carotid hold can generally be more easily applied. For many years, the Los Angeles Police Academy had trained officers in the use of both.[9]

The carotid hold is designed to encourage the subject to submit to control but also, if necessary, to render the subject unconscious. It is derived from the sport of judo. An officer applies the hold from a position behind the subject and places one arm around the subject's neck, holding the wrist of that arm with the other hand. The officer's chest is brought flush against the subject's back. In the carotid hold, the lower forearm and bicep muscles apply pressure to the carotid arteries, located on either side of the neck.[10] The bar armhold, which is less commonly used, involves an officer putting pressure on the front of the suspect's neck.

The carotid hold constricts the flow of oxygenated blood through the carotid arteries, thereby diminishing the supply to the brain. When the brain is sufficiently deprived of oxygen, the subject becomes unconscious.[11] Normally, unconsciousness will occur within fourteen seconds. Depending on the "position of the officer's arm and the force applied, the victim's voluntary or involuntary reaction, and his state of health, an officer may inadvertently crush the victim's larynx, trachea, or thyroid. The result may be death caused by either cardiac arrest or asphyxiation."[12]

After the L.A. police allowed Lyons to go, he later learned that in a sense he had been lucky. Before this incident, sixteen men in Los Angeles had died from police use of the chokehold, almost all, like him, African American. Lyons sued the City of Los Angeles for a court order, an injunction, to keep police officers from using the chokehold, except if necessary to protect an officer's safety. Lyons sought not to eliminate the ability of police to use the chokehold altogether but rather to limit their use of it and to keep it from being applied in situations like his own.

The case was assigned to federal district court judge Robert Tagasuki. When he was twelve years old, Tagasuki and his family had been interned in the Tule Lake War Relocation Center—they were among the 110,000 Japanese Americans interned during World War II. Perhaps shaped by this experience, Judge Tagasuki was known to be especially compassionate, both off the bench and on. In the mid-1980s he organized a free course to help law students who had failed the bar exam to get past that hurdle. The bar exam is administered twice a year, and until he died in 2009, Judge Tagasuki taught this course before every bar exam and recruited faculty (including me) to teach without compensation.

Judge Tagasuki presided over Lyons's case and heard the powerful and extensive evidence that Lyons's lawyer presented about the dangers of police use of the chokehold. One witness for the plaintiff, Dr. Alex Griswold, stated that "pressure on both carotid sheaths also result[s] in pressure, if inadvertent or unintended, on both vagus nerves. . . . Stimulation of these nerves can activate reflexes . . . that can result in immediate heart stoppage (cardiac arrest)."[13]

Other experts described the hold's effects in equally vivid terms: "[V]iolent struggle is 'very definitely' likely to ensue with the victim seeking to 'flee or escape.' The victim's face turns blue, becoming cyanotic (lacking oxygenated blood), and he goes into a spasmodic state of convulsions. The victim's eyes roll back and he will sometimes 'jerk,' his body 'wriggles,' his feet kick up and down and his arms move about wildly."[14] Thus for a person being choked, the involuntary physical reaction is to struggle, and that causes the police to choke harder until the individual is rendered unconscious. The person being choked will often urinate and defecate upon losing consciousness. Although the City of Los Angeles tried to minimize the danger, it ultimately conceded that the hold was risky: "The City does not deny that it is possible to injure seriously or even kill someone using the control holds; they are not failsafe."[15]

Attorneys for Lyons also presented evidence to Judge Tagasuki that L.A. police officers' use of the chokehold had a significant racial dimension. According to statistics later submitted to the Supreme Court, an African American man was twenty times more likely to be subjected to a police chokehold than a white man.[16] In Los Angeles, Black men were 9 percent of the population, but they accounted for 75 percent of the deaths resulting from the use of chokeholds.[17]

When L.A. police chief Daryl Gates was questioned about why a disproportionate number of victims of the chokehold had been African American, he infamously and absurdly declared that it was because of physiological differences between Black people and "normal people," stating that "veins or arteries of Blacks do not open up as fast as they do in normal people."[18] Gates, who served as chief from 1978 until 1992, espoused taking a very hard-line, aggressive, paramilitary approach to policing. This single quote speaks volumes about his racial attitudes.

Judge Tagasuki ruled in favor of Adolph Lyons and granted him the requested injunction to keep police from using the chokehold except when necessary to protect an officer's life or safety. The city appealed to the U.S. Court of Appeals for the Ninth Circuit, arguing that Lyons had lacked "standing" to sue because he could not show that he personally was likely to be choked again in the future. Standing is the legal rule that limits who can bring a lawsuit in federal court. A person must personally be injured in order to sue; the rule keeps the federal courts from having to resolve purely ideological disputes and ensures that the plaintiff is the appropriate person to litigate the issue.

Lyons had obviously been injured by the L.A. police officer who choked him. He explained to the court that since that episode, every time he went outside he was afraid he could be stopped by a police officer and be choked again. But the city argued that that was not enough to allow Lyons to sue, and it insisted that he not be given standing to seek an injunction because it was speculative as to whether he ever would be choked again.

The federal court of appeals rejected the city's argument and agreed with Judge Tagasuki's ruling, explaining that "in this case, the threat of future injury to not only Lyons, but to every citizen in the area is much more immediate. To be subject to these strangle-holds, a citizen need only be stopped for a minor traffic violation while driving an automobile, as shown by the alleged facts in this case."[19] The court of appeals explained that courts had to be able to end unconstitutional police practices and bar government actions that violated the law. The court concluded its opinion by explaining how important it was for federal courts to enforce the Constitution: "as long as we refuse to allow anyone to attack their constitutionality here, we tell the citizen that there is no guardian of his constitutional rights. That is a principle that has no foundation either in the Constitution or in our beliefs about what a government ought to be."[20]

The City of Los Angeles continued to aggressively defend the police use of the chokehold and ultimately sought Supreme Court review. The Court agreed to hear the case, and in a 5–4 decision, it reversed the federal court of appeals and ordered Lyons's suit dismissed. The Court accepted the city's argument that Lyons lacked standing to sue in federal court because he could not show that he personally was likely to be put in a chokehold by an LAPD officer in the future. In other words, a person who has been harmed by an illegal government action cannot sue for an injunction to halt the practice unless the individual can demonstrate that he or she is personally likely to suffer that specific injury again.

The justices in *Lyons* divided along ideological lines: the five most conservative ruled in favor of the city and against Adolph Lyons. Throughout American history, ideology has mattered enormously in Supreme Court decisions about police: those identified as conservatives have consistently refused to interpret the Constitution to limit police behavior. The Court's conservative justices never have acknowledged the enormous effect of race on how policing is done. Except for a brief time during the Warren Court in the 1960s, the majority of justices have been quite conservative on policing issues.

In *Lyons,* Justice Byron White wrote the majority opinion, joined by Chief Justice Warren Burger and Justices Lewis Powell, William Rehnquist, and Sandra Day O'Connor. White had been appointed by President John F. Kennedy, but he was no liberal. He had been one of two dissenting justices in *Roe v. Wade,* which upheld a woman's right to abortion,[21] and in *Miranda v. Arizona,* which said that police must warn those being interrogated in police custody of their rights to remain silent and to have an attorney present.[22] A former All-American college and then professional football player, White was an imposing presence. I met him a few times and remember most his crushing handshake and stern demeanor. Chief Justice Burger and Justices Powell and Rehnquist had been appointed to the Court by President Richard Nixon, and Justice O'Connor, the first woman to ever serve on the Court, had been appointed by President Ronald Reagan. These justices, throughout their tenure on the Court, could be counted on to vote in favor of the police and against the constitutional claims of those suspected and accused of crimes.

Justice White wrote for the Court that "Lyons' standing to seek the injunction requested depended on whether he was likely to suffer future injury from the use of the chokeholds by police officers."[23] In other words, Lyons could not sue for an injunction unless he could demonstrate that he was likely to be personally choked again by L.A. police officers. Lyons could sue the individual police officer who choked him for monetary damages, the Court held, but his having been choked once did "nothing to establish a real and immediate threat that he would again be stopped for a traffic violation, or for any other offense, by an officer or officers who would illegally choke him into unconsciousness without any provocation or resistance on his part."[24]

Lyons's attorneys had argued that even if Lyons could not show that he was likely to be choked again in the future, he still was harmed as long as the LAPD authorized the use of chokeholds, in that he feared he could be choked again. In light of his harrowing experience, they said, this continuing fear should be regarded as a sufficient injury to permit a suit for an injunction. The Court expressly rejected this argument as a sufficient basis for standing: "It is the reality of the threat of repeated injury that is relevant to the standing inquiry, not the plaintiff's subjective apprehensions. The emotional consequences of a prior act simply are not a sufficient basis for an injunction absent a real and immediate threat of future injury by the defendant."[25] That is, even a person who has been seriously injured by an unconstitutional police practice cannot sue to enjoin its use unless the individual can show that he or she is likely to be subjected to it again. Simply put, as a result of the majority's ruling, no one will ever be able to go to court and seek an injunction to stop the police from using the chokehold, or other unconstitutional practices, because no one will ever be able to demonstrate that he or she is likely to be subjected to it again in the future.

Writing for himself and three other justices, Justice Thurgood Marshall wrote a strong dissent, making the crucial point that the majority's ruling meant that no one ever could sue to stop even the most outrageous of police practices. Marshall, the first African

American ever to serve on the Supreme Court, had a truly legendary career. In the 1940s and '50s he served as the executive director of the NAACP Legal Defense and Educational Fund and directed its strategy to challenge segregation. He also represented many criminal defendants, including before the Supreme Court. He argued thirty-two cases before the Court, including *Brown v. Board of Education*, and won in twenty-nine of them. In 1961 President Kennedy named him a judge on the U.S. Court of Appeals for the Second Circuit. He served there for four years until President Lyndon Johnson named him U.S. solicitor general, the Justice Department's lead lawyer at the Supreme Court. In 1967 President Johnson made Marshall the first Black Supreme Court justice, a position he held until 1991, when he retired and was replaced by Clarence Thomas.

Marshall played a key role on the Court on issues of race; among the justices he served with, he alone had experienced the discrimination that comes from being Black in America. He alone had represented victims of discrimination, including those on death row, in courts across the country as well as in the Supreme Court. Unlike any justice before or since, he was familiar with how policing was actually done in small southern towns.

The *Lyons* dissenters, like the federal court of appeals in the case, were primarily concerned that denying Lyons standing would mean that no one ever would have the ability to seek an injunction to stop any illegal government practice at all. Justice Marshall began his dissent by declaring: "Since no one can show that he will be choked in the future, no one—not even a person who, like Lyons, has almost been choked to death—has standing to challenge the continuation of the policy. The City is free to continue the policy indefinitely as long as it is willing to pay damages for the injuries and deaths that result."[26]

Justice Marshall's dissent lamented that the Court's decision would effectively close federal courthouse doors to challenges to unconstitutional policies where it was unknowable which specific person would be hurt by them in the future. He concluded his dissent by stating, "Under the view expressed by the majority today, if the police adopt a policy of 'shoot to kill,' or a policy of shooting one out of ten suspects, the federal courts will be powerless to enjoin its continuation. The federal judicial power is now limited to levying a toll for such a systematic constitutional violation."[27]

The impact of *Lyons* has been profound. Today no one can challenge the chokehold, or its disproportionate use against Black men, because no one can show that he or she is likely to be stopped and choked in the future. Imagine that a police department subjects women to strip searches when they are brought to a jail for even minor offenses, such as traffic violations. A woman who suffered this humiliation and degradation could not bring a lawsuit for an injunction because she would be unable to demonstrate that she was likely to be stopped, arrested, and stripped again in the future. In fact, lower courts have dismissed such challenges in exactly this situation.[28]

· · · · · · · · · ·

IN THE ALMOST FOUR DECADES since *Lyons*, the Supreme Court and the lower courts have repeatedly dismissed suits brought by citizens for injunctive relief against police departments because the plaintiff could not demonstrate a likelihood of future personal injury and therefore lacked standing. Citizens have brought lawsuits requesting injunctions to regulate police use of the chemical Mace, and challenging a state practice of paying officers a bonus if an arrest they made led to a conviction, and, yes, attempting to halt strip searches in county jails of those arrested for minor crimes. Based on *Lyons*, however, courts have dismissed them all.[29] Lower federal courts have dismissed requests for injunctions to stop warrantless wiretaps, intrusive TSA screening protocols at airports, and unreasonable searches near the Mexican border.[30]

Victims of unconstitutional police misconduct cannot sue to stop an abusive practice unless they can show that they are personally likely to be subjected to it again in the future. Rarely can they meet this burden. Thus federal court injunctions to enforce the Constitution to stop police abuses and racist policy are almost impossible.

Citizens can still challenge government practices, such as in schools or prisons, that predictably will affect certain individuals, by bringing suits for injunctions to halt the practices. A school that requires daily prayers by its students can be sued to enjoin the practice because it is known who will be affected every day. By contrast, the courts cannot stop a government policy or practice that will harm unidentifiable people in the future, even when a person who has suffered from that policy in the past brings the suit. A victim may sue for damages, but even then, in civil rights cases, he or she will face many obstacles to recovering monetary relief: the absence of city liability for the actions of its officers,[31] the immunities accorded to individual government officers,[32] and the small amount of monetary damages available for violations of many constitutional rights.[33] Suits for injunctions are greatly restricted, even against a police practice that is clearly unconstitutional and widespread, even when it is applied in a racist manner, and even when it is sure to result in further injuries or even deaths.

· · · · · · · · · ·

THE *LYONS* CASE could have arisen in any of countless cities across the country. Most cities at the time trained their police officers to use the chokehold as a way of subduing suspects.[34] And other police departments also engaged in abusive practices, such as racial profiling, that might have led to suits for injunctive relief.[35] But the fact that the case arose from the LAPD, with its long and notorious history of racism and of use of excessive force, hardly seems coincidental.[36] The very events that gave rise to the case must be understood as the product of the LAPD and its culture, one that was even glorified in television programs like *Dragnet.*

Every police department has a culture—unwritten rules, mores, customs, codes, values, and outlooks—that creates its policing environment and style. The LAPD's underlying culture was what drove its serial scandals as well as its defense of officers' ability to use chokeholds all the way to the Supreme Court. In 1991 a commission to investigate the LAPD, chaired by Warren Christopher (who later became a U.S. secretary of state), called the department's culture "unnecessarily aggressive and confrontational" and identified it as the central barrier to effective reform.[37] David Dotson, a former assistant LAPD chief, wrote that the problems in the department were "cultural in nature, the result of an institutional mind-set first conceived in the 1950s."[38]

The prime driver of LAPD culture was authoritarian control of the streets. In the 1950s, LAPD chief William Parker instilled this philosophy, authorizing the use of force to ensure control. Parker, who served as chief for thirty-nine years, was notoriously racist. During the Watts riots in 1965, which were precipitated by police abuses in the Black community, Parker said those who participated were behaving like "monkeys in a zoo."[39] During the riots, Parker said on television, "It is estimated that by 1970, 45 percent of the metropolitan area of Los Angeles will be Negro. . . . If you want any protection for your home and family . . . you're going to have to get in and support a strong Police Department. If you don't, come 1970, God help you." Earlier in his tenure, Parker had attributed criminal activity among Latinos to their "not being too far removed from the wild tribes of . . . the inner mountains of Mexico."[40] Parker imbued the LAPD with his militaristic, racist approach to policing.

In 2000 I wrote a report on the LAPD, in which I stated: "The LAPD's street patrolling culture is hard to miss. It can be summed up as a 'confront, command and arrest' or 'proactive' paramilitary style of policing. It relies on 'command presence.' Within the Department, the LAPD officers prize aggressive crime suppression that projects omnipresent intimidation and total command of the streets."[41] The department culture was one that would shield and laud Dirty Harry and shun Frank Serpico. It was thus hardly surprising that a lawsuit about a citizen's ability to sue a city and a police department to stop aggressive practices would have arisen in Los Angeles.

Notwithstanding the Supreme Court's decision in *Lyons,* public pressure mounted against police using the chokehold, and in 1982 the L.A. Board of Police Commissioners on its own permanently prohibited its use except where necessary to protect officers' safety. But less than a decade after the Court's decision in *Lyons,* the controversy flared again, in dramatic fashion.

In 1991 police had stopped Rodney King, an unarmed African American man, on suspicion of drunk driving and ordered him out of his car. Four officers beat him for seven minutes while twenty-one other officers watched.[42] A bystander captured the beating on videotape, revealing that King was struck with batons between fifty-three and fifty-seven times. Afterward the officers acknowledged the beating in a computer exchange among themselves:

> Sgt. Stacey Koon: "You just had a big-time use of force . . .
>   Tazed and beat the suspect of CHP pursuit big time."
> Headquarters: "Oh well . . . I'm sure the lizard didn't deserve
>   it . . . ha-ha."
> From officers Laurence Powell and Timothy Wind's patrol car:
>   "Oops."
> Another unit responds: "Oops what?"
> From Powell and Wind: "I haven't beaten anyone this bad in a
>   long time."[43]

The image of the horrifying beating was repeatedly broadcast on national and local television stations. The four officers were prosecuted in California state court, but in April 1992 a jury acquitted them. The day the acquittal was announced, devastating riots erupted across Los Angeles. A year later the four officers were prosecuted in federal court, and two were convicted.

Interestingly, both sides of the debate over police reform saw a direct link between the Rodney King beating and the Supreme Court's decision in *City of Los Angeles v. Lyons*. Critics of the decision perceived *Lyons* as delivering a clear message to officers that they were free to use excessive force. David Rudovsky, a civil rights attorney and a professor at the University of Pennsylvania Law School, said *Lyons* sent "a fairly direct message. You don't have to worry because the courts are not going to do a lot—we'll find some technical reason. The tipoff that the message has been received is that the L.A. police brag about it."[44]

For their part, the officers who beat King also said that the *Lyons* litigation was responsible for their actions, but for a very different reason: denying officers the ability to use the chokehold meant that they had to resort to physical force to subdue King.[45] If only the chokehold had been available, they said, they would not have needed to beat King into submission.

Although Los Angeles stopped police from using the chokehold, most other cities did not. Its use would lead to the deaths of George Floyd and Eric Garner and so many others. Federal legislation to outlaw it has been proposed but has not been enacted, and it continues to be used in many police departments in the United States. Because of the Supreme Court's decision in *City of Los Angeles v. Lyons* it is impossible to use litigation to end, or even limit, police use of chokeholds.

2

Confronting the Realities of Race and Policing

I T WAS NOT COINCIDENTAL THAT ADOLPH LYONS WAS
Black. Nor was it coincidental that Michael Brown, Eric Garner, Walter Scott, Laquan McDonald, George Floyd, and Breonna Taylor were Black. All these unarmed individuals were killed
by police officers. Their names have received public attention, but
we have no way of knowing how many others have died or suffered
serious injuries because of excessive police force in recent years, let
alone over the course of American history.

Race has infected policing in the United States since its founding.[1]
African Americans and Hispanics are more likely to be stopped by
police than whites for the same behavior, more likely to be arrested,
and more likely to be subjected to police violence.[2] As former president Barack Obama explained: "A large body of research finds that,
for similar offenses, members of the African American and Hispanic
communities are more likely to be stopped, searched, arrested, convicted, and sentenced to harsher penalties."[3] Black men make up about
13 percent of the U.S. male population but nearly 35 percent of all
U.S. men with a prison sentence of more than one year. Black people
are incarcerated in state prisons at 5.1 times the rate of white people.[4]

Study after study has documented that people of color are far
more likely to be stopped by police than are white individuals. In
2015 *The New York Times* studied the records of police stops in

Greensboro, North Carolina, choosing that city because its detailed police records were available. The investigation found that police "used their discretion to search black drivers or their cars more than twice as often as white motorists—even though they found drugs and weapons significantly more often when the driver was white."[5] Also in 2015 a study of the San Francisco Police Department found that while African Americans make up 15 percent of the population, they are more than 42 percent of those searched after a stop.[6]

In 2016 Black males between fifteen and thirty-four were nine times more likely than other Americans to be killed by law enforcement officers.[7] They were killed at four times the rate of young white men.[8] Hispanic men are nearly twice as likely to be killed by police as white men.[9] The U.S. Civil Rights Commission concluded that "while people of color make up fewer than 38 percent of the population, they make up almost 63 percent of unarmed people killed by police."[10] Overall, civilian deaths from shootings and other police actions are vastly higher in the United States than in other developed nations.[11]

And even when death does not result, excessive police force, especially directed at racial minorities, remains a serious problem, causing physical and psychological injuries. We have seemingly endless accounts of police unnecessarily striking suspects, especially men of color, with batons, using tasers, applying chokeholds, and employing far more force than needed under the circumstances. The Center for Policing Equity found that "one in five Americans interacts with law enforcement yearly. Of those encounters, one million result in use of force. And if you're Black, you are two to four times more likely to have force used than if you are White."[12] The center's study found "that the overall mean use-of-force rate for all black residents was 273 per 100,000, which is 3.6 times higher than the rate for white residents (76 per 100,000) and 2.5 times higher than the overall rate of 108 per 100,000 for all residents. For those who were arrested, the mean rate of use of force against blacks was 46 for every one thousand arrests, compared with 36 per thousand for whites."[13] A 2018 study found that during stops police "were twice as likely to threaten or use force" against people of color than white people.[14]

Nor is this new. More than fifty years ago, in the mid- and late 1960s, unrest erupted in cities across the United States: violent riots killed forty-three in Detroit and twenty-six in Newark. To identify the cause of the violence, President Johnson created an eleven-member commission, chaired by Illinois governor Otto Kerner. The commission broadly examined race in the United States, including how policing was done in major cities. Most of the uprisings, it found, had been triggered by police incidents.

The Kerner Commission's 1968 *Report of the National Advisory Committee on Civil Disorders* presented a searing portrayal of policing and race. "To some Negroes," it wrote, "police have come to symbolize white power, white racism, and white repression. And the fact is that many police do reflect and express these white attitudes. The atmosphere of hostility and cynicism is reinforced by a widespread belief among Negroes in the existence of police brutality and in a 'double standard' of justice and protection—one for Negroes and one for whites."[15] The commission warned that "our nation is moving toward two societies, one black, one white—separate and unequal," and it explained powerfully that the "the abrasive relationship between the police and minority communities has been a major and explosive source of grievance, tension, and disorder."[16]

Since 1968 the Kerner Commission's findings and recommendations have been consistently ignored. One could read its report today and think it had just been written and was describing America in the early twenty-first century.

The earlier one looks at American history, the more one finds that police were openly racist.[17] Early police enforced the laws that enslaved Blacks and segregated the races. In southern slaveholding states, the early police forces were slave patrols, made up of white volunteers empowered to use vigilante tactics to enforce laws supporting slavery. Slave patrols "located and returned enslaved people who had escaped, crushed uprisings led by enslaved people and punished enslaved workers found or believed to have violated plantation rules."[18] During Jim Crow, police enforced laws that segregated every aspect of life in the South and elsewhere.

There always have been, and are now, racist police officers; a recent study has documented police officers with ties to white supremacist groups.[19] After incidents of serious police abuse, cities and police departments invariably respond by blaming the misconduct on aberrant officers, a few "bad apples." But this explanation ignores the cultures in police departments, like that of the LAPD, that encourage excessive force and racist policing.

· · · · · · · · ·

IN 1998—fifteen years after the Supreme Court's decision in *Lyons*—Los Angeles police officer Rafael Pérez was caught stealing cocaine from a police evidence room and replacing it with flour. He pleaded guilty, and in exchange for a lighter prison sentence, he provided prosecutors with information about police misconduct within the antigang unit of the LAPD's Rampart Division, named after a predominately Hispanic neighborhood in Los Angeles.

Pérez's information revealed a deeply disturbing pattern of policing that violated the most basic civil rights of young African American and Latino men. A mentality had developed, he explained, that gangs presented a crisis requiring extraordinary police efforts at control. Rampart officers came to assume that all Latino and African American men between fifteen and fifty who had short hair and wore baggy pants were gang members, and that that warranted any efforts on their part to remove them from the streets. So they planted evidence to frame innocent people and lied in courts to gain convictions.

As a result of Pérez's testimony and the investigations that followed it, more than one hundred convictions were overturned. One such case was that of Javier Ovando, who had the misfortune of having a verbal spat with Pérez and his partner, Nino Durden. The officers shot Ovando and then planted a gun on him so they could say they had acted in self-defense. Pérez and Durden lied in court about what happened. Ovando, who was left permanently paralyzed, was sentenced to twenty-three years in prison. The judge observed that the sentence was justified, in part, because Ovando had shown no remorse. When Pérez later told the truth about what had occurred, Ovando was released from custody and received a sizable settlement from the city. But obviously, no amount of money could compensate for what Officers Pérez and Durden had done to him.

After the Rampart scandal came to light, in 2000, the Los Angeles Police Protective League, the police union, asked me to write an independent report on the LAPD and the Rampart scandal.[20] Working with six other civil rights attorneys, I spent six months examining the LAPD, interviewing about one hundred police officers and many judges, former judges, prosecutors, and defense lawyers. In the process, I learned a great deal about police culture. Many of the officers I met impressed me; several told me that the day they got their badge was the proudest day of their lives.

But I also learned that police culture affects even the best-intentioned officers. The Rampart scandal, I became convinced, was the result of the long-standing culture within the department. Time and again, officers expressed to me the need to ensure control on the streets in a way that reminded me of how the chokehold came to be used in Los Angeles and why it had been employed against Adolph Lyons.

A "code of silence" in the department, I learned, kept police officers from reporting misconduct by other officers. Several officers told me that they feared that if they reported a violation by another cop, no one would "protect their back" the next time they needed it. I learned a new expression, "freeway therapy." Officers who reported misconduct on the part of other officers, I was told, would be transferred to the precincts farthest away from where they lived, often a two-hour drive on Los Angeles freeways.

From the police academy to the daily briefings, officers were taught how policing was to be done on the streets of Los Angeles. The racism was often explicit. But police officers, even those who would vehemently deny being racist, live in a society infected by rac-

ism, and they often have unconscious biases. I heard this as I listened
to police officers describe the neighborhoods where they worked and
how suspects of different races were treated.

Los Angeles, of course, is not unique. Civil rights lawyer Bryan
Stevenson explains that "people of color in the United States, particularly young black men are burdened by a presumption of guilt and
dangerousness."[21] Black Lives Matters reminds us that racism, both
conscious and unconscious, affects policing in the United States, and
it reminds us to say the names of those who have died from police
violence across the country, disproportionately people of color.

3

The Supreme Court's Essential Role in Enforcing the Constitution and Controlling Police

D ISCUSSIONS OF THE PROBLEMS IN AMERICAN POLICING usually do not focus on the Supreme Court. The Court, after all, does not hire or train or supervise or discipline police officers. It does not set budgets for police departments or manage their operations. Today as Americans increasingly focus on police behavior in the streets, its connection to Supreme Court rulings is not apparent. But the Constitution contains crucial provisions relevant to policing, and what the Supreme Court says about them, or more importantly does not say, has an enormous effect on what police do every day. The Constitution places constraints on police, but unless those constraints are enforced, the rights of criminal suspects and defendants all too often become illusory.

Why is it important to focus on the Supreme Court in discussing policing? To start with the obvious, the Court and the judiciary are the bodies that have the power to enforce the Constitution. Many constitutional provisions, especially in the Bill of Rights, are concerned with regulating police. The Fourth Amendment, for example, bars police from engaging in unreasonable searches or arrests: "The right of the people to be secure in their persons, houses, papers, and effects, against unreasonable searches and seizures, shall not be violated, and no warrants shall issue, but upon probable cause, supported by oath or affirmation, and particularly describing the place to be searched, and the persons or things to be seized." Even a Supreme Court that normally eschews imposing limits on police conduct has held that excessive police force is a "seizure" that violates the Fourth Amendment.[1]

The Fifth Amendment protects the privilege against self-incrimination, declaring that "nor shall [any person] be compelled in any criminal case to be a witness against himself." This has been understood to mean that a person cannot be coerced into incriminating him- or herself, including when being interrogated by the police. This was the provision that the Warren Court famously interpreted in *Miranda v. Arizona* in 1966, to require that police warn suspects in custody that they have a right to remain silent and a right to an attorney when they are subjected to police interrogation.[2]

The Sixth Amendment regulates many aspects of the criminal justice system. It creates a right to counsel for criminal defendants, the right of defendants to confront their accusers, the right to a public trial, and the right to trial by jury. It reads: "In all criminal prosecutions, the accused shall enjoy the right to a speedy and public trial, by an impartial jury of the State and district wherein the crime shall have been committed, which district shall have been previously ascertained by law, and to be informed of the nature and cause of the accusation; to be confronted with the witnesses against him; to have compulsory process for obtaining witnesses in his favor, and to have the Assistance of Counsel for his defence."

The Fifth and Fourteenth Amendments, respectively, provide that neither federal nor state government can deprive any person "of life, liberty, or property, without due process of law." The Supreme Court has said that this principle, too, constrains police, as when it ruled that involuntary confessions and unduly suggestive police lineups violate due process of law.

The Eighth Amendment prohibits excessive bail and also forbids cruel and unusual punishment. The Fourteenth Amendment provides that "nor shall any State . . . deny to any person within its jurisdiction the equal protection of the laws." For decades after the amendment was adopted in 1868, the Court refused to enforce this provision, but it is the constitutional provision that prohibits racial discrimination and should be a basis for stopping race-based policing.

That many provisions in the Bill of Rights involve law enforcement and criminal justice is not accidental. No government possesses any power more important than the authority to take away a person's liberty or even life. Only the government has this authority, and it vests it in police officers on the street and more generally in the criminal justice system. In many countries throughout history, this power has been abused: police have exercised arbitrary power that costs people their liberty or their lives. Hence the Framers of the Constitution in Philadelphia in 1787, and the drafters of the Bill of Rights in 1791, sought to limit government power and protect individuals from arbitrary actions. They included many protections against law enforcement in the Bill of Rights because they knew that people could not trust elected or appointed government officials to be their only safeguard against overzealous police.

The Supreme Court exists, above all, to enforce the Constitution. Long ago in 1803, in *Marbury v. Madison,* the Court explained that the Constitution exists to limit government, and those limits are meaningful only if they are enforced.[3] The Constitution often would be ignored without the judiciary. Under the Articles of Confederation, which preceded the Constitution after the Revolutionary War, the United States had neither federal courts nor a federal judicial power. Article III of the Constitution created the Supreme Court and authorized the creation of the lower federal courts because the Framers believed that the enforcement of federal law, including the Constitution, could not be left exclusively to the state judiciaries or to the political processes.

· · · · · · · · ·

THE CENTRAL FOCUS of this book is to assess the Court's record
in enforcing the provisions of the Constitution that are meant to constrain police, protect liberty, and ensure equality. It has most often
been a record of failure. In *Lyons* and many other cases, the Court
has failed in its fundamental duty to enforce the Constitution. It
has made it difficult, if not impossible, for people to sue to stop or
seek redress for police conduct that violates the Fourth, Fifth, Sixth,
Eighth, or Fourteenth Amendment. This failure to prevent or remedy
unconstitutional police behavior is especially problematic because
the American political process has also consistently failed to address
the problems of abusive and racist policing.

We are at a moment, thanks especially to Black Lives Matter,
when the pressure to change policing is great; some even advocate
defunding or abolishing the police. Historically, though, the political
process has not significantly regulated police conduct; judicial action
and enforcement have usually been necessary for police reform.

One reason is that public pressure generally favors more aggressive
law enforcement to stop crime, not protection of the rights of suspects
and criminal defendants. After all, when was the last time any state or
city adopted a law to expand the rights of criminal suspects or criminal defendants? When was the last time a state adopted a law to protect prisoners' rights? As the constitutional law scholar Barry Friedman
observes, "Legislatures avoid regulating the police because they don't see
any advantage in doing so."[4] Historically, the political pressure has overwhelmingly been in one direction: for aggressive, even overly aggressive,
law enforcement. This has resulted in the country's tremendous over-
criminalization. The United States has 5 percent of the world's population but 25 percent of the world's prisoners.

Another reason the political process does not generally regulate
police conduct is that the victims of police misconduct are disproportionately individuals of color, and the political process has historically
been far less responsive to their needs.[5] In 1938, in a footnote,[6] the
Court observed that the political process does not provide adequate

safeguards for "discrete and insular" minorities, by which it meant especially people of color. So judicial action is essential to protect vulnerable minorities, the people at greatest risk for police abuse.

Another problem with relying on the political process to control police conduct is that day-to-day violations of rights are largely invisible to the public. We all hear about the high-profile tragic shootings and deaths, like those of George Floyd and Breonna Taylor and Eric Garner and Michael Brown. But the day-to-day pattern of racially discriminatory police stops, abusive frisks, and unnecessary use of tasers and batons rarely comes to general public attention.

The high-profile instances attract public attention especially where video of the police abuse exists, but my study of the LAPD found that even the existence of videos rarely leads to the sustained action needed to reform policing. In Los Angeles, events followed a pattern over decades. A highly publicized incident of police abuse would be followed by a study and recommendations for reform. Some of the proposals would be adopted, but most would be ignored. Then the city would declare a victory over the problem of police abuse until the next incident. The cycle started in the 1950s: after a high-profile incident, a commission carried out a study, made a report, and issued recommendations—some were adopted, most were not; the city declared victory and moved on. Similarly, the 1965 Watts riots were followed by a report by the McCone Commission, and the 1991 Rodney King beating was followed by a report by the Christopher Commission. The 2000 Rampart scandal was followed by my and other reports, and so on.

I believe that the pattern in Los Angeles is typical of many major cities where a high-profile incident is followed by a short-lived focus on police abuses. The same thing happened nationally with the 1968 Kerner Commission: the urban uprisings led to a commission, a thorough report, and detailed recommendations for change, but little was actually done.

This context explains why disciplinary mechanisms created

within police departments are so often inadequate, especially when dealing with the day-to-day constitutional violations that occur on the streets. Even when police use excessive force that takes innocent people's lives, the department often finds that the officer acted within department policy, and it imposes no discipline. The attitudes of those who serve on those police disciplinary boards, like those within police departments, are tremendously insular. In 2000, when I was doing my study of the LAPD after the Rampart scandal, then LAPD chief Bernard Parks said to my face, "You can't criticize this department until you stand up to the bullets." This is the attitude of many police departments, and boards of review often lean toward accepting the stories of officers and rejecting the stories of victims. They will bend over backward to find that even serious police misconduct is "within policy."

· · · · · · · · ·

TO BE CLEAR, police departments are sometimes reformed without judicial action, and sometimes those reforms work. But meaningful change generally requires court action and court enforcement. In Los Angeles, significant reforms in policing did not occur until the city and the U.S. Department of Justice reached a consent decree—a legally binding and judicially enforceable agreement.[7] The consent decree mandated a system for tracking police discipline and requiring officers to record the race of those stopped. Although the consent decree certainly did not make LAPD into a perfect police department, by all accounts it greatly improved policing in the city.[8]

Thus, constraining the police and protecting people's rights greatly depends on the Supreme Court. The Court's interpretations of the Constitution create the rules that police must follow in their searches, their arrests, their interrogations, and their procedures for identifying suspects. Police receive regular training and are often very familiar with Court decisions. A few years ago the Court held that evidence gained as a result of an illegal stop is admissible if police then learn that there is an arrest warrant for the person who was stopped.[9] Several months later the inspector general of a police department in a large city told me that the officers quickly reacted to this decision by engaging in more frequent illegal stops knowing that if they discovered that the person stopped had an outstanding warrant, they could search the person. Anything incriminating could be used as evidence, and if nothing was found, the officers would just let the person go.

Supreme Court rulings have powerful impact, as occurred when the Court gave police the legal authority to stop and frisk individuals. "Stop and frisk" is the power of police to stop a person who is suspected of criminal activity and to the pat down the person if the police suspect the individual has a weapon. The Fourth Amendment explicitly requires police to have probable cause for all "seizures" of a person—which includes any stop where the person is not free to leave—and for all "searches" of a person. But in 1968, in *Terry v. Ohio,* the Court for the first time held that police could stop individuals—unquestionably a "seizure"—without needing to meet the Fourth Amendment standard for probable cause.[10] Since *Terry,* it has been sufficient for police to have "reasonable suspicion"—an easier standard to meet—that a person has committed a crime. It is often forgotten that it was the Warren Court, the most liberal in American history, that decided the *Terry v. Ohio* case and thereby greatly expanded police power.

It was inevitable that the police power permitted by *Terry* would be used in a racially discriminatory fashion. Between January 2004 and June 2012, the New York Police Department conducted over 4.4 million *Terry* stops. The use of this power increased sharply over that period, as the number of stops per year rose from 314,000 in 2004 to a high of 686,000 in 2011.

The detailed statistics on police stops are available to us as a result of a 2013 lawsuit against the NYPD.[11] They reveal the extent of racial discrimination in New York City policing. In 52 percent of the 4.4 million stops, the person stopped was Black, in 31 percent the person was Hispanic, and in 10 percent the person was white. To put this in context, in 2010, New York City's resident population was roughly 23 percent Black, 29 percent Hispanic, and 33 percent white.

Nor were the stops or frisks often justified in terms of what was gained. Stops are supposed to take place only because police have a reasonable suspicion that a person has committed a crime. But only 6 percent of all stops resulted in an arrest, and only 6 percent resulted in a summons. The remaining 88 percent of the 4.4 million stops resulted in no further law enforcement action.

Frisks are allowed only if police have a reasonable suspicion that the person has a weapon. Of all the stops, 52 percent were followed by the officer frisking the person stopped. A weapon was found after only 1.5 percent of these frisks. In other words, in 98.5 percent of the 2.3 million frisks, no weapon was found. Weapons were seized in 1.0 percent of the stops of Blacks, 1.1 percent of the stops of Hispanics, and 1.4 percent of the stops of whites.

Every police stop risks the possibility that the officer will use force; here, too, race played a large role in New York City. In 23 percent of the stops of Blacks, and 24 percent of the stops of Hispanics, the officer recorded using force. The number for whites was 17 percent.

The same pattern—the disproportionate use of power to stop against people of color—has been found in other cities as well. A 2019 study of the Los Angeles Police Department looked at the 385,000 drivers and passengers that officers pulled over from July 1, 2018, to the end of April 2019.[12] Of those stopped, 27 percent were Black, in a city that is about 9 percent Black in population. About 47 percent of those pulled over were Latino, which is roughly equivalent to their share of the population. About 18 percent of those stopped were white, when 28 percent of the city is white.

The basis for the stop also varied based on the race of the driver. A broken taillight or tinted windows was listed as the reason for more than 20 percent of vehicle stops involving Blacks and Latinos, but 11 percent of stops involving whites. Moreover, "Blacks and Latinos were more than three times as likely as whites to be removed from the vehicle and twice as likely to either be handcuffed or detained at the curb."[13] This finding is consistent with studies done all over the country that reveal how much policing is based on race.

Every interaction with the police has the potential to escalate into police violence. And as illustrated by what happened to Adolph Lyons, who was stopped for a malfunctioning taillight, far too many interactions have done exactly that.[14] Under the current rules as declared by the Supreme Court (as explained in later chapters), police can stop virtually any person at any time; each stop is frightening for the individual and has the possibility to escalate into a violent confrontation.

. . . .

SUPREME COURT DECISIONS matter enormously for how policing is done on a daily basis throughout the country. The Court can constrain the police by interpreting the Constitution to create clear rules and by providing remedies for violations of rights. Or it can enable police arbitrariness and bias by limiting the rights of criminal suspects and criminal defendants and by failing to provide remedies when there are constitutional violations. The Court also can empower the police by being silent and doing nothing in the face of abusive police practices, even those that risk conviction of innocent people and the use of excessive force.

My thesis is that through most of American history, the Court has usually refused to impose constitutional checks on police or to provide adequate remedies for police misconduct. Instead, it has created a series of legal rules that fail to protect citizens' constitutional rights and that facilitate and even encourage racist policing.

Over the course of American history, with the brief exception of the Warren Court, the Court has overwhelmingly ruled in favor of police and against the rights of criminal defendants and civil rights plaintiffs. It has contributed directly and significantly to the problems of policing in two important ways. First, it has narrowed the scope of rights that people have when dealing with the police. If there is no constitutional limit to police power, and politically imposed limits are absent, then police can do whatever they want. Overall, the Court has interpreted protections against unreasonable searches and arrests narrowly, compelled self-incrimination, and accepted faulty identification procedures.

Second, the Court has restricted the remedies available to those whose constitutional rights have been violated. A right is meaningless in the absence of a way to enforce it. *City of Los Angeles v. Lyons* is one example of a case where the Court limit remedies for police misconduct, in this instance by preventing injunctions to stop police from violating the Constitution. The Court did not deny that the chokehold constitutes excessive force in violation of the Fourth Amendment, but it effectively said that no court can issue an injunction to stop the practice. Similarly, the Court has greatly limited the ability of victims of police misconduct to sue police departments or police officers for monetary damages. Another possible remedy for police misconduct is for courts to exclude illegally obtained evidence, but the Court increasingly has gutted this remedy too.

Nor can the Court's failure be defended by arguing that it has simply been following the original meaning of the Constitution. We are highly unlikely ever to know the specific intentions of the Framers, and even if we did, I doubt they would have much relevance for judicial decision making today. Police forces as we know them did not exist until the mid-nineteenth century. It makes no sense to inquire into the original meaning of the Fourth Amendment with regard to "stop and frisk," let alone electronic surveillance or DNA testing. Nor is it useful to ask how the Framers would have protected people from coercive interrogation in police stations or from police lineups that too often lead to innocent people being convicted. These practices did not exist in 1791, when the Bill of Rights was adopted.

Rarely do even the most conservative self-avowed originalist justices try to justify their decisions regarding criminal procedure in originalist terms.

Long ago in 1819, Chief Justice John Marshall wrote that "we must never forget that it is a Constitution we are expounding," a Constitution "meant to be adapted and endure for ages to come."[15] Historically, the Supreme Court's decisions about police must be seen, not as the result of following a mythical original understanding, but as consistent value choices to favor police power over individual rights. This is the context in which we must see the Supreme Court in relation to policing in the United States.

For the first century and a half of American history, the Court rarely imposed any limits at all on police behavior even though racist and abusive policing was widespread. Only during the Warren Court era, from 1953 to 1969, did the Court, for the first time, significantly expand the rights of criminal suspects and attempt to provide protection against illegal searches and arrests, coerced confessions, and suggestive police identification procedures. In addition, the Court greatly expanded the two remedies for police misconduct: it required illegally obtained evidence to be excluded from use at trial (the exclusionary rule), and it allowed citizens to bring civil suits to recover monetary damages for police misconduct. Not coincidentally, the Court's most liberal era in American history was also a time when the justices were especially concerned about racial issues, including in policing.

But these decisions came under intense public criticism, especially from law enforcement, who said that their ability to control crime was being greatly limited. The Court was accused of handcuffing the police and letting guilty people go free. The Court likely felt this pressure, which partially explains why in *Terry v. Ohio* in 1968 it greatly expanded the ability of police to engage in stops and frisks. In 1968 Richard Nixon campaigned for president, in large part, against the Warren Court, which he frequently attacked for "handcuffing the police." His promises of "law and order" often had an explicitly racial dimension, as he proclaimed his opposition to school busing to achieve desegregation and condemned the racial disturbances in many American cities.

After Nixon became president, he was able to appoint four justices to the Court between 1969 and 1971, including the new chief justice, Warren Burger, who had been a vocal critic of the Warren Court's decisions protecting criminal suspects and defendants. These four justices, along with the Warren Court's dissenters who remained on the bench, quickly halted the protection of the rights of criminal suspects and greatly narrowed, and sometimes expressly overruled, the Warren Court's decisions. The Burger Court, which lasted from 1969 until 1986, returned to the historical pattern and rarely limited police searches, arrests, interrogations, or identification procedures but did limit remedies for police constitutional violations.

The Rehnquist Court, from 1986 until 2005, and the Roberts Court, since 2005, have gone much further than the Burger Court in narrowing the constitutional rights protecting individuals from the police and in restricting remedies for police misconduct. It is appropriate to look at the Rehnquist and Roberts Courts together in this area because their jurisprudence has been the same: empower the police. Both Courts have made civil suits for police misconduct very difficult and have gutted the remedy of excluding evidence that is the product of illegal police behavior.

The Supreme Court before 1953, the Burger Court, and the Rehnquist and Roberts Courts all failed to enforce the constitutional provisions that limit police conduct. Instead, the Supreme Court consistently has empowered police, with powers that are so often used in a racially biased manner. But it does not have to be this way. The book concludes by examining what might be different in the future and how to get there.

At this writing in late 2020, when it comes to race and policing in the United States, we are at a crucial moment in history. Six percent of American adults said that in May and June 2020 they

"attended a protest or rally on issues related to race or racial equality."[16] That is, 15 million people went to a protest in the midst of a
lethal pandemic. I fear that if we squander this energy for reform,
if no major reform comes of it in terms, then resentments and anger
will only grow, perhaps exponentially. But I am hopeful that the
current attention to policing can lead to major changes, by police
departments, by cities, by state legislatures, by Congress, and maybe
even by the Supreme Court.

Part II

A MINIMAL JUDICIAL ROLE

The Court and Policing Before 1953

A police lineup at the Detective Bureau in Chicago, 1929. *(Photo by* Chicago Sun-Times/Chicago Daily News *collection/Chicago History Museum/Getty Images)*

4

Why the Supreme Court Ignored Policing for Much of American History

F ROM THE ADOPTION OF THE CONSTITUTION IN 1787 until well into the twentieth century, the Supreme Court issued few decisions dealing with issues of policing. The first came in the late nineteenth century, but even until the mid-twentieth century, they were relatively scarce compared to the last seventy years. One naturally asks why such a profound change occurred. The answers are starkly revealing, providing significant insight into how policing increased, and how some initial attempts were made to limit it.

Twenty-first-century Americans may have a hard time imaging this, but prior to the second half of the nineteenth century, our cities had no police forces. Law enforcement was loosely organized, primarily made up of night watches and constables who worked for the courts.[1] The night watch's primary role was to stay alert during the nighttime hours and raise alarm in case of a fire. They were supposed to patrol the city at night, tend to street lamps, break up fights, and arrest suspicious people. They reported to a head constable. In smaller towns, the night watch was enlisted only during times of war.[2] Sheriffs were common in more rural areas and in the territories as America expanded westward. At the time when the Bill of Rights was adopted, as the Supreme Court explained in 1967, "there were no organized police forces as we know them today. . . . The accused confronted the prosecutor and the witnesses against him, and the evidence was marshalled largely at the trial itself."[3]

Constables and sheriffs worked directly for the civil and criminal courts and were either supported by a salary or, more commonly, paid fees per task they completed.[4] For example, victims of crimes often paid fees to constables to get them to start the legal process.[5] Constables and sheriffs thus had some of the characteristics of police today, but they were also quite different in that they were not employed by city governments and were not formally organized in departments.

During the first half of the nineteenth century, law enforcement was considered the responsibility of the whole community or of the specific victims who had suffered a transgression. After a crime occurred, the victims were expected to come to the court to seek a remedy.[6] To provide an incentive for community action, localities posted public notices offering bounties and rewards for the captures of wrongdoers.[7] In some instances, posses of citizens were summoned to catch offenders or to control disorderly crowds. Community members were involved to the extent that anyone could act in the capacity of a constable without formally being designated as such, especially when a constable or a sheriff called upon them to assist with law enforcement.[8] In the territories, as in the Old West, a sheriff imposed justice. Countless Hollywood westerns have overly dramatized these individuals, but many of those depictions did not diverge much from the reality of the powerful sheriff who acted to keep law and order.

Furthermore, the society made no effort to detect, control, or prevent crime. Sheriffs, constables, and night watches did almost nothing in this regard. Criminal law enforcement was almost entirely reactive because cases were adjudicated only when a victim came forward claiming, for example, to have been robbed or assaulted.[9] Since the system depended on victims coming forward, the cases were criminal in nature but essentially civil in form: civil legal proceedings are instigated not by government actors but by private individuals.[10]

Most search warrants were issued for the purpose of recovering stolen goods.[11] In order to start the process, all the victim had to do was say that he or she had reason to believe that a certain individual had stolen something and had it in his or her possession. Magistrates apparently did not evaluate the facts to ascertain whether there was probable cause.[12] If a search warrant was issued, a constable would accompany the victim to the accused person's premises to search for the stolen items.[13]

This system of law enforcement was inefficient, and night watches were often ridiculed. But it was cheap to administer.[14] It was also unchecked by the courts or by the Supreme Court. The Fourth Amendment, for example, should have applied to warrants that were issued and searches that were done. But for the first century of American history, if anyone did challenge the constitutionality of such actions, the cases did not make it to the Supreme Court.

Those who today call for the abolition of police point to the racist origins of policing in much of the United States. Indeed, slave patrols developed in the South around 1704 and are considered the precursor to formal police forces in southern cities.[15] The slave patrols were neither haphazard nor ill-planned; they were efficient organizations for protecting the institution of slavery.[16] The patrols were under government control. In 1802 North Carolina placed its slave patrols entirely in the control of its state courts. In 1806 Tennessee developed a system where town commissioners appointed slave patrols for incorporated and unincorporated municipalities. In 1821 in Louisiana, parish governments were given complete control of slave patrols, and in 1831 incorporated towns in Mississippi were given control of patrols.[17] As police departments began to form, in at least eight states they were put under the same governing body as the slave patrols.[18] One historian has observed that southern cities had virtual standing armies tasked with slave control.[19]

The slave patrols were responsible for preventing slave uprisings, tracking and returning runaway slaves, and preventing slaves from leaving their plantations without a travel permit from their masters.[20] Slave patrols had unfettered powers to search houses to look for runaway slaves and to search slave quarters.[21] Some localities allowed slave patrols to whip free blacks who were out without their "free papers."[22]

As officers of the government, members of slave patrols were in theory obligated to act in compliance with constitutional requirements, such as the Fourth and Fifth Amendments. But history records no Supreme Court decisions that apply these constitutional limits to the actions of slave patrols. To the contrary, the Supreme Court aggressively enforced the Constitution's fugitive slave clause. Found in Article IV, Section 3, this provision states: "No Person held to Service or Labour in one State, under the Laws thereof, escaping into another, shall, in Consequence of any Law or Regulation therein, be discharged from such Service or Labour, but shall be delivered up on Claim of the Party to whom such Service or Labour may be due." In other words, the Constitution required that a slave who escaped to a free state be returned to his or her owner.

The Fugitive Slave Act, adopted by the second Congress in 1793, required that judges return escaped slaves to their owners. In *Prigg v. Pennsylvania* in 1842, the Supreme Court heard the case of a state law that prevented the use of force or violence to remove a person from the state to return the individual to slavery.[23] The Court declared the Pennsylvania law unconstitutional, relying on the fugitive slave clause and the Fugitive Slave Act to invalidate it. Writing for the Court, Justice Joseph Story—one of the most respected justices in history—held that the Constitution prohibited states from interfering with the return of fugitive slaves. Story, the youngest person to ever become a justice, at age thirty-two, served on the Court for thirty-three years. His treatise on the Constitution was regarded with reverence and is still quoted to this day. Yet, in *Prigg,* he handed down a decision in favor of the power of slave owners that deserves full-throated condemnation.

Justice Story explained that the purpose of the fugitive slave clause "was to secure to the citizens of the slaveholding states the complete right and title of ownership in their slaves, as property, in every state in the Union into which they might escape from the state where they were held in servitude."[24] Indeed, the fugitive slave clause "was so vital . . . that it cannot be doubted that it constituted a fundamental article, without the adoption of which the Union could not have been formed."[25] Thus, the Court concluded that "we have not the slightest hesitation in holding that under and in virtue of the Constitution, the owner of a slave is clothed with entire authority, in every state in the Union, to seize and recapture his slave."[26] Likewise, states could punish those who harbored fugitive slaves.[27] The Court came down emphatically on the side of slave owners and against slaves and those who provided them assistance. The Pennsylvania law had simply prohibited the use of force or violence in returning slaves; surely government always has an interest in stopping violence, but the Court nonetheless declared this law unconstitutional.

At no point prior to the Civil War did the Supreme Court significantly limit slavery or even raise serious questions about its constitutionality.[28] In fact, the Court did the opposite, most notably in *Dred Scott v. Sanford*, in 1857, in which it declared that slaves were the property of their owners and not U.S. citizens. It also declared unconstitutional the Missouri Compromise, which had prohibited slavery in northern territories.[29] To further protect the institution of slavery, it empowered slave patrols and eschewed constitutional limits on them.

· · · · · · · · ·

SCHOLARS WHO STUDY the history of police forces have no consensus about when they began.[30] The British Parliament created the world's first military-style police force in 1829, to keep order and investigate crimes.[31] But Americans strongly resisted replacing the constable system with organized police forces, likely because of fear of government power. Still, the replacement ultimately occurred. Eric Monkkonen, an expert on police history, identifies four key changes in the shift to organized police.[32] First, the new forces had a hierarchical structure with command and communications resembling the military. Second, where sheriffs and constables had been under local judicial authority, the police were placed under cities' executive authority. In time, states would develop their own forms of police, such as highway patrols, and the federal government developed its law enforcement agencies as well. Third, uniforms made police visible to the public and easier to control by a central command. And fourth, police were expected to actively patrol to prevent crime from happening and to catch criminals.[33]

The advent of salaried police forces dramatically changed the role of prosecutors. Previously, a robbery victim had to decide if a prosecution was worth it and, if so, pay a fee to a constable. But with a salaried police force in place, prosecutions could be based on evidence uncovered by police.[34] This entire shift in law enforcement occurred without the Supreme Court placing any limits or even issuing any opinions on it.

Between 1850 and 1880, uniformed police departments were created all over the country.[35] Recurring riots in many cities seem to have been a key factor.[36] The riots occurred for many reasons. In 1863 in New York City, a riot erupted from a protest against the military draft. After the Civil War, race-based riots occurred in Memphis, New Orleans, and elsewhere. By the 1870s, labor protests were often turning violent.

In the early years of formal police forces, recruits underwent no training; there were no settled procedures for how police officers should conduct searches or make arrests. Left on their own, they developed their own strategies for performing these tasks, often with no reference to constitutional requirements.[37] Sometimes those strategies were violent. Citizens frequently complained, and newspapers published accounts of police violence.[38] Citizens who were injured by police were often charged with resisting arrest, leading us to infer that they had not been doing anything wrong in the first place.[39]

Additionally, police sought to establish their legitimacy by going into dangerous gang-run neighborhoods and "beating senseless" known gang members and suspected criminals.[40] Police also began to use violent methods during investigations and interrogations. When police began conducting interrogations, they initially gave suspects warnings about their right to remain silent, but "by 1875 they were brazenly refusing to provide the warnings, and by the mid-1880s they were torturing confessions out of suspects."[41]

The new forces' key tasks were guiding and fixing traffic problems, giving directions, finding and returning lost children, helping out victims of sudden accidents, and escorting drunks home or to the station. Police also provided nightly lodging to homeless drifters and operated city soup kitchens. They enforced public health measures. Until 1881, police in New York City were responsible for street cleaning.[42] Around 1890, however, these public welfare responsibilities began to wane as reformers pushed the police to focus more on crime and especially on those committing felonies. Available data about arrests suggest that by the 1890s the police were shaking off their welfare responsibilities and concentrating more exclusively on arresting felons and preventing crime.[43]

A key figure in changing policing was Theodore Roosevelt, who served as president of the New York Police Department's board of commissioners from 1894 to 1896.[44] New York mayor William Strong, upon discovering widespread graft and corruption in the NYPD, appointed Roosevelt to clean it up. Roosevelt changed the qualifications for becoming a police officer; previously hiring had been based entirely on political affiliations or friendships. He instituted ethical standards and imposed discipline on officers who violated them. Not surprisingly, he was met with intense resistance, but other cities soon copied Roosevelt's reforms. His initiatives were intended primarily to deal with corruption and to create a more professional police force, not to discourage excessive force or racist policing.

. . . .

ONE SEARCHES THE nineteenth-century historical record in vain for cases in which the Supreme Court enforced constitutional protections limiting police conduct, such as the Fourth Amendment's limits on searches and seizures, and the Fifth Amendment's privilege against self-incrimination. Their absence indicates that such matters did not come to the Supreme Court. Likely, this reflected a widespread perception, as explained below, that the Bill of Rights did not limit what officers of state and local governments could do. But the absence of Supreme Court decisions meant that police operated with no constitutional limits; their conduct could remain unchecked even to the point of abuse.

To be sure, a handful of cases made their way to the Supreme Court that involved police officers. Most involved the question of when a sheriff could be held liable for negligence; none involved challenges to abusive police practices or violations of constitutional rights. In *Long v. Palmer, Smith, & Co.* in 1842, a Mississippi sheriff was holding a prisoner for an unpaid debt; the prisoner escaped. The Court ruled that under a state statute, the sheriff was liable for the debt, as he had either negligently or purposefully allowed the prisoner to escape.[45] Similarly, in *Walker v. Robbins* in 1852, a deputy marshal—a police figure common in territories before they became states—said that he had served a summons on a defendant, but he lied; he had not done so. The Court held that the marshal was responsible for any damages derived from the conduct of his deputy.[46]

Notably, none of these cases were about violations of constitutional rights. The Court was not interpreting or enforcing the Fourth, Fifth, and Sixth Amendments. It was not limiting the police in any meaningful way. Slave patrols in the early nineteenth century were often brutal, especially to slaves and former slaves, but never did the Court address this issue; nor did it address the issue of police violence later in the century.

There is another important reason why the Supreme Court dealt with almost no cases of criminal procedure in the nineteenth century, and many fewer than one would expect in the early twentieth. The Bill of Rights—including the Fourth, Fifth, and Sixth Amendments—was deemed to apply *only to the federal government*, not to state and local governments. And relatively little policing was done at the federal level until the creation of the Federal Bureau of Investigation in 1908, the advent of Prohibition in 1920, and J. Edgar Hoover's appointment as head of the FBI in 1924. Although federal law enforcement existed in the first half of the twentieth century, most policing, then and now, was done at the state and local level. Only in the 1960s did the Court find that the requirements of the Fourth, Fifth, and Sixth Amendments applied to state and local police as well as federal law enforcement officials. This explains why the vast majority of cases involving these amendments are from the last seventy years and not from the first 160 years of American history.

To us, it seems strange that the Bill of Rights—the enumeration of our most cherished constitutional rights—was thought for such a long time to apply only to the federal government. But early in American history, the Supreme Court expressly ruled that the Bill of Rights' protection of individual liberties limited only the federal government, not state or local governments or their officers. In *Barron v. Mayor & City Council of Baltimore* in 1833, the Court expressly held that the Bill of Rights restricted federal actions, not state or local conduct.[47] John Barron, a prominent Baltimore wharf owner, sued the city for taking his property without just compensation in violation of the Fifth Amendment. He alleged that the city ruined his busy wharf in Baltimore Harbor by taking sand and dirt from a road construction project and depositing it in the water. He said this made the water too shallow to dock most vessels. The Maryland state court had ruled in Barron's favor and awarded him $4,500 to compensate him for his losses.

The issue before the Supreme Court was whether the takings clause of the Fifth Amendment—which says that the government can take private property for public use but must pay just compensation—applied to the City of Baltimore. Chief Justice John Marshall, writing for the Court, began by declaring: "The question . . . is . . . of great importance, but not of much difficulty."[48] The Court reversed Barron's victory in the lower court and explained that the Bill of Rights was clearly intended to apply only to the federal government: "The constitution was ordained and established by the people of the United States for themselves, for their own government, and not for the government of the individual states." Justice Marshall said that if the Framers had intended the Bill of Rights to apply to the states, they would have explicitly said so.[49]

In a way it is surprising that such a ruling came from John Marshall, who served as chief justice from 1801 to 1835. Throughout his time on the Court, Marshall was the architect of expanded power of the federal government. He authored landmark decisions establishing the power of the federal courts to declare laws and presidential acts unconstitutional, and greatly enlarging the powers of Congress.[50] One would think that Marshall, who never seemed to care much about "states' rights," would have wanted state and local governments to comply with the Bill of Rights. Yet to him—and he had participated in Virginia's constitutional convention and in the ratification of the Bill of Rights—it was clear that the Framers meant for the Bill of Rights to apply only to the federal government. Thus in *Barron*, the Court concluded that the Fifth Amendment was "intended solely as a limitation on the exercise of power by the government of the United States, and is not applicable to the legislation of the States."[51] *Barron* meant that the Bill of Rights—including the provisions limiting searches and seizures, protecting the right against self-incrimination, and safeguarding due process of law—applied only to the federal government.

From a modern perspective, it is troubling that under the U.S. Constitution, state and local governments were free to violate and even ignore basic constitutional rights. Yet at the time of its decision, *Barron* made sense because of faith in state constitutions and because of the widely shared understanding that the Bill of Rights applied only to the federal government.[52] States had their own constitutions. Many had provisions limiting police conduct that were similar or identical to those in the U.S. Constitution, but we have no indication that they were used to impose significant constraints on policing. State courts were no more likely than the Supreme Court to constrain police searches and interrogations.

· · · · · · · · ·

NOT UNTIL the late nineteenth century, after more than one hundred years of American constitutional history, did the Supreme Court even suggest that the Bill of Rights—including the provisions protecting the rights of criminal suspects and criminal defendants— might apply to state and local governments. The Fourteenth Amendment, adopted in 1868, states, in part, that no state can deprive any person of life, liberty, or property without due process of law. At the end of the nineteenth and the beginning of the twentieth century, the Court suggested that at least some of the Bill of Rights provisions are part of the "liberty" protected from state interference by the Fourteenth Amendment's due process clause.

Why did the Supreme Court finally make this suggestion? It was a conservative Court that wanted to protect the rights of property owners from the government. To accomplish this, it applied constitutional provisions safeguarding property rights to state and local governments. In 1897 in *Chicago, Burlington & Quincy Railroad Co. v. City of Chicago,* the Court ruled, without much explanation, that the due process clause of the Fourteenth Amendment prevents states from taking property without just compensation.[53]

In 1908 in *Twining v. New Jersey,* the Court expressly recognized the possibility that the due process clause incorporates provisions of

the Bill of Rights and thereby applies them to state and local governments.[54] The criminal defendants claimed that a state court had violated their constitutional rights by instructing the jury that it could
draw a negative inference from their failure to testify at trial. The
Court rejected this claim but said that some of the Bill of Rights
provisions included in the first eight amendments might be applied
to state and local governments "because a denial of them would be
a denial of due process of law. . . . If this is so, it is not because those
rights are enumerated in the first eight Amendments, but because
they are of such a nature that they are included in the conception of
due process of law."[55]

For example, in *Gitlow v. New York* in 1925, the Court for the
first time said that the First Amendment's protection of freedom of
speech applies to the states through its incorporation into the due
process clause of the Fourteenth Amendment.[56] In 1919 the socialist
politician and journalist Benjamin Gitlow was convicted for publishing a "left wing manifesto," under a state law that made it a crime to
advocate the violent overthrow of government by force or violence.
Gitlow challenged the law, but the Court rejected his challenge and
upheld his conviction, ruling that his speech was not protected by the
First Amendment. But importantly, the Court also said that freedom
of speech, which the First Amendment protects from abridgement by
Congress, is also safeguarded by the due process clause from impairment by the states.[57]

Two years later, in *Fiske v. Kansas,* the Court for the first time
found that a state law regulating speech violated the due process
clause.[58] Harold B. Fiske, who had distributed literature for the
Industrial Workers of the World (IWW), was convicted in state court
of seeking to overturn America's industrial structure by force or violence. The evidence against him was the preamble from the IWW's
mission statement, which pointed to differences between the working and employing classes and said that the struggle would persist
until the workers took over production and abolished the wage system. Fiske acknowledged his membership in the IWW but said he

believed it sought to achieve its objectives through peaceful means. Fiske was convicted in state court, but the Supreme Court overturned the conviction and said that his speech was protected by the First Amendment.

Not until 1932 did the Supreme Court first find that a person had a right to a lawyer provided for by the government when being tried in state court for a crime where there was a possible death sentence. *Powell v. Alabama* involved the infamous "Scottsboro Boys" trial.[59] Nine African American teenagers charged with raping two white women on a train were convicted at trial without the assistance of an attorney and with a jury from which all Blacks had been excluded. The trial occurred just days after the alleged assault, with lynch mobs outside the courthouse. The "Scottsboro Boys" were found guilty and sentenced to death. The Supreme Court reversed their convictions, concluding that the due process clause of the Fourteenth Amendment protects fundamental rights from state interference and that this can include Bill of Rights provisions. The Court held that in a capital case "it [is] clear that the right to the aid of counsel is of this fundamental character."[60]

For the first 142 years of American history—from 1791, when the Sixth Amendment was ratified, until 1932—a state could try a person for a capital crime and sentence the defendant to death without providing him or her with a lawyer. But even after *Powell,* the Court refused to find that defendants in state court had a right to counsel in noncapital cases. In *Betts v. Brady* in 1942, the Court held that the government did not have to pay for an attorney for an indigent criminal defendant who faced a possible prison sentence.[61] Smith Betts, an unemployed farmhand, was tried for robbery in Maryland state court and requested a lawyer. The court refused to appoint one and insisted that he be tried without counsel. Betts, who was forty-three years old, was convicted and sentenced to eight years in prison. He argued that his conviction violated his Sixth Amendment right to a lawyer. The Supreme Court disagreed and said that "while want of counsel in a particular case may result in a conviction lacking in such

fundamental fairness," it could not say that the Sixth Amendment
"embodies an inexorable command" that those tried for crimes in
state court must be provided lawyers.[62] Not until *Gideon v. Wainwright* in 1963 did the Court hold that states must provide counsel
for anyone being tried for a crime where they face a possible prison
sentence.[63]

· · · · · · · · ·

THE COURT'S REFUSAL to apply the Bill of Rights to the states to
protect criminal defendants continued well into the twentieth century.[64] In the mid-1940s, Admiral Dewey Adamson was charged with
murder in California. At trial he did not take the witness stand in his
own defense, and the prosecutor told the jury that they could infer
his guilt from that. The law was clear that making that inference in
federal court violated the Fifth Amendment privilege against self-
incrimination; a jury could not presume guilty a criminal defendant
who refused to testify and invoked this constitutional right. But the
Supreme Court, in its 5–4 decision in *Adamson v. California* in 1947,
ruled that this key right under the Fifth Amendment did not apply
to the states. It did not provide the defendant "freedom from giving testimony by compulsion in state trials."[65] In other words, the
privilege against self-incrimination, long regarded as a fundamental
right in the criminal justice system, did not apply in state courts.
Two years later, in *Wolf v. Colorado,* the Court held that the crucial
mechanism for enforcing the Fourth Amendment, the exclusionary
rule—the requirement that evidence gained by police violation of the
Fourth Amendment cannot be used at trial—did not apply to state
and local police.[66]

Why did it take so long—until the Warren Court in the 1950s
and especially the 1960s—for the Court to say that state and local
governments, including their police, have to comply with the Bill of
Rights? Justice Hugo Black (who served on the Court from 1937 to
1971) long argued unsuccessfully that the entire Bill of Rights should
be applied to state and local governments. It is interesting that Black,

a southerner from Alabama, the place long known for states' rights arguments, led the fight to limit state and local power. Black had been a member of the Klan earlier in his life and was a U.S. senator from Alabama when President Franklin Roosevelt named him to the Court. He may have had a sense from personal experience of the importance of limiting state police powers. Also, Black was known for wanting to interpret the Constitution based on the plain meaning of its text, and he believed that the privileges or immunities clause of the Fourteenth Amendment—which provides that no state may deprive any citizen of the "privileges or immunities of United States citizenship"—was meant to apply all of the Bill of Rights to the states.[67] But those on the other side of the debate argued that its drafters and ratifiers did not intend for the Fourteenth Amendment to apply the Bill of Rights to the states. In 1949, in a famous article that Supreme Court justices would come to rely on, Stanford Law professor Charles Fairman examined the history of the Fourteenth Amendment and forcefully argued that the original intent was not to apply the Bill of Rights to the states.[68]

The debate over applying the Bill of Rights to the states was also about federalism and states' rights. Applying the Bill of Rights to the states would impose a substantial set of restrictions on state and local governments, including on their police forces. As long as the Fourth, Fifth, and Sixth Amendments did not apply, state and local police would not need to comply with the amendments' constraints on searches, arrests, interrogations, and trials. Not surprisingly, opponents to applying the Bill of Rights to the states argued based on federalism, that it was desirable to preserve state and local governing autonomy by freeing states and localities from the application of the Bill of Rights. Justice Felix Frankfurter, a staunch opponent of applying the Bill of Rights, stressed that states should not be constrained.[69] But those who favored applying the Bill of Rights to the states countered that history shows many instances where states and state courts have not adequately protected rights; safeguarding precious liberties should not rest on faith in the states. They said the

Supreme Court and the federal courts should ensure the protection of basic liberties, including from infringement by state and local governments.

· · · · · · · · ·

IN THE TWENTIETH CENTURY, as federal law enforcement increased, the Supreme Court considered the meaning of these constitutional provisions for policing by the federal government. Prohibition, which was imposed by constitutional amendment in 1920, dramatically increased the scope of federal law enforcement and provided the basis for many of the cases in which the Supreme Court initially defined the meaning of the Fourth and Fifth Amendments.

Enforcing the prohibition of alcohol required enormous law enforcement efforts. Courts across the country were "flooded" with Prohibition cases to such an extent that Judge Learned Hand—who served as a federal judge from 1909 until 1961 and was one of the most respected jurists in history—opposed Prohibition because it was turning federal courts into low-level criminal courts.[70]

Wesley Oliver, in his influential book *The Prohibition Era and Policing,* observes that "Prohibition brought out the worst in law enforcement."[71] In 1920, when Prohibition began, most people did not doubt that the police had the authority to search where and how they wanted. The reforms in policing in the late nineteenth century, such as implemented by the Roosevelt Board in New York City, had focused on preventing police from using their positions for political or financial gain.[72] The concern was about limiting police corruption, not about stopping abusive police behavior.[73] But enforcing Prohibition often led to abusive police behavior. A proliferation of "indiscriminate" warrantless searches across the country destroyed personal property and perpetrated violence against those searched.[74] According to a New York City magistrate in 1922, "[r]aid after raid is being brought into these courts despite the fact that magistrates have been declaring them illegal. The police are running roughshod over the rights of the people."[75]

As a result, on a more positive note, police departments during Prohibition went from being self-regulated organizations to "being the subjects of substantial judicial oversight. From 1920 to 1940, *state* courts began to define the appropriate scope of search and seizures and to punish violations."[76] But the Supreme Court rarely reviewed these state court decisions because the key Bill of Rights provisions had not yet been applied to state and local governments. Also, of course, state courts varied tremendously in their willingness to limit police conduct and in their concerns about race and the rights of Blacks.

During this time police interrogations sometimes veered into confessions elicited through physical coercion and even torture so severe that the Supreme Court took action.[77] State courts were often unwilling to exclude confessions from being used as evidence no matter what the police had done to extract them.[78] In *Wan v. United States* in 1924, the Supreme Court held that a confession that resulted from coercion was inadmissible.[79] However, state courts disagreed, and most did not view coerced confessions as inadmissible in criminal prosecutions.[80] Supreme Court review of these state court decisions generally was not possible because key constitutional rights had not yet been applied to the states. The Court's overall silence allowed these police practices and state court decisions to continue unchecked.

At the turn of the twentieth century and continuing through Prohibition, police began to utilize wiretapping in their investigations. Much as the public had accepted police violence prior to Prohibition, citizens generally were not put off by the idea that the police were listening to phone calls or intercepting telegraph messages. Prior to Prohibition, for example, New Yorkers learned that the NYPD had been tapping phone lines, but they seem to have accepted this practice as a necessary tool for fighting crime.[81]

In fact, challenges to law enforcement actions during Prohibition led to some of the major Supreme Court cases about police. Prohibition ended in 1933, but the federal law enforcement agencies that were created to enforce it largely continued to exist, and their actions led to cases before the Court. But before the Warren Court applied the Bill of Rights to the states in the 1950s and '60s, the Court was unable to consider challenges to most policing in the United States which is done at the state and local levels of government.

· · · · · · · · ·

THERE IS A THIRD REASON, perhaps more subtle, why so few Supreme Court cases dealt with police conduct in the nineteenth century and only a modest number in the early twentieth: there were few avenues by which issues about policing could get to the Court. One way an issue of policing might get there was for victims of police misconduct to sue the police for monetary damages. If the suit was brought under federal law, the Supreme Court could review the case. But to this day, no federal law authorizes suits for monetary damages against federal law enforcement officers, or other federal officials, who infringe constitutional rights. In 1971 the Court allowed such suits in a limited way.[82] The federal law authorizing suits against state and local police officers—42 U.S. Code Section 1983—was adopted in 1871 but was infrequently used until a 1961 Supreme Court decision allowed Chicago police officers to be sued for an abusive and unconstitutional search.[83]

In the rare instances when civil suits based on tort claims reached the Supreme Court, the justices limited the liability that could be imposed on the police. In 1855 *South v. State of Maryland for Use of Pottle*, Jonathan Pottle brought a suit against the sheriff.[84] He alleged that when a mob was coming for him to demand money, he sought the sheriff's protection, but the sheriff refused to protect him.[85] The Court said that a sheriff has two roles: the judicial role of carrying out matters like recovering stolen property and the public role of preserving the peace.[86] The latter is similar to what we would think of as policing today. As for the former, the Court said that a sheriff could be civilly sued "where he acts ministerially, and is bound to render certain services to individuals, for a compensation in fees or salary, he is liable for acts of misfeasance or non-feasance to the party who is injured by them." The Court stressed that sheriffs are paid to perform these tasks by those wanting their services, like a creditor wanting the sheriff to attach the property of a debtor. The Court said that a sheriff should be liable when he was not doing what he was compensated to do.

But the Court held that in the role of preserving public peace, a sheriff can be held liable only through criminal indictment, not through civil liability.[87] It found that civil actions were not appropriate against sheriffs as "no instance can be found where a civil action has been sustained against [a sheriff] for his default or misbehavior as conservator of the peace, by those who have suffered injury to their property or persons through the violence of mobs, riots, or insurrections." In effect, the Court broadly declared what today we would call "absolute immunity" for law enforcement officers from civil liability. It limited a key potential judicial check on the police and restricted opportunities for the Court to hear cases challenging unconstitutional police actions of all types, no matter how egregious.

A second way the Supreme Court may hear constitutional challenges to law enforcement conduct is when a convicted person seeks a writ of habeas corpus, a court order that the person is being held in violation of the Constitution and laws of the United States. Although Congress authorized courts to issue such writs for federal prisoners in 1789, it did not authorize them for state prisoners until 1867. Judges, though, limited what criminal defendants could raise in a habeas corpus petition. The Court held that the law authorizes courts to issue writs of habeas corpus only if the court that convicted the defendant lacked jurisdiction and not if the conviction violated the defendant's constitutional rights.[88] A defendant was limited to arguing that the court that convicted him had no authority to hear the case and could not claim that the court's ruling was inconsistent with the Constitution. And not until 1953, when the Court was becoming more sensitive to the problems for Blacks tried for crimes in southern courts, did the Court say that a person convicted in state court could use habeas corpus in federal court to relitigate issues already raised and presented at trial and on appeal.[89] Until then, the scope of habeas corpus and its utility as a vehicle for the federal courts to protect constitutional rights was quite narrow because the constitutional issues almost always had been presented by the criminal defendant to the state court.

A third way the Supreme Court may hear constitutional challenges to police behavior was open only to people convicted in federal court. They could argue that their conviction was unconstitutional, including because of the actions of the police, and seek Supreme Court review. In the first half of the twentieth century, a number of cases came to the Court this way, especially cases arising from police investigations to enforce Prohibition. (In the next chapter, I examine these initial Court decisions about policing and what they did, and did not do, to control the police.)

Nor did the Court acknowledge or give any attention to the racism that existed, often openly, in police departments. In occasional cases—the Scottsboro Boys case, *Powell v. Alabama* in 1932, and some involving abusive police interrogations—the racism was so overt that it could not be ignored. But in the first century and a half of American history, no more than a handful of cases mentioned, let alone tried to deal with, race and policing. Then and now, the justices have not openly recognized the existence of racism in the criminal justice system or of the ways it profoundly affects policing in the United States. The Emancipation Proclamation and the Thirteenth Amendment ended slavery, and the Fourteenth Amendment assured due process of law and equal protection. But for Blacks facing the police, and often the courts, these constitutional achievements often were little more than empty words on paper.

5

Judicial Silence on Constitutional Protections and Remedies Before 1953

S A RESULT OF THE LATE NINETEENTH-CENTURY growth of local police forces, and the increase in federal law enforcement during Prohibition, the Supreme Court issued more decisions that interpreted the constitutional provisions intended to limit police conduct. It would be wrong to say that the Court did nothing at all to constrain police misconduct, but also an error to say that it did much. Prior to the Warren Court, which began in 1953, the Court construed the Fourth Amendment's limits on police conduct narrowly; it protected the privilege against self-incrimination, but only from egregious police abuse; and it applied the rule that evidence gained illegally by the police could not be used against a criminal defendant only to federal law enforcement, not to state and local police.

Notably, the Court made no effort to deal with the problem of police identification procedures, which led to the conviction of many innocent individuals. In 1932 legal scholar Edwin Borchard, in *Convicting the Innocent,* reported that among sixty-five cases in which innocent persons were convicted, twenty-nine were the result of an inaccurate eyewitness identification.[1] But in not a single case did the Supreme Court hold that the police conducted a lineup or a photo identification in a way that offended the Constitution, even though it was well known that the police often conducted them in a highly suggestive manner, resulting in wrongful convictions.

It is important to look carefully at what the Court said about the Constitution and policing before 1953, because it created the foundation for everything the Court has done in this area since then. What the Court did not do is perhaps even more important; silence from the Court meant that it imposed no limits on police conduct.

The Prohibition Against Unreasonable Searches and Seizures

From its earliest treatment of the Fourth Amendment until 1967, near the end of the Warren Court,[2] the Supreme Court took a narrow view of the scope of the Fourth Amendment, saying it applied only if police physically trespassed on property. In other words, as long as police did not physically intrude on a person's property, they did not need to get a warrant or have probable cause for their actions. This minimalist interpretation enabled the police to engage in searches in countless ways without needing to be concerned with the requirements of the Fourth Amendment.

In fact, for ninety-five years after the ratification of the Fourth Amendment, no Supreme Court case interpreted it as imposing limits on police searches and seizures; the Court hardly ever mentioned it. The seminal Court case involving the Fourth Amendment was *Boyd v. United States* in 1886, which involved the government's seizure of thirty-five cases of plate glass as part of customs enforcement.[3] Boyd, the owner, argued that this seizure violated the Fourth Amendment.

The Court said that the meaning of the Fourth Amendment should be understood by looking at English history. Even though the Fourth Amendment was almost a century old, there were no Court precedents about it, so the Court looked to earlier English law decisions. In England, it explained, when police were looking for evidence of a crime, courts granted "general warrants" for them to search people's houses and papers. No suspicion was required that a specific person being searched had committed a crime or had evidence of a crime. The Court described the strong reaction against general warrants. The English decision in *Entick v. Carrington* in 1765, it observed, was a pivotal moment changing this law.[4] That case was an action against trespassers who entered a person's home in November 1762 and broke open his desks and boxes and searched and examined his papers. The English court found this to be an impermissible trespass, and the Supreme Court in *Boyd* described it as one of "the landmarks of English liberty" that "was welcomed and applauded by the lovers of liberty in the colonies as well as in the mother country."[5]

This case, the Court said, was the key to understanding the Fourth Amendment: "every American statesman, during our revolutionary and formative period as a nation, was undoubtedly familiar with this monument of English freedom, and considered it as the true and ultimate expression of constitutional law."[6] This case was "in the minds" of those who drafted the Fourth Amendment, the Court said, and should be understood as the explanation "of what was meant by unreasonable searches and seizures."

What then did the Fourth Amendment mean? From the Court's perspective, it was entirely about preventing physical intrusions on a person's property without a warrant or probable cause. As the Court later explained in *Boyd,* the amendment was historically directed against general warrants that allowed searching everyone in a geographic area. And it was intended "to prevent the use of governmental force to search a man's house, his person, his papers, and his effects, and to prevent their seizure against his will."[7]

In one sense, this interpretation imposed a limit on police, but in another way it was quite enabling of law enforcement power. It limited police conduct by imposing a requirement of individualized suspicion for a search—they may search a person only if there is a basis for believing that individual has committed a crime or has evidence of a crime. This principle of individualized suspicion remains core to the Fourth Amendment to this day and is at issue in matters such as whether the government can impose random drug tests on individuals[8] or stop and examine everyone at checkpoints.[9]

In historical perspective, though, *Boyd* also was very empowering of police in that it meant that unless they physically trespassed, their action did not constitute a search—and no warrant or probable cause was required. One of the Court's most significant Fourth Amendment decisions in the first 170 years of American history was *Olmstead v. United States* in 1928.[10] Like so many cases of that era, *Olmstead* arose out of Prohibition. The seventy-two defendants were indicted and prosecuted for conspiring to violate the National Prohibition Act by unlawfully possessing, transporting, importing, and selling "intoxicating liquors." The Court said the defendants employed over fifty people, had many boats to transport liquor from British Columbia, a large "underground cache for storage and a number of smaller caches in that city, the maintenance of a central office manned with operators, and the employment of executives, salesmen, deliverymen dispatchers, scouts, bookkeepers, collectors, and an attorney."[11] The enterprise was, to say the least, very lucrative.

Roy Olmstead, the business's general manager, invested the most money to get it started and was seen as the leader of the operation. Police gained key evidence by wiretapping telephones. They tapped wires outside the houses of four individuals and those leading to their main office.[12] The Court stressed that "[t]he insertions were made without trespass upon any property of the defendants. They were made in the basement of the large office building. The taps from house lines were made in the streets near the houses."[13] For many months thereafter, the police listened in on conversations through these wiretaps. Through them they gained the crucial evidence against Olmstead and the other defendants for violating the Prohibition Act.

The question presented to the Court was whether this police wiretapping constituted a search and thus violated the Fourth Amendment because no warrant had been obtained. The Court, in a 5–4 decision, ruled that it was not a search, and no warrant had been needed, because the wiretapping had not involved a physical trespass on the property.

The Supreme Court was very conservative at this time. Beginning in the 1890s, the Court's majority was deeply committed to upholding an unregulated economy and regularly invalidated economic regulations. In 1905 the Court struck down a New York law that limited bakers to working no more than sixty hours a week or ten hours a day,[14] and in 1923 it declared unconstitutional a law requiring that women be paid a minimum wage.[15] In 1918 it invalidated the first federal law prohibiting the use of child labor.[16] But the Court was also conservative morally and politically: even as it was limiting congressional power to regulate the economy, it upheld federal laws prohibiting gambling and prostitution.[17] The year before its decision in *Olmstead*, the Court upheld the ability of states to impose involuntary sterilization on those it deemed to be intellectually disabled. In some of its most offensive language ever, it declared that "three generations of imbeciles are enough."[18]

In *Olmstead*, Chief Justice William Howard Taft wrote the opinion for the Court. Taft had been U.S. president from 1909 until 1913 and remains the only former president ever to serve on the Supreme Court. President Warren Harding nominated him to be chief justice in 1921. Taft was a larger-than-life figure in every way, including physically: standing just under six feet tall, he weighed over three hundred pounds. He was said to have a strong and imposing personality and to have managed the Court aggressively. Writing for the Court in *Olmstead*, he said: "The amendment does not forbid what was done here. There was no searching. There was no seizure. The evidence was secured by the use of the sense of hearing and that only. There was no entry of the houses or offices of the defendants."[19] The Fourth Amendment did not apply, the Court explained, since the police had eavesdropped by tapping into wires that were physically outside the home: "The intervening wires are not part of his house or office, any more than are the highways along which they are stretched."[20]

Justice Brandeis wrote a dissenting opinion, which is among the most admired opinions in American history. Brandeis, the Court's first Jewish justice, had been a prominent lawyer in Boston before becoming a justice in 1916. As an attorney, he had been involved in many progressive causes and was referred to as "the people's lawyer." His confirmation to the Court was bitterly contested, involving blatant anti-Semitism. I have always regarded Brandeis as one of the best and most eloquent writers ever to serve on the Court.

In his dissent in *Olmstead*, Brandeis stressed that the Constitution had to be adapted to changing circumstances and new technology. The fact that the Framers of the Fourth Amendment did not contemplate telephones or wiretapping should not prevent constitutional limits from being applied. Justice Brandeis wrote powerfully of the importance of protecting privacy from government intrusion: "The makers of our Constitution . . . sought to protect Americans in their beliefs, their thoughts, their emotions and their sensations. They conferred, as against the government, the right to be let alone—the most comprehensive of rights and the right most valued by civilized men." Thus "[t]o protect, that right, every unjustifiable intrusion by the government upon the privacy of the individual, whatever the means employed, must be deemed a violation of the Fourth Amendment."[21]

No one disputed that requiring the police to get a warrant before wiretapping would limit law enforcement and could hinder police investigations. But Justice Brandeis directly answered this concern: "It is, of course, immaterial where the physical connection with the telephone wires leading into the defendants' premises was made. And it is also immaterial that the intrusion was in aid of law enforcement." In one of the most eloquent opinions even written, he gave us an important reminder for all times: "Experience should teach us to be most on our guard to protect liberty when the government's purposes are beneficent. Men born to freedom are naturally alert to repel invasion of their liberty by evil-minded rulers. The greatest dangers to liberty lurk in insidious encroachment by men of zeal, well-meaning but without understanding."[22]

The conservative *Olmstead* decision, handed down in 1928, remained the controlling interpretation of the Fourth Amendment until 1967 when the Warren Court, in *Katz v. United States,* overruled it, holding that electronic eavesdropping is a search even if there is no physical trespass.[23] For those thirty-nine years, police could engage in wiretapping or other forms of eavesdropping without a warrant or probable cause so long as they did not enter a person's property.

In *Goldman v. United States,* handed down fourteen years after *Olmstead,* the Court found that the Fourth Amendment was inapplicable when the police put a listening device to a wall but did not trespass on the property.[24] Martin Goldman, an attorney, was suspected of engaging in bankruptcy fraud. The police got a building superintendent to allow them to install a listening device on the other side of a wall to Goldman's office. The device actually didn't work, but the police also placed a "dectaphone" against the wall.[25] Using this second device, the agents were able to overhear, and have a stenographer transcribe, several conversations in Goldman's office. Goldman was convicted on the basis of evidence gained through this eavesdropping.

The Court ruled that this eavesdropping did not violate Goldman's Fourth Amendment rights because police had made no trespass or a physical intrusion onto Goldman's property. Relying explicitly on *Olmstead,* the Court said the eavesdropping did not constitute a search within the meaning of the Fourth Amendment.

A decade later in 1952, in *On Lee v. United States,* the Court held that there was no search when an undercover agent entered a suspect's apartment with a hidden transmitter.[26] The undercover agent said he had been invited into the apartment, so "no trespass was committed."[27] The Court said that the Fourth Amendment did not protect the conversation and said that the use of "bifocals, field glasses or the telescope to magnify the object of a witness' vision is not a forbidden search or seizure, even if they focus without his knowledge or consent upon what one supposes to be private indiscretions."[28] This case was brought at the height of the McCarthy era, when merely being suspected of being a Communist was enough for people to lose their jobs. The Court's decision, approving such spying without a warrant or probable cause, reflected the repression of the times.

The Court's approach was formalistic: a physical trespass, however small, generally was a search, but without a trespass there was no search and the Fourth Amendment did not apply at all. In *Silverman v. United States*, the Court found that when a spike microphone was inserted into a party wall and intruded a small amount into the suspect's side of the wall, that was a search because it was "an actual intrusion into a constitutionally protected area."[29]

Actually, even after *Boyd* in 1886, not all trespasses were searches. In *Hester v. United States* in 1924, the Supreme Court held that a trespass onto the "open fields" of a person's property was not a search and the Fourth Amendment did not apply.[30] Justice Oliver Wendell Holmes, writing for the Court, declared that the "special protection accorded by the Fourth Amendment to the people in their 'persons, houses, papers and effects,' is not extended to open fields."[31] In fact, that is the law to this day: the Fourth Amendment applies to a person's home and the area—the curtilage—immediately around it, but not to the open fields on a person's property that is beyond the curtilage. No warrant or probable cause is required for the police to search in open fields even when a trespass occurs.

Especially as technology developed for wiretapping and electronic surveillance, *Olmstead* became very important in empowering law enforcement. It gave the police the power to gather information without the judicial checks of having to obtain a warrant or meet the constitutional standard of probable cause. And because the Fourth Amendment did not apply, any evidence gained was admissible against the defendant in court. In hindsight, it is surprising and disturbing that this restrictive approach to the Fourth Amendment lasted so long. Perhaps it survived because it allowed the justices to draw a clear line: without a trespass, the Fourth Amendment did not apply. That line also helped police as electronic eavesdropping technology advanced. The Court's interpretation of the Fourth Amendment did not change until the advent of a Court with a very different attitude toward the Constitution and the desire to protect rights from police intrusion.

The Privilege Against Self-incrimination

Fully a century after the Bill of Rights was enacted, including the Fifth Amendment's protection of the privilege against self-incrimination, the Supreme Court finally expressed concern about physically coercive police interrogations that led to confessions. The shocking cases that came before the Court usually involved Black suspects who confessed after being tortured by the police. Confronted with such police abuse, the Court had no choice but to enforce the Constitution.

The Court first dealt with the issue of confessions and the privilege against self-incrimination in 1884 in *Hopt v. People*.[32] Frederick Hopt was convicted of murder and sentenced to death in large part because a police detective testified that in his few minutes with Hopt, he had heard the man confess. Hopt argued that to use his statements against him violated his Fifth Amendment privilege against self-incrimination. The Court rejected this argument: "[a] confession, if freely and voluntarily made, is evidence of the most satisfactory character."[33] Hopt's confession was admissible, the Court said, because no "such inducements, threats, or promises" prompted his statement.[34] *Hopt* thus established that confessions are admissible, and that the privilege against self-incrimination does not matter if the suspect's confessing statements are voluntary.

Subsequently, the Court found that some confessions were involuntary and thus inadmissible as evidence. In *Bram v. United States* in 1897, it reaffirmed the general rule that a "confession must be free and voluntary—that is, not produced by inducements engendering either hope or fear."[35] Applying this standard, the Court found that John Bram's confession to a shipboard murder was not voluntary and therefore was inadmissible. Before Bram was questioned, the Court explained, the police detective took Bram from his jail cell to a private office and stripped him. Bram allegedly made the self-incriminating statements "either while the detective was in the act of so stripping him, or after he was denuded."[36] Allegedly, the detective told Bram that another man, a sailor, had said that Bram committed the murder. Bram replied, "He could not have seen me. Where was he?" The detective replied that the sailor had been at the wheel. Bram said, "Well, 'he could not see me from there.' "[37] The Court said that under the circumstances of the police questioning, this statement should not be regarded as voluntary. Bram's statement was deemed to have been obtained in violation of his privilege against self-incrimination, and his conviction was overturned.

Similarly, in *Wan v. United States* in 1924, the Court found the police practices so egregious as to make a confession involuntary.[38] On January 31, 1919, District of Columbia police learned that three men who lived at the Chinese Educational Mission had been murdered. A witness, a student at the mission, told police that he had seen Ziang Sun Wan there. The witness told the police that Wan lived in New York City. Police went to New York, taking the witness with them. The police broke into the room where Wan was staying, and though they had no warrant, they thoroughly searched Wan's possessions.

Wan, a twenty-five-year-old native of China, had been in the United States since 1916. At the time when the police found him in New York, he was suffering from the Spanish flu. The police asked him to go back to D.C. with them, but he said he was too sick. When the police told him that he was the suspect in a triple murder, he consented to go to D.C. When they arrived in Washington, Wan was not arrested but was taken to a secluded hotel room. Three detectives questioned him for five to six hours.

Wan, who remained very sick, was held incommunicado in the hotel room for a week without formal arrest. Every minute of the day and night, at least one police officer was in the room with him. All day long—and once after midnight—police questioned him. The Court said that on the eighth day of Wan's custody, the "questioning took a more excruciating form" as Wan was taken to the place where the murders occurred and "continuously for ten hours, . . . [he] was led from floor to floor minutely to examine and re-examine the scene of the triple murder and every object connected with it, to give explanations, and to answer questions. . . . From seven o'clock in the evening until five o'clock in the morning the questioning continued."[39]

At 5:20 a.m. the next day, Wan was taken from the mission to the station house and placed formally under arrest. There the interrogation resumed. The next day—his tenth day in detention—Wan was returned to the mission and was again questioned for many hours. On the eleventh day, Wan was formally interrogated at the station house by the detectives in the presence of a stenographer and made incriminating statements. On the twelfth day, the verbatim typewritten report of the interrogation (which was twelve pages long) was read to Wan in his cell at the jail. There he signed the report and initialed each page.

The confession was the only evidence against Wan. Based on it, he was convicted and sentenced to death. The court of appeals affirmed and said that a confession made by one competent to act is deemed voluntary. But the Supreme Court reversed, relying on its earlier decision in *Bram* to say that a confession gained by "compulsion must be excluded whatever may have been the character of the compulsion, and whether the compulsion was applied in a judicial proceeding or otherwise."[40] Under the circumstances of Wan's interrogation, the Court said, his confession could not be deemed voluntary: the

"undisputed facts showed that compulsion was applied."[41] It overturned his conviction.

Wan's interrogation occurred at a time of great anti-Chinese
racism, which was likely an important unstated part of the police
treatment of him. A dozen years later, in a series of cases, the Court
overturned the convictions of Black criminal defendants who had
been convicted on the basis of coerced confessions. In the 1930s the
Court for the first time acknowledged and dealt with the egregious
racism in the country's criminal justice system, such as in the Scottsboro Boys case in 1932 and in *Brown v. Mississippi* in 1936. The
Court's silence before then had been a refusal to even acknowledge
that racism.

Brown v. Mississippi was the first time the Supreme Court overturned a state court conviction on the ground that a confession had
been involuntary; it was thus an important decision about protections from extreme abusive police practices, especially directed at
people of color.[42]

On March 30, 1934, in Mississippi, a white man, Raymond Stewart, was murdered. The white deputy sheriff, Dial, accompanied
by others, went to the home of Arthur Ellington, a Black man, and
took him to the home of the victim. A number of other white men
gathered and accused Ellington of committing the murder. Ellington
denied having anything to do with it.

Members of the crowd, with the assistance of the deputy, hung
him by a rope from the limb of a tree. They let Ellington down, then
hung him again, "and when he was let down the second time, and
he still protested his innocence, he was tied to a tree and whipped."[43]
Ellington still did not confess. He was released and went home in
intense pain from his beating.

A day or two later, Deputy Sheriff Dial arrested Ellington. On
the way to the jail, Dial stopped and severely whipped Ellington and
told him the whipping would continue until he confessed. Ellington
then agreed that he would confess to any statement that the deputy
dictated.[44]

Two other area Black men, Ed Brown and Henry Shields, received similarly horrific treatment from Deputy Sheriff Dial. On the night of April 1, Dial took them into custody and, accompanied by a number of other white men, made Brown and Shields remove their clothes. "They were laid over chairs and their backs were cut to pieces with a leather strap with buckles on it."[45] They were told that the whipping would continue until they confessed to the murders. They ultimately confessed.

Brown, Shields, and Ellington were indicted on April 4. They pleaded not guilty. The court appointed an attorney to defend them. The trial began the next morning, April 5. Signs of the rope on Ellington's neck were still plainly visible. He, Brown, and Shields repeated everything that the deputy sheriff told them to say. On April 6 the three defendants were found guilty and sentenced to death. The only evidence against them was their confessions.[46]

The Supreme Court overturned their convictions. It noted that the trial court knew how the confessions had been obtained, yet it had nonetheless convicted the defendants and sentenced them to death. The Court declared that "[t]he conviction and sentence were void for want of the essential elements of due process."[47] The case was sent back to the trial court. The three defendants, rather than risk a retrial and the death penalty, pleaded "no contest" to manslaughter. They respectively spent six months, two and a half years, and seven and a half years in prison. The prosecutor in the case, who obtained their convictions by using confessions gained from torture, was John Stennis, who would later serve as a U.S. senator for forty-two years.

The Court did impose a limit on police conduct in *Brown v. Mississippi,* but we will never know how many others, especially individuals of color, suffered similar treatment and got no relief from the Court. Nor will we ever know how many individuals were pressured into making false confessions, even if they were not tortured. The restriction on police in *Brown* was important, but a wide array of abusive police interrogation techniques remained unrestrained. Although some state courts found confessions to be coerced and not voluntary, many, as reflected by *Brown* and so many other cases, imposed no limits.[48]

Based on *Wan v. United States* and *Brown v. Mississippi*, the Supreme Court in a handful of other cases found confessions to be involuntary. They all involved egregious police misconduct, and they usually involved white police officers and Black suspects.

In *Chambers v. Florida* in 1940, four young African American men had been convicted of murder. They confessed after being subjected to six days of police questioning and being kept awake all night.[49] They said that they had been subjected to physical abuse, which the sheriffs denied. The Court, citing *Brown v. Mississippi*, said the confessions had not been voluntary and hence had to be excluded. Justice Hugo Black eloquently concluded the Court's opinion: "Due process of law, preserved for all by our Constitution, commands that no such practice as that disclosed by this record shall send any accused to his death. No higher duty, no more solemn responsibility, rests upon this Court, than that of translating into living law and maintaining this constitutional shield deliberately planned and inscribed for the benefit of every human being subject to our Constitution—of whatever race, creed or persuasion."[50]

Ward v. Texas, in 1942, concerned William Ward, an African American man, who was convicted for the murder of Levi Brown, a white man, in rural eastern Texas.[51] The crucial evidence against Ward was his confession. Ward was arrested without a warrant, "taken from his home town, driven for three days from county to county, placed in a jail more than 100 miles from his home, questioned continuously, and beaten, whipped and burned by the officer to whom the confession was finally made."[52] Ward was told that if he did not confess, there would be mob violence. Although the sheriffs denied it, one of the officers at the jail said he saw cigarette burns on Ward.

The Court overturned Ward's conviction, saying that the "effect of moving an ignorant negro by night and day to strange towns, telling him of threats of mob violence, and questioning him continuously" had led Ward to say that he would be glad to make any statement that the county attorney wanted. The Court said this confession had not been free and voluntary but was the product of coercion and duress.[53]

The Court found that confessions were obtained in ways that violated the privilege against self-incrimination, but only in these egregious cases. It never found psychological or even less extreme physical coercion to be constitutional violations. Nor did it acknowledge, let alone address, the underlying role of race in police interrogations. The Court's silence about all this meant that police faced minimal checks as they questioned suspects.

Remedies for Police Misconduct

Rights are meaningless unless there are remedies to their violation. Unless adequate remedies are in place, nothing will deter police from violating constitutional rights, and nothing can be done to help those whose rights have been violated.

Before the Warren Court began in 1953, two basic remedies for police misconduct developed, and they remain the primary remedies to this day. One is the exclusionary rule, which states that evidence gained by unconstitutional police actions must be excluded from trial. The other remedy is the criminal or civil liability of police officers under federal law. Of course, states can create their own liability under state criminal or tort law, but such cases would not come to the Supreme Court, which is limited to deciding federal law issues. Both of these remedies saw important developments before 1953, and the Warren Court built on them in imposing greater limits on police conduct.

The first remedy, the exclusionary rule, is often traced back to the 1892 Supreme Court decision *Counselman v. Hitchcock,* which held that the privilege against self-incrimination protects a person from being required to incriminate himself or herself before a grand jury.[54]

In a criminal case, it said, the government cannot compel grand jury testimony to obtain information, then use that information to gather evidence against a defendant.[55] Ever since, the law has been that the privilege against self-incrimination "prohibits the derivative use, as well as the direct use, of compelled utterances."[56] In other words, prosecutors cannot benefit from using evidence obtained as a result of constitutional violations.

In *Chambers, Brown, Counselman,* and other cases regarding coerced confessions, the Court insisted on excluding unconstitutionally obtained information from use as evidence at trial. The Court overturned the convictions that had been obtained with such evidence; the state then had to release the individual or try the person again, without the tainted evidence. The latter was sometimes impossible because frequently there was no other evidence. The Court first announced this as a remedy for searches in violation of the Fourth Amendment in *Weeks v. United States* in 1914.[57]

Police arrested Fremont Weeks, a shipping employee in Missouri, for engaging in illegal gambling. While Weeks was being held at the police station, officers went to his home. They did not have a search warrant; nor did they have Weeks's permission to enter. A neighbor told them where they could find a key, and they used it to enter the house. The officers thoroughly searched Weeks's house and seized various things they found there. Later that day they returned, again without a warrant, and someone let them in. They again thoroughly searched Weeks's room and took away things they found.

The Court said the police violated Weeks's Fourth Amendment rights by entering, searching, and seizing documents without a warrant. Therefore that evidence should not have been admissible at trial, the Court declared: "To sanction such proceedings would be to affirm by judicial decision a manifest neglect, if not an open defiance, of the prohibitions of the Constitution, intended for the protection of the people against such unauthorized action."[58] In other words, where courts rely on evidence that government agents obtain by violating constitutional rights, they participate in or become complicit in unconstitutional actions.

Ever since the Warren Court expanded the application of the exclusionary rule, it has been enormously controversial. Those attacking it lament that it allows guilty, and sometimes even dangerous individuals, to go free. But when the Supreme Court created the exclusionary rule, it did not mention that concern. It primarily focused on the unfairness of convicting someone with illegally obtained evidence and on the undesirable taint to the judiciary of convictions based on such evidence. Later, the exclusionary rule was defended as a way of deterring police misconduct. In fact, in recent years, the Roberts Court has dramatically narrowed the scope of the exclusionary rule, saying that its sole purpose is to deter police misconduct. It is often forgotten that the exclusionary rule traces back more than a century to a quite different foundation.

The exclusionary rule had one very important limit: it did not apply to state or local police. The evidence gained as a result of their violations of the Fourth Amendment, no matter how outrageous, was admissible at trial. After the Supreme Court applied the exclusionary rule to the federal government in 1914, it made no effort to require that state courts follow it as well. Most did not. In 1949 the Court noted that thirty-one states rejected the exclusionary rule in state courts; only sixteen applied it.[59] Thus in the majority of states, evidence that police gained as a result of illegal searches and arrests was admissible against a criminal defendant.

In *Wolf v. Colorado* in 1949, the Court considered whether to apply the exclusionary rule to the states through the due process clause of the Fourteenth Amendment.[60] The case involved a doctor who was convicted for conspiracy to perform abortions, which were then outlawed. Police obtained the evidence against the doctor through an illegal search. The Court, in an opinion written by Justice Felix Frankfurter, rejected the argument that state courts were obligated to exclude evidence gained as the result of an illegal search:

"We hold . . . that in a prosecution in a State court for a State crime the Fourteenth Amendment does not forbid the admission of evidence obtained by an unreasonable search and seizure."[61] Not for another thirteen years, or 170 years after the adoption of the Fourth Amendment, would the Court require that all U.S. courts must exclude evidence gained through such police misconduct.

. . . .

IN ADDITION TO the exclusionary rule, a second remedy exists to potentially deter police violations of the Constitution: the possibility that police officers have civil liability and could even face criminal prosecution. But before the 1970s, civil liability for police officers under federal law was almost nonexistent, no matter how egregious their misconduct. Under state law, one might possibly bring a tort suit against police officers in state court. But these suits seem not to have been brought very often, let alone successfully. It is impossible to imagine that a Black individual who had been subjected to abusive police conduct would be able to successfully sue a white police officer in a state court in Alabama or Mississippi or other southern or even northern states. Especially in the South, judges were elected and knew that ruling in favor of civil rights plaintiffs would doom their judicial careers. Besides, Blacks were systematically excluded from juries.

In the most egregious instances, where police officers violated not only a person's civil rights but also a criminal statute, federal criminal prosecution was possible. But not until 1945, in *Screws v. United States,* did the Court hold that police officers can be criminally prosecuted under federal law for violating the constitutional rights of suspects, and given the horrific facts, it is astounding that the decision was 5–4.[62] Criminal prosecutions of police officers are exceedingly rare. Even today, indicting and gaining a conviction against a police officer is unusual. The four officers charged with beating Rodney King in Los Angeles in 1991 were acquitted in state court, and when re-prosecuted in federal court, only two were convicted. The officer who killed Michael Brown in Ferguson, Missouri, in 2014 was not indicted. In 2020 only one of the officers responsible for the death of Breonna Taylor in Louisville, Kentucky, was indicted, and that was on relatively minor charges.

The facts of *Screws v. United States* are very disturbing but reflect abusive behavior that was all too common. M. Claude Screws was the sheriff of Baker County, Georgia. Together with Frank Jones, a police officer, and Jim Bob Kelley, a special deputy, they arrested Robert Hall, who was Black, on suspicion of stealing a tire. Late one night they came to his home and took him in handcuffs to the station house. As Screws, Jones, and Kelley were pulling Hall from the car, they began "beating him with their fists and with a solid-bar blackjack about eight inches long and weighing two pounds."[63]

In a story that still has resonance today, the officers later claimed that Hall had used insulting language and reached for a gun, but no gun ever was found, and Hall was in handcuffs. After they knocked Hall, still handcuffed, to the ground, they beat him for fifteen to thirty minutes until he was unconscious. They then dragged him feet first into the jail, threw him onto the floor of a cell, and left him to die. Someone eventually called an ambulance to take Hall to the hospital. He died there within an hour without ever regaining consciousness.

The officers were prosecuted under a federal statute, adopted in 1866, that made it a crime for government officials or those acting with state authority to violate the constitutional rights of individuals on the basis of race. The maximum punishment was a fine of not more than $1,000 or imprisonment for not more than a year or both. The defendants were convicted in federal court, lost in the federal court of appeals, and sought Supreme Court review.

The Supreme Court ruled that the police officers were acting "under color of law" even though they were clearly violating both the Constitution and Georgia state law. Surprisingly, three justices— Owen Roberts, Felix Frankfurter, and Robert Jackson—dissented and would not allow federal law to be used in such instances. They said the sole remedy should be under state law. They believed that

"Georgia alone has the power and duty to punish."[64] They did not address or even allude to the unlikelihood that Georgia, in 1945, would prosecute white police officers for their treatment of a Black suspect, even treatment that proved lethal.

These three justices likely thought of themselves as civil libertarians. Roberts had consistently voted with the conservatives until 1937, when he dramatically switched sides and cast the decisive votes to uphold New Deal programs and to allow state laws protecting workers and consumers. Frankfurter, while a Harvard law professor, had fought publicly for justice for Nicola Sacco and Bartolomeo Vanzetti, two men who were wrongly convicted and executed. As a justice, though, Frankfurter was a conservative who frequently professed the need for judicial restraint and consistently ruled against interpreting the Constitution to limit police conduct.

And in 1944, when the Supreme Court upheld the evacuation of Japanese Americans from the west coast during World War II, Jackson had dissented.[65] Following the war, Jackson would serve as the chief U.S. prosecutor at the Nuremberg trials of Nazi war criminals. But in 1945 he was unwilling to allow a federal criminal prosecution of the police officers in *Screws* even when they killed a man in cold blood. For these three justices, deferring to state governments— federalism—was more important than enforcing federal civil rights law. Their attitude reflects a Supreme Court that so often in American history has subordinated constitutional rights, and especially the rights of people of color, to empowerment of police.

Screws was important for opening the door to federal criminal prosecution of police, and it paved the way for allowing civil suits as well. But the reality is that from 1787 to 1953, federal criminal prosecutions and federal civil liability for police officers were extremely rare.

· · · · · · · · ·

IN HINDSIGHT, it is stunning that in the nineteenth century the Supreme Court heard virtually no cases in which it interpreted the constitutional provisions protecting criminal suspects and criminal defendants. Never did the Court acknowledge the racism that, from the earliest days of American history, pervaded police departments and infected much policing. Even after organized police forces developed, the Court did not impose significant constraints on police until the Warren Court. Surely that was not because police always complied on their own with the Fourth, Fifth, and Sixth Amendments. The justices lived in a society that largely accepted what the police were doing, and they, too, seemed to share that sentiment.

But the importance of the Supreme Court's silence should not be underestimated. By declining to enforce the Constitution's limits on police conduct, the Court was empowering police and letting officers know that they could violate the Constitution with impunity. And by failing to limit racist policing, the Court allowed it to continue unchecked.

We have no way of knowing how many people like Robert Hall were killed at the hands of police. We have no way of knowing how many people were beaten or had their constitutional rights violated. We have no way of knowing how many innocent people were convicted, imprisoned, and even put to death because of police misconduct. But everything that we do know says that the number was significant, especially for people of color.

Part III

THE WARREN COURT

Finally Enforcing Constitutional Protections and Remedies

6

"Each Era Finds an Improvement in Law for the Benefit of Mankind"*

Applying the Bill of Rights to State and Local Police

O N MAY 23, 1957, THREE ARMED CLEVELAND POLICE officers arrived at Dollree Mapp's home, having received a tip that Virgil Ogletree was hiding in her house.[1] Ogletree was a rival of the gambling racketeer Don King (who would later become famous as a boxing promoter). Three days earlier King's home had been bombed, and Ogletree was wanted for questioning. Mapp, an African American woman who was divorced from a former boxer, and her daughter lived on the upper floor of the two-family dwelling. She rented the lower floor to boarders. Police thought Ogletree was hiding in the apartment of the downstairs tenant.

Upon arriving at the house, the officers knocked on the door and demanded entrance. Mapp called her lawyer, who told her not to admit the officers unless they showed her a search warrant. Based on this advice, she refused to let them enter. It is not clear why Mapp

---

* Clarence Earl Gideon spoke these words to his lawyer, Abe Fortas, and they appear on Gideon's tombstone, which was placed on his grave by the American Civil Liberties Union.

was so resistant to allowing the police to enter or why she could so easily reach a lawyer.

The officers stayed outside the house. About three hours later four, or perhaps even more, officers arrived, and they again sought entrance. The officers knocked and announced their presence. When Mapp did not come to the door immediately, the officers forced the door and entered. Mapp's lawyer was present outside the house, but the police would not let him see her or enter the house.

At the moment when the police broke into the hall, Mapp was coming down the stairs from the upper floor on her way to the front door. Following the advice of her lawyer from their phone conversation, Mapp—whose life experience likely had taught her to be wary of police—demanded to see a search warrant. An officer held up a paper that he claimed was a warrant. Mapp grabbed it and stuck it in her blouse. An officer struggled with Mapp and took the paper back. It later came out that it was not a warrant; none ever had been obtained.

The officer handcuffed Mapp "because she had been belligerent"— a familiar term when police rationalize such an arrest—in not giving back the "warrant."[2] Mapp reported that an officer had "grabbed" her and "twisted [her] hand," and that she "yelled [and] pleaded with him" because "it was hurting."[3] In handcuffs, Mapp was forcibly taken upstairs to her bedroom, where the officers looked through her photo album and her personal papers. They searched through a dresser, a chest of drawers, a closet, and some suitcases. They searched through her child's bedroom, the living room, and the kitchen. They then searched the basement, where they found a trunk and searched it too.

In a suitcase in Mapp's bedroom, the police found four books, including Jimmy Harrington's *Memories of a Hotel Man*—now considered vintage 1930s erotica—that they thought to be obscene. Mapp was arrested for possessing obscene material and was prosecuted for this crime. She was convicted and sentenced to one to seven years in prison. Mapp said that these books and also other things that police found in the suitcase, such as evidence of illegal gambling activity, had been left there by a former tenant.

The police were at Mapp's house to look for a man who was wanted in connection with a bombing. Since the alleged suspect was not, for lack of a better term, a Houdini-like contortionist, he could not plausibly have been hiding in places the police searched, like the photo album, the dresser drawers, and the suitcase. Although the police did find Virgil Ogletree in the lower-floor apartment, they nonetheless searched every part of Dollree Mapp's apartment, not to mention the contents of her drawers and suitcases. And they did all this without a search warrant.

When the case came before the Supreme Court, the issue was whether the evidence used against Mapp at trial—the contents of the suitcase—should be excluded because the police search unquestionably violated the Fourth Amendment's prohibition of unreasonable searches and its requirement for a valid warrant. No one in the litigation denied that the police in their search violated the Fourth Amendment. The issue was the nature of the remedy and also whether the evidence could be used against Mapp because it was the fruit of an illegal search. As explained in Chapter 5, in *Wolf v. Colorado* in 1949, the Court held that the exclusionary rule—the requirement that evidence obtained as the result of an illegal search be excluded from use against a criminal defendant—did not apply to state and local governments.[4]

· · · · · · · · ·

BY 1961, when the Supreme Court decided *Mapp v. Ohio,* its composition had changed greatly, especially with the appointment of Chief Justice Earl Warren in 1953 and Justice William Brennan in 1956. In *Mapp,* the Court overruled *Wolf* in a 6–3 decision and held that evidence obtained in violation of the Fourth Amendment must be excluded from use at trial regardless of whether the police are federal, state, or local employees. The exclusionary rule, which had hitherto applied to Fourth Amendment violations only by federal law enforcement, would now apply to state and local governments as well.[5]

Justice Tom Clark, who had been appointed to the bench by President Harry Truman and was never regarded as a liberal, wrote for the Court and declared that the "same sanction of exclusion" should apply against state and local police. He spoke forcefully of the need for keeping evidence that had been gained illegally from being used and said that without the exclusionary rule the prohibition of searches and seizures would be "valueless and undeserving of mention in a perpetual charter of inestimable human liberties." Unless evidence gained in violation of the Fourth Amendment was excluded, he continued, "the freedom from state invasions of privacy would be so ephemeral and so neatly severed from its conceptual nexus with the freedom from all brutish means of coercing evidence as not to merit this Court's high regard as a freedom 'implicit in the concept of ordered liberty.' "[6]

The Court said that the exclusionary rule is an "essential part" of the Fourth Amendment.[7] It is meant to deter police from engaging in illegal searches or arrests because of the knowledge that any evidence gained as a result could not be used at trial. Also, it is meant to shield the courts from being tainted by convictions of people based on evidence gained through police misconduct. The Court spoke of the imperative of "judicial integrity"[8] and quoted the eloquent 1927 words of Justice Louis Brandeis: "Our government is the potent, the omnipresent teacher. For good or for ill, it teaches the whole people by its example. . . . If the government becomes a lawbreaker, it breeds contempt for law; it invites every man to become a law unto himself; it invites anarchy."[9] The federal government had operated under the exclusionary rule for over a half-century, the Court noted, and that had not hampered its law enforcement efforts. The Court rejected the claim that applying the exclusionary rule to state and local police would unduly hinder their work.

Mapp v. Ohio was important in another way as well: it ushered in the Warren Court's significant expansion of the rights of crim-

inal suspects and criminal defendants. The conventional understanding is that the Warren Court was the only Court in American
history that consistently and significantly limited police behavior and
expanded the rights of people suspected or accused of crimes. This
is largely true, but it also oversimplifies history because both at the
beginning and at the end of this period, the Warren Court also took
important steps to empower the police. Only for a relatively short
time during the 1960s did the Court seek to change police conduct
and expand constitutional rights under the Fourth, Fifth, and Sixth
Amendments.[10]

   During these years, the Court imposed significant restrictions on
policing in the United States. Starting in 1962, the Court had a liberal majority, and it continued until the resignations of Chief Justice
Earl Warren and Justice Abe Fortas in 1969. This was an exceptional
period in American history, so far never again witnessed, in which
the majority of the justices were concerned about protecting criminal defendants from police and were especially attentive to racial
issues in society. It does not seem coincidental that Dollree Mapp
was Black.

· · · · · · · · · ·

ANY UNDERSTANDING of the Warren Court must start with its
chief.[11] Earl Warren, born in 1891, grew up in Bakersfield, California, and attended the University of California, Berkeley School of
Law. Warren spent much of his career as a prosecutor, serving as a
deputy district attorney and then a district attorney. He was elected
attorney general of California in 1938. As attorney general during
World War II, he supported the forced relocation and incarceration
of Japanese Americans from the west coast, for which he is much
criticized.[12] Some 110,000 Japanese Americans—aliens and citizens,
adults and children—were uprooted from their lifelong homes and
placed in what President Franklin Roosevelt himself referred to as
concentration camps.[13] Warren played a key role in urging this policy, claiming that the absence of any domestic sabotage by Japanese

only showed the deviousness of their plotting. Warren wrote to officials in Washington that "there is more potential danger among the group of Japanese who were born in this country than the alien Japanese."[14] Given this background, it was surprising that he would later lead the Court's efforts to constrain the police and to expand the rights of those accused of crimes.

Warren was elected governor of California in 1942. In 1948 he was the Republican candidate for vice president, running on the ticket with Thomas Dewey. In 1952 he sought the Republican presidential nomination that went to Dwight Eisenhower. As part of Warren's endorsement for Eisenhower, Warren was reportedly told that he would be nominated to the Supreme Court at the first opportunity.[15] In the summer of 1953, Chief Justice Fred Vinson died of a heart attack, and Eisenhower apparently initially balked at replacing him with Warren.[16] But he ultimately kept his word and made a recess appointment of Warren to be chief justice on October 5, 1953. Warren was formally nominated on January 11, 1954, and was confirmed by the Senate on March 1, 1954. Just two and a half months later, on May 17, the Supreme Court handed down its unanimous opinion in *Brown v. Board of Education,* which declared unconstitutional state laws requiring segregated public schools.[17] Warren wrote the opinion in what is regarded as one of the most important Supreme Court decisions in American history.

Although nothing in Warren's background would have predicted that he would become a liberal Supreme Court justice, he was never conservative in the mold of California politicians like Richard Nixon and Ronald Reagan. Nixon came to prominence in the late 1940s for his red-baiting and strong anti-Communist views; Reagan, a former actor, would run for governor by running against permissiveness and against student protesters. Warren represented a more moderate part of the Republican Party.

He joined a Court where all the other justices had been appointed by Franklin Roosevelt or Harry Truman. But it would be a mistake to assume that all of them were liberal, especially in the area of policing and criminal justice. Justice Jackson and especially Justice Frankfurter often voted in a quite conservative direction. Frankfurter dissented in *Mapp v. Ohio* and in some of the Warren Court's most significant decisions expanding the judicial protection of voting rights.[18] Frankfurter was an enigma, a liberal Harvard law professor who as a justice was committed to judicial restraint and protecting states' rights.[19] Jackson died in October 1954, so he and Warren did not serve together on the Court for long.

When Warren arrived, the Court had two reliably liberal justices: William O. Douglas and Hugo Black. Douglas had been appointed by President Roosevelt in 1939 to take the seat of Justice Louis Brandeis. Only forty years old when confirmed, Douglas had been a Yale law professor and chairman of the Securities and Exchange Commission. He would serve on the Court for more than thirty-six years, until 1975—the longest tenure of any Supreme Court justice ever. Douglas was controversial for his outspoken liberal views and also for his personal life, having been divorced three times and married four times.[20] He consistently voted for limiting police power, sometimes in lone dissents.[21] In *Terry v. Ohio,* for example, only Justice Douglas dissented from the Court's expansion of police power to stop and frisk individuals without needing to have probable cause.

Douglas was usually joined by Justice Hugo Black, who had been a U.S. senator from Alabama when Roosevelt appointed him to the Court in 1937. He often sided with the liberal justices in voting for racial equality, freedom of speech, and especially in applying Bill of Rights protections to state and local governments. At least until his last years on the bench, Black was a consistent, crucial vote for limiting police power. But it also should be remembered that Black wrote, and Douglas joined, the opinion in *Korematsu v. United States* in 1944, which upheld the forced relocation of Japanese Americans from the west coast during World War II.[22] *Korematsu,* one of the worst Supreme Court decisions in American history, reveals that even the civil libertarians on the Court were prepared in some cases to uphold sweeping exercises of government power, based entirely on race, to detain people who were innocent of any crime.

The tensions among these four justices—Frankfurter, Jackson, Douglas, and Black—were enormous. It was said that they were like scorpions in a bottle.[23] This made it all the more remarkable that Warren, soon after arriving at the Supreme Court, found a way for all nine justices to agree in *Brown v. Board of Education*. Warren, who had spent his career as a politician, saw the need for unanimity in this landmark ruling to end segregated schools and persuaded reluctant justices to join his opinion holding that separate can never be equal in public education.[24]

In 1956 Warren, Black, and Douglas were joined by a fourth liberal justice, when Eisenhower nominated New Jersey Supreme Court justice William Brennan.[25] Justice Sherman Minton, a Truman appointee, retired in October, less than a month before the November presidential election. Eisenhower felt pressure to appoint a Catholic; there had been no Catholic on the Court since Justice Frank Murphy, a liberal, died in 1949. Also, appointing Brennan, a Democrat, gave Eisenhower the chance to seem bipartisan. In our deeply polarized time, it is hard to imagine a president appointing a justice from the other political party. Eisenhower made Brennan a recess appointment to the Court on October 15, just weeks before the election. Although it could not have been predicted, Brennan remained a staunch liberal, in criminal justice and every area, until he retired in 1990. Brennan also was notable for his ability to sometimes put together coalitions to reach unexpected liberal results, likely through a combination of persuasive legal arguments and great personal charm.[26]

During this era, Warren, Douglas, Black, and Brennan were part of the majority in every important decision expanding the rights of criminal defendants. But it takes five votes to get a majority, and they did not have a consistent fifth in the first years of the Warren Court. Eisenhower's other picks—Republicans John Marshall Harlan, Charles Evans Whittaker, and Potter Stewart—were much more likely to rule for the police than to expand the constitutional rights of criminal suspects and defendants. In *Mapp v. Ohio,* for example, Justice Harlan wrote the dissent, arguing that state courts should decide for themselves whether to exclude evidence gained from illegal police searches; he was joined by Justices Frankfurter and Whittaker. In the famous decision *Miranda v. Arizona* , Harlan and Clark dissented; Whittaker was no longer on the bench.[27] Whittaker had struggled with the burdens of being a Supreme Court justice and was notorious for his indecisiveness, suffering a nervous breakdown in 1962. He resigned from the Court, saying it was due to exhaustion and stress.

Not until that year, when Felix Frankfurter retired and President Kennedy nominated Arthur Goldberg, did the Court have a consistent fifth vote to significantly change the law with regard to policing. Goldberg, who had been a prominent labor lawyer in Chicago and then Kennedy's secretary of labor, joined Warren, Black, Douglas, and Brennan to create the liberal Warren Court. Goldberg, for example, wrote the majority opinion in the important 1964 case *Escobedo v. Illinois,* which expanded the right to counsel of those accused of crimes.[28]

Goldberg served on the Supreme Court for only three years. President Johnson persuaded him to resign from the bench to become United Nations ambassador, apparently convincing him that he had a unique opportunity to end the Vietnam War and bring world peace. Goldberg's departure allowed Johnson to appoint his close friend Washington lawyer Abe Fortas to the Court. Fortas, a prominent and highly regarded attorney, had argued the landmark *Gideon v. Wainwright* case, which held that state courts must provide counsel to all defendants who are tried for crimes where there are possible prison sentences.[29] Fortas spent four years on the Court, and like Goldberg, he was a consistent liberal vote.

For a short time, at the end of this era, the Court had a sixth liberal justice: Thurgood Marshall was confirmed in 1967. The vacancy had opened when President Johnson named Ramsey Clark to be U.S. attorney general. Clark's father was a sitting Supreme Court justice, Tom Clark. A Truman appointee, Clark felt that his being on the Court while his son was attorney general would create a conflict of interest in too many cases. After all, the Department of Justice is involved in a significant percentage of the cases heard by the Court. Interestingly, both of the vacancies that emerged on the Court during Johnson's presidency were ones he manufactured: by persuading Goldberg to depart and inducing Clark to retire.

To fill Clark's seat, Johnson appointed Thurgood Marshall, the first African American to serve as a Supreme Court justice. Marshall, who was fifty-nine when appointed, had a legendary career and is one of the small number of justices who would have had a major place in history even if he had never served on the Court. He had been the architect of the NAACP's effort to end segregation and had argued, and won, many landmark cases, including *Brown v. Board of Education*. No justice before or since had accomplished more as a lawyer or had more renown before going on the Court. Yet his confirmation became a fierce battle as southern senators strongly resisted putting a Black man on the Court.

· · · · · · · · ·

WHEN COMMENTATORS refer to the liberalism of the Warren Court, especially in the area of criminal justice, they are speaking of the period from 1962 until 1969. Warren and Fortas left the bench in 1969 and were replaced by two Nixon appointees, Warren Burger and Harry Blackmun. At that point, the Warren Court was ended, both in name and in jurisprudence. But what occurred in those seven years was remarkable.

That seven-year period was the only time in American history when the Court had a solid liberal majority. The fact that it had never happened before, and has not happened since, is crucial to understanding the Court and more generally, the American legal system. In those few years, the Court changed the law in many areas, such as civil rights, civil liberties, voting rights, and privacy. But in no area was the impact of that liberal majority more notable than in criminal justice. It has shaped perceptions of the Supreme Court ever since. Liberals have continued to turn to the courts for social progress, inspired by what was accomplished during the Warren Court era. Conservatives have railed against liberal judicial activism, even though since 1969 the Court consistently has had a majority of justices appointed by Republican presidents and their activism—striking down laws and overruling precedents—has very much been in a conservative direction.

The Warren Court's most significant change in criminal justice, one that we take largely for granted today, was the application of the Bill of Rights to the states. Originally the Bill of Rights, as explained earlier, was thought to apply only to the federal government. State and local governments were governed by their own constitutions and laws, which sometimes protected rights guaranteed in the Bill of Rights but often did not. In the late nineteenth century, the Supreme Court opened the door to applying the Bill of Rights to the states by saying that the Fourteenth Amendment protects "liberty" from state infringements and this includes those parts of the Bill of Rights which the Court deems to be fundamental. Termed *incorporation,* the idea is that the word *liberty* in the amendment's due process clause "incorporates" these rights and protects them from violation by state or local governments. But until the Warren Court, and really not until the 1960s, the Court used this authority only sparingly. The result was that the constraints on policing found in the Constitution did not apply to state and local law enforcement.

The Warren Court, which saw major problems in policing at the state and local levels, changed that. In *Mapp v. Ohio* in 1961, it held that the exclusionary rule, as a constitutional remedy for Fourth Amendment violations, is incorporated into the Fourteenth Amendment and hence applies to state and local police officers as well.

That same year, in *Irvin v. Dowd,* the Court for the first time held that the Sixth Amendment right to an impartial jury applies in state court.[30] In a small town in Gibson County, Indiana, Leslie Irvin had been convicted of murder and sentenced to death. But in advance of his trial, the case was substantially publicized, which might have induced the jurors to believe that the defendant was guilty. In fact, eight of the twelve jurors thought the defendant was guilty before the start of the trial.[31] The Court, noting a "pattern of deep and bitter prejudice" throughout the community, overturned the conviction and remanded the matter for a new trial.[32]

What began as a trickle with *Mapp* soon turned into a flood of decisions by the Warren Court, reflecting its conviction that no level of government should be able to violate the fundamental liberties contained in the Bill of Rights. In *Robinson v. California* in 1962, the Court held for the first time that the Eighth Amendment's prohibition of cruel and unusual punishment applies to state laws.[33] Lawrence Robinson, a Black man, had been convicted under a California law that made it a criminal offense for a person to "be addicted to the use of narcotics." He was convicted, not for selling or even possessing illegal drugs, but for having needle marks on his arms and scars indicating he was a drug user. The Court stressed that Robinson had been convicted for the status of being a drug addict and not for any observed illegal conduct. The Court said that constituted cruel and unusual punishment: imprisoning a person for drug addiction, "even though he has never touched any narcotic drug within the State or been guilty of any irregular behavior there, inflicts a cruel and unusual punishment in violation of the Fourteenth Amendment."[34] In *Robinson*, by applying the prohibition of cruel and unusual punishment to the states, the Court laid the groundwork for challenging the constitutionality of prison conditions, lengthy prison sentences, and the death penalty.

· · · · · · · · ·

OF ALL THE Warren Court's decisions finding Bill of Rights provisions to be incorporated, the most important, by far, was that of *Gideon v. Wainwright* in 1963.[35] Two years earlier someone had broken into a pool hall and bar in Panama City, Florida, and stolen five dollars in change and a few bottles of beer and soda from the pool room. Clarence Earl Gideon, age fifty-one, was charged with the crime. Gideon, who had dropped out of school after eighth grade, had a number of prior convictions for theft and larceny. He occasionally worked as an electrician but was indigent and could not afford a lawyer. He requested that an attorney be appointed to represent him, but the trial court refused, and none was provided to him.

Earlier, in *Powell v. Alabama* in 1932, the Court had affirmed the right of defendants to counsel as provided by the due process clause, but only in cases where the defendant faced a possible death sentence.[36] In *Betts v. Brady* in 1942, the Court had ruled 6–3 that the Sixth Amendment right to counsel did not apply in state courts except in cases where a death penalty was sought.[37] Because Gideon did not face a death sentence, based on *Betts,* the Florida court said Gideon had no right to a lawyer paid for by the state government.

So Gideon represented himself at trial. He was convicted of theft, and the judge sentenced him the maximum of five years in prison. After losing his appeals in the Florida courts, he filed a handwritten petition for Supreme Court review. The Court decided to hear his case and appointed the renowned Washington attorney (and later Supreme Court justice) Abe Fortas to represent him. Only lawyers can appear before the justices, and in situations like this, where a nonlawyer has a case granted by the Supreme Court, the Court appoints an attorney to handle the matter.

In *Gideon v. Wainwright*, the Court unanimously held that the government is obligated to provide an attorney not only to criminal defendants who face the death penalty, but also to those who face imprisonment. Justice Black took the rare opportunity to convert a dissent into a majority opinion; his dissent in *Betts v. Brady* laid the foundation for his majority opinion in *Gideon v. Wainwright.* Justice Black powerfully declared in *Gideon*: "[R]eason and reflection require us to recognize that in our adversary system of criminal justice, any person haled into court, who is too poor to hire a lawyer, cannot be assured a fair trial unless counsel is provided for him. This seems to us to be an obvious truth." The right of one charged with a crime to counsel is fundamental and essential to fair trials, the Court explained. "The noble ideal" that "every defendant stands equal before the law . . . cannot be realized if the poor man charged with crime has to face his accusers without a lawyer to assist him."[38]

After the Supreme Court overturned Gideon's conviction, the case was sent back to the Florida courts for a new trial. Gideon, now represented by a lawyer, was acquitted. His experience was typical: *Gideon*'s assurance of counsel to all facing a prison sentence has undoubtedly meant, in the years since, that many who otherwise would have been convicted and imprisoned, some wrongly, have remained free. Many people who before *Gideon* might have been arrested were not because police now knew that that individual would be represented by counsel. In a criminal justice system where almost all cases are disposed of by guilty pleas—97 percent in federal court and 94 percent in state court—the presence of defense attorneys frequently makes an enormous difference in the nature of the plea deal and the length of the sentence.

None of these effects can be measured. It is impossible to know how many people have been acquitted who would have been convicted, or how many cases were not brought, or how many sentences were not imposed. But nor can these benefits be denied by anyone with even a passing familiarity with the criminal justice system. In a society where race so correlates with poverty, *Gideon*'s assurance of counsel has unquestionably benefited Black and Brown criminal suspects and defendants.

The importance of *Gideon* as a symbol also cannot be overstated. An adversary system of justice requires some semblance of equality between the two sides. *Gideon* is a crucial attempt to make that requirement a reality. It holds that anyone, however poor, who faces the power of the state to take away his or her liberty is entitled to representation. The Constitution imposes many prohibitions on what government can do, but it creates relatively few affirmative duties.

Gideon v. Wainwright does just that, requiring that government pay for a lawyer for those who cannot afford one.

Yet while *Gideon* is rightly celebrated, the shortcomings in its implementation must be lamented. A decade and a half ago, on the fortieth anniversary of *Gideon,* an American Bar Association study concluded: "Forty years after *Gideon v. Wainwright,* indigent defense in the United States remains in a state of crisis, resulting in a system that lacks fundamental fairness and places poor persons at constant risk of wrongful convictions. . . . Funding for indigent defense services is shamefully inadequate."[39] As an attorney who sometimes handles criminal appeals, I have represented clients who I believed to be innocent who were convicted because of grossly ineffective assistance of counsel,[40] and some who received death sentences.[41] As Senator Patrick Leahy has remarked: "Too often individuals facing the ultimate punishment are represented by lawyers who are drunk, sleeping, soon-to-be disbarred or just plain ineffective. Even the best lawyers in these systems are hampered by inadequate compensation and insufficient resources to investigate and develop a meaningful defense."[42]

What explains *Gideon*'s flaws? Most of all, American society has failed to adequately fund the right to counsel that *Gideon* promised.[43] In 2009 the National Right to Counsel Committee reported that "inadequate financial support continues to be the single greatest obstacle to delivering 'competent' and 'diligent' defense representation."[44] Many excellent public defender services exist, but they carry "astonishingly large caseloads."[45] Appointed counsel, who represent criminal defendants in the absence of public defenders, are often paid so little that only those attorneys who cannot find other clients are available, and their compensation is so inadequate as to provide insufficient incentives for them to perform the needed work.[46]

The Court imposed on states the duty to provide counsel without providing a funding source. It was left to each state, and in many instances each county, to find ways to fund attorneys for indigent criminal defendants.[47] In the decades following *Gideon,* this burden

rose tremendously as a result of an enormous increase in criminalization, prosecution, and incarceration. Nationally, five times more
prisoners are incarcerated today than just a few decades ago.[48] The
U.S. incarceration rate is among the world's highest, five to ten times
higher than rates in other industrialized nations.[49] The war on drugs
in the 1980s played a huge role in dramatically increasing incarceration, as did punitive laws like "three strikes," which required mandatory life imprisonment for a third felony conviction, and mandatory
minimum sentences for many offenses. In other words, regardless of
whatever burden on state treasuries the *Gideon* Court might have
envisioned, the dramatic growth in criminal laws and criminal prosecutions in the decades since have made that burden vastly greater
than expected.

Among the many interests that compete for scarce government
resources, indigent criminal defendants are hardly a powerful political constituency.[50] The inadequacy, often gross inadequacy, of
the funding of defense counsel for them is hardly surprising. The
Supreme Court left it to the states to provide defense counsel, and
states often will choose the most inexpensive way to meet this obli-
gation. This pattern has important implications for limits on policing
because the criminal defense lawyer's job is to assert the constitutional rights of his or her client.

· · · · · · · · · ·

IN THE SIX YEARS after *Gideon,* the Warren Court continued
to find that provisions of the Bill of Rights apply to state and local
governments. In 1964 in *Malloy v. Hogan,* the Court held that the
privilege against self-incrimination was incorporated into the due
process clause.[51] A New Jersey state court judge had asked William Malloy to answer questions about his alleged involvement
in gambling, but Malloy refused to answer, invoking his privilege
against self-incrimination. The judge held him in contempt. The
Supreme Court had held twice before that the privilege against self-
incrimination does not apply to state and local governments.[52] Now

when it ruled in *Malloy,* in an opinion written by Justice Brennan, the Court expressly overruled those previous decisions. It found that state and local courts must comply with the Fifth Amendment's privilege against self-incrimination.

In 1965 the Court held that the confrontation clause—the right to confront one's accusers and adverse witnesses—applies in state courts as well as federal.[53] And in *Klopfer v. North Carolina* in 1967, the Court held that the Sixth Amendment right to speedy trial was also incorporated into the due process clause.[54] In the tumultuous year 1968, as the Warren Court neared its end, it held in *Duncan v. Louisiana* that the Sixth Amendment right to a jury trial in a criminal case applies to the states.[55] The right to trial by jury, the Court explained, is meant to "prevent oppression by the Government" and is "essential for preventing miscarriages of justice and for assuring that fair trials are provided for all defendants."[56]

By the end of the Warren Court, almost all the provisions of the Bill of Rights had been deemed incorporated and found to apply to the states. Later the Court found that the Second Amendment right to bear arms[57] and the Eighth Amendment right against excessive fines applies to the states as well.[58] Today, there are only three provisions of the Bill of Rights that have never been incorporated and that still do not apply to state and local governments: the Third Amendment right to not have soldiers quartered in a person's home, the Fifth Amendment right to grand jury indictment in criminal cases, and the Seventh Amendment right to jury trial in civil cases. Incorporation began in the late nineteenth century, but especially for the rights of criminal suspects and criminal defendants, most of the application to the states of these provisions occurred during the Warren Court.

The decisions applying the Bill of Rights to state and local governments now seem unassailable and are hardly criticized. I have rarely heard anyone call for these decisions to be reconsidered or overruled.[59] The Bill of Rights is regarded as the charter of fundamental rights that all Americans possess. It is unthinkable that state and local governments could violate them and not be held account-

able. Yet it is important to remember that it was not until the Warren Court, in 1961, that unconstitutionally obtained evidence had
to be excluded in state court; not until 1963 that states had to provide an attorney in cases involving possible prison sentences; and
not until 1964 that states were required to recognize the privilege
against self-incrimination. Because many of these provisions limit
police conduct, they are critically important ways in which the Warren Court advanced the rights of criminal suspects and defendants.
And this crucial aspect of the Warren Court's jurisprudence has not
been eroded over time. None of these decisions about incorporation
have been overruled or even narrowed.[60]

7

Both Limiting and Empowering Police

The Warren Court and the Fourth Amendment

I N 1967 AND 1968, THE WARREN COURT WAS RESPONSIBLE for expanding the scope of Fourth Amendment protections more significantly than ever before in American history, but also for greatly enlarging police power. The two cases, *Katz v. United States*[1] and *Terry v. Ohio*,[2] were enormously important in shaping what police do and in how courts approach the Fourth Amendment, and they remain so to this day. That the Warren Court's civil libertarian majority, in *Katz*, dramatically increased the protections of the Fourth Amendment was not surprising, but that it also expanded police power by authorizing police to engage in "stop and frisk" without probable cause, in *Terry*, is a puzzle that must be addressed.

Charles Katz, a preeminent college basketball handicapper, lived in an apartment building on Sunset Boulevard in Los Angeles. On most days he would walk from his building down the street to a cluster of three public telephone booths. He would enter one of these booths and place telephone calls, usually to Miami and Boston, during which he would transmit wagering information. In February 1965 he stepped into one of the phone booths to place some bets on basketball games. He had no idea that police were listening in on his call, let alone that he was initiating a chain of events that would dramatically change the law concerning the Fourth Amendment.

The FBI suspected Katz of being part of a multicity gambling operation.[3] FBI agents were investigating his gambling activities and gathering evidence. They focused on the phone booths, but they did not get a warrant to listen in on his calls. Because of the Supreme Court's 1928 decision in *Olmstead v. United States*, they did not need a warrant unless they physical trespassed on Katz's property.[4]

Instead, the agents asked the telephone company to put one of the telephone booths out of order. It agreed. The agents then affixed an electronic listening and recording device on top of and between the two remaining booths. They could then hear Katz's conversations regardless of which of the two remaining booths he used. The FBI stationed one agent outside Katz's apartment to observe him when he left. That agent notified another agent, who then activated the listening device on the phone booths.

The elaborate wiring system worked—the FBI overheard and recorded Katz's conversations. Katz was arrested for violating federal gambling law. His lawyer moved to suppress the evidence as having been gained in violation of the Fourth Amendment. His motion contained an amusing typo: "a man has as much right to bet alone in a public telephone booth as in his own home."[5]

The federal district court, following clear Supreme Court precedent, found that there had been no search because there had been no trespass on Katz's property. Katz was convicted and appealed. The federal court of appeals agreed.

But the Supreme Court, in one of the most significant Fourth Amendment decisions in American history, reversed and overturned the earlier precedents that held that a search requires a physical invasion of a person's property. In an opinion written by Justice Potter Stewart, the Court said that the earlier decisions "have been so eroded by our subsequent decisions that the 'trespass' doctrine there enunciated can no longer be regarded as controlling."[6] Stewart, an Eisenhower appointee, is perhaps most famous for having declared about obscenity that he couldn't define it, but "I know it when I see it."[7] Overall Stewart, over the course of his career, was much more likely to side with police than with those suspected and accused of crimes. We know now that initially there were just four votes to overrule *Olmstead,* and it appeared that an evenly divided Court was going to split 4–4 and affirm Katz's conviction. There were only eight justices because Justice Thurgood Marshall, who had just been confirmed, could not participate because he had been involved in the case in his prior role as the solicitor general. But Stewart's law clerk, Laurence Tribe (later to become a preeminent constitutional law scholar and Supreme Court advocate), drafted an opinion that focused on the Fourth Amendment's protection of privacy and explained why *Olmstead* needed to be overruled.[8] Tribe's approach persuaded Stewart and ultimately seven of the eight justices.

The Court said in *Katz* that by listening to and recording Katz's words, the government had violated his privacy, and "the fact that the electronic device employed to achieve that end did not happen to penetrate the wall of the booth can have no constitutional significance."[9] The Fourth Amendment protects people, not property, the Court stressed. A person's Fourth Amendment rights do not depend on where he or she is at the time of the government intrusion, nor on whether a physical trespass occurs. The Court concluded: "These considerations do not vanish when the search in question is transferred from the setting of a home, an office, or a hotel room to that of a telephone booth. Wherever a man may be, he is entitled to know that he will remain free from unreasonable searches and seizures."[10]

The Court, though, did not elaborate on how to determine what constitutes a search under this standard. Justice Harlan did this in a concurring opinion, and this opinion has been the controlling standard for the Fourth Amendment ever since. Harlan, a Republican appointed by Eisenhower, championed what he saw as judicial restraint and often dissented in Warren Court decisions limiting police. Yet in *Katz* he was with the majority, and he said that Fourth Amendment protection against a search has a "twofold requirement, first that a person have exhibited an actual (subjective) expectation of privacy and, second, that the expectation be one that society is prepared to recognize as 'reasonable.' "[11]

. . . .

THERE IS MUCH to praise in the Court's approach and Justice Harlan's standard. In determining whether a "search" exists for purposes of the Fourth Amendment, the test focuses the inquiry on privacy, where it should be, rather than on trespass onto property. Under the Court's approach in *Katz*, wiretapping and electronic eavesdropping qualify as searches, even if the police carry them out without physically entering a person's premises.

This test is the reason the Fourth Amendment applies to the technology of the twenty-first century. In 2018 in *Carpenter v. United States,* the Supreme Court held that when police obtain a large amount of stored cellular location information about a person, that is a search.[12] The *Carpenter* decision, one of the most significant in applying the Fourth Amendment to the technology of the twenty-first century, is very much based on *Katz.* The Court held that police may obtain cellular location information—information that can be used to determine where a person was at a particular time—only if they have a warrant based on probable cause or if emergency circumstances justify allowing the search without a warrant. The ruling is a strong affirmation of the right to privacy under the Fourth Amendment.

Timothy Carpenter was suspected of committing a series of armed robberies; perhaps ironically, given the case, some of the stores he robbed were RadioShacks, a chain that sold do-it-yourself electronic components. The FBI went to his cell phone companies and got the cell phone tower records—the cell site location information—that revealed his location and his movements for 127 days. The FBI obtained this information without a warrant from a judge.[13] The cell tower information was crucial evidence used to convict him and to sentence him to 116 years in prison.

Every time we use our cell phone—to send and receive calls or texts or emails or access the internet—it connects to cell towers. In fact, even if we are not using the phone, if it is simply turned on, it is connecting to cell towers. The records—generated hundreds and sometimes thousands of times per day—include the precise GPS coordinates of each tower as well as the day and time the phone tried to connect to it. Through this information, our location may be determined and our movements tracked at almost any point in time. Police frequently use this technology: in 2016 Verizon and AT&T alone received about 125,000 requests for cellular information from law enforcement agencies.

The issue before the Supreme Court in *Carpenter v. United States* was whether the Fourth Amendment requires police to obtain a warrant to access this information. In *Carpenter* there was no phys-ical trespass; under the Court's approach to the Fourth Amend-ment before *Katz,* that meant there would have been no search. But the Court based its 5–4 decision squarely on *Katz* and the Fourth Amendment's protection for the reasonable expectation of privacy. It reversed the lower courts and ruled in favor of Carpenter. Chief Jus-tice Roberts wrote the opinion, joined by Justices Ginsburg, Breyer, Sotomayor, and Kagan. That Roberts joined the liberal justices may seem surprising, but just a few years earlier it was Roberts who wrote the opinion for the Court holding that police can look at the contents of a suspect's cell phone only if there is a warrant or if an emergency makes it impossible to get one.[14] Roberts stressed that a person's cell phone contains the "privacies of life," and an enormous amount of personal information can be gained by looking at its content.

Likewise, in *Carpenter,* Roberts stressed that accessing a person's cellular location information for a long period of time intrudes on privacy. Tracking the location of a cell phone for 127 days "provides an all-encompassing record of the holder's whereabouts, . . . which reveals the familial, political, professional, religious, and sexual associations."[15] Roberts stressed once more that location tracking lets police learn the privacies of a person's life.

The Court's rulings limiting police authority to look at the contents of a cell phone or to obtain cellular location information have caused me to remark, and not in jest, that one can predict the Supreme Court's decisions concerning the Fourth Amendment based on whether the justices can imagine it happening to them. All the justices own cell phones, but rarely are they or their children subjected to police stops.

• • • • • • • • •

THE VIRTUE OF the *Katz* approach to the Fourth Amendment is its focus on privacy and its capacity to be extended to situations like that in *Carpenter*. The central insight of *Katz,* that the Fourth Amendment protects persons and not property, surely is right. The disadvantage of *Katz* is the inherent difficulty in determining what constitutes a reasonable expectation of privacy and when courts should recognize that a person has a legitimate subjective expectation of privacy. Justice Harlan's approach requires both: the person must have a subjective expectation of privacy, and that expectation must be one that society regards as reasonable.

But how are these criteria to be applied and decided? Can the government, pursuant to this test, extinguish privacy under the Fourth Amendment just by telling people not to have any expectations in a particular situation? How can a society where ever less seems to be private determine what expectation of privacy is "reasonable"? Is it an empirical question of what people actually expect? If so, how would that be determined? Or is it just a sense by the Court of what people should expect? If so, how is that to be determined? And how is it to be decided whether a person has exhibited a sufficient desire for privacy to qualify it as a subjective expectation?[16]

At times, the *Katz* test has been used in a troubling way to deny Fourth Amendment protection, when the Court concludes that a "reasonable expectation of privacy" was absent. One such case was *Florida v. Riley* in 1989.[17] Michael Riley lived in a mobile home in Pasco County, Florida, where he kept a greenhouse on his property, some ten to twenty feet behind the mobile home. A wire fence surrounded both the mobile home and the greenhouse, and the property was posted with a DO NOT ENTER sign. The greenhouse was covered by corrugated roofing panels, some translucent and some opaque. At the time relevant to this case, two of the panels, amounting to about 10 percent of the roof area, were missing. A police helicopter flew four hundred feet over the property and peered into the greenhouse through the missing panels. The officers spotted marijuana plants growing there.

The Court held that the search did not fall within the meaning of the Fourth Amendment. Despite Riley's efforts to protect his privacy on the ground, the Court said that he had no reasonable expectation of privacy from observation by a helicopter or a low-flying airplane.[18]

Similarly, in *California v. Greenwood* in 1988, the Court held that when police searched a person's garbage that was left on the street for pickup, there was not a search, and no warrant was required.[19] The defendant had placed their garbage on the street "for the express purpose of having strangers take it" and so "could have had no reasonable expectation of privacy in the inculpatory items that they discarded."[20] Once more the Court used the *Katz* reasonable-expectation-of-privacy test to rule in favor of police. The Court has said that "[w]hat a person knowingly exposes to the public, even in his own home or office, is not a subject of Fourth Amendment protection."[21]

Having established that people have no reasonable expectation of privacy for what is in public or even what third parties see, the Court held in *Smith v. Maryland* in 1979 that police do not need a warrant to install a device with the phone company that records all the phone numbers that a person calls or returns calls from.[22] People have no legitimate expectation of privacy in the numbers they dial on their telephones, the Court explained, because when they use the telephone, they voluntarily convey those numbers to the telephone company: "a person has no legitimate expectation of privacy in information he voluntarily turns over to third parties."[23]

The point is that the reasonable-expectation-of-privacy test has often been used to help police and to the detriment of criminal defendants. In 2018, Justice Clarence Thomas sharply criticized the *Katz* test and explicitly said that he would overrule it and would find a search only if the government invades property rights. The test "has no basis in the text or history of the Fourth Amendment," he wrote, and quoted those who called it "an unpredictable jumble," "a mass of contradictions and obscurities," "riddled with inconsistency and incoherence," "flawed to the core," and "inspired by the kind of logic that produced Rube Goldberg's bizarre contraptions." He concluded "the *Katz* test is a failed experiment."[24]

But if *Katz* is ever overturned, what would be the alternative to its focus on privacy? How would the legal system then decide what constitutes a search under the Fourth Amendment? Justice Thomas would go back to the law as it was before 1967 and determine searches based on whether police physically trespassed. But today police rely on technology that gathers information without needing a physical intrusion, so it would make no sense to require such an intrusion in order for the Fourth Amendment to apply. The focus on police trespass was very problematic when it was created, and it makes no sense at all in a world where the police can use stored cellular information and drones to gather information. The *Katz* test, focusing on the reasonable expectation of privacy, for better and for worse, is likely to continue to the be the central criterion in determining whether Fourth Amendment protections apply.

· · · · · · · · ·

IF IN *KATZ* the Warren Court substantially expanded the scope of Fourth Amendment protections and limited police, the same cannot be said for *Terry v. Ohio*.[25] Quite the contrary, in *Terry*, in 1968, the Court greatly expanded the powers of police and contributed significantly to race-based policing. It often is forgotten that *Terry* was decided by the Warren Court, with a solid liberal majority. In fact, the Court's opinion was written by Chief Justice Earl Warren, a year before he stepped down from the bench. Even liberal heroes like William Brennan and Thurgood Marshall joined the majority opinion.

By 1963, Martin McFadden had been a policeman in Cleveland, Ohio, for thirty-nine years and a detective for thirty-five. On October 31, in plain clothes, he was patrolling a downtown vicinity for shoplifters and pickpockets, as he had done for decades. At approximately two-thirty in the afternoon, as he would later testify, he saw two Black men, John Terry and Richard Chilton, standing on the corner of Huron Road and Euclid Avenue. Officer McFadden had never seen the two men before, he would later say, and could not explain what first drew his attention to them: "when I looked over they didn't look right to me at the time."

McFadden decided to watch them. One of the men walked down Huron Road, past some stores. The man paused for a moment and looked into a store window, then walked on a short distance. Then he turned around and walked back, pausing to look into the same store window. He rejoined his companion at the corner, and the two conferred briefly. Then the second man went through the same series of motions, strolling down Huron Road, looking in the window, walking on a short distance, turning back, peering in the store window again, and returning to the corner to confer. The two men repeated this ritual alternately five or six times apiece. At one point, while they were standing together on the corner, a third man approached and engaged them briefly in conversation, then left them.

This went on for ten to twelve minutes, and then Terry and Chilton walked off together. McFadden later testified that he suspected the two men of "casing a job, a stick-up," and that he considered it his duty as a police officer to investigate further. McFadden followed Chilton and Terry and saw them stop to talk to the same man who had conferred with them earlier on the street corner. McFadden approached the three men, identified himself as a police officer, and asked for their names. McFadden then grabbed Terry, spun him around so that they were facing the other two, and patted down the outside of his clothing. McFadden felt what seemed to be a pistol in the left breast pocket of Terry's overcoat. He reached inside the overcoat pocket but was unable to remove the gun. At this point, keeping Terry between himself and the others, the officer ordered all three men to enter the store, apparently so he could question and frisk them. As they went in, McFadden removed Terry's overcoat completely, took a .38-caliber revolver from the pocket, and ordered all three men to face the wall with their hands raised.

McFadden proceeded to pat down the outer clothing of the other two men. He discovered another revolver in the outer pocket of Chilton's overcoat, but no weapons on the third man. The officer testified that he patted the men down only to see whether they had weapons and that he did not put his hands beneath the outer garments of either Terry or Chilton until he felt their guns. McFadden seized Chilton's gun, asked the store proprietor to call a police wagon, and took all three men to the station, where Chilton and Terry were formally charged with carrying concealed weapons.

The men, through their lawyers, asked the court to exclude the guns from being used as evidence against them on the ground that McFadden's frisk violated the Fourth Amendment. Doubtless Terry and Chilton were "seized" when McFadden stopped them: they were not free to leave; they obviously could not just walk away from the armed police officer. Doubtless McFadden searched the men; that was how he found the guns. The Court acknowledged that "it is nothing less than sheer torture of the English language to suggest that a careful exploration of the outer surfaces of a person's clothing all over his or her body in an attempt to find weapons is not a 'search.' "[26] The Court also recognized the tremendous intrusion of such frisks: "Moreover, it is simply fantastic to urge that such a procedure performed in public by a policeman while the citizen stands helpless, perhaps facing a wall with his hands raised, is a 'petty indignity.' It is a serious intrusion upon the sanctity of the person, which may inflict great indignity and arouse strong resentment, and it is not to be undertaken lightly."[27]

The Fourth Amendment explicitly requires that all searches and seizures be based on "probable cause." That standard was clearly not met here. The men had done nothing but walk down the street in a way that made McFadden suspicious, but that is neither a crime nor evidence of a crime.

Thus, the issue before the Supreme Court was whether police can stop and frisk a person without having to meet the Fourth Amendment standard of probable cause. The Court said that in resolving this issue, it needed to balance the interests of law enforcement and public safety against the intrusion a person suffers when being stopped and frisked. The Court came down solidly on the side of the police. Chief Justice Warren wrote for the Court that "the proper balance" allows police to conduct "a reasonable search for weapons for the protection of the police officer, where he has reason to believe that he is dealing with an armed and dangerous individual, regardless of whether he has probable cause to arrest the individual for a crime."[28]

In other words, police do not need to have probable cause to seize a person by stopping him or her. Nor is it required that the officers have probable cause to frisk the person. As long as an officer has "reasonable suspicion" that the person has committed or might commit a crime, there can be a stop. And as long as an officer has "reasonable suspicion" that the person might have a weapon, there can be a frisk.

The Court concluded by declaring that a police officer who observes unusual conduct that leads him to believe that "criminal activity may be afoot and that the persons with whom he is dealing may be armed and presently dangerous" may pat down the person to see if there are weapons. Chief Justice Warren left no ambiguity: "Such a search is a reasonable search under the Fourth Amendment, and any weapons seized may properly be introduced in evidence against the person from whom they were taken."[29]

· · · · · · · · ·

AS A MATTER of constitutional law and in its effects on policing, *Terry v. Ohio* was a terrible decision. First, the Fourth Amendment clearly specifies that "probable cause" is the standard for searches and arrests. Terry and Chilton were searched and arrested, but no one, not even the State of Ohio, claimed that there was probable cause. As Justice Douglas argued in his dissent, the Fourth Amendment allows no basis for any other standard.[30] The Court said it was choosing this lower standard by balancing law enforcement interests against privacy interests. But never did the Court explain why the traditional standard of probable cause—with its long history and its enshrinement in the Constitution—was insufficient to meet the needs of law enforcement. Also, the Court assumed but did not justify why the "balancing" inquiry was an appropriate basis for abandoning the long-standing constitutional standard. The Court was saying, in effect, that a standard prescribed in the Constitution, one that had been followed since 1791 when the Fourth Amendment was adopted, could be abandoned if on balance a different standard were in some way better. That radical proposition had potentially enormous consequences for all constitutional rights, but the Court never justified it.

Nor did the Court explain why it chose to strike the balance in favor of police. It recognized that stops and frisks are intrusive and degrading, but nonetheless it said that they were allowed without probable cause. The concern (and it was borne out by later cases) was that whenever the Court balanced law enforcement needs against protecting privacy, the former would always win out and leave little of individual rights.

Second, the Court did not define "reasonable suspicion" in 1968 in its Terry decision, and it has not done so since. It often has said that "reasonable suspicion" requires less than probable cause but more than a mere hunch.[31] But that gives little guidance to police officers in the field needing to decide when someone can be stopped and frisked. In 2020 the Court said there is no precise definition of reasonable suspicion: "In fact, we have stated that reasonable suspicion is an 'abstract' concept that cannot be reduced to 'a neat set of legal rules,' and we have repeatedly rejected courts' efforts to impose a rigid structure on the concept of reasonableness."[32]

This ambiguity gives police officers enormous latitude in deciding whether there is reasonable suspicion. Police can easily stop almost anyone at any time as long as they can articulate some basis for suspicion, even if they make it up after the fact to justify the admissibility of evidence against the criminal defendant, and courts are reluctant to exclude evidence. Police can easily frisk anyone if they later say they saw a bulge that could have been a weapon. It thus became very easy for police to stop anyone and do a frisk. If they find nothing, the person can leave. If they find something, they can make up a basis for suspicion.

Third, the Court predictably opened the door to racialized policing. Everything we know about policing—then and now—tells us that when American police have unfettered discretion, they will use it to the detriment of people of color. The Court's majority opinion recognized this point in only one sentence: "The wholesale harassment by certain elements of the police community, of which minority groups, particularly Negroes, frequently complain, will not be stopped by the exclusion of any evidence from any criminal trial."[33] But this completely misses the point. Even if the application of the exclusionary rule will not stop police from harassing people of color, that does not mean that the Court should increase the latitude of the police to use race as a basis for police searches and seizures. There are two distinct questions: Do people have the right to be free from stops and frisks unless there is probable cause, and if so, what is the remedy when the police violate this right? The Court recognized the problem of police harassment based on race, but then said that because the remedy of the exclusionary rule might not stop it, the Court would empower the police to stop and frisk without probable cause. Having recognized the problem of race-based policing, the Court should have acted to control it, not to increase it.

Even though it was completely predictable that stop and frisk would be used in a racially discriminatory manner, the Court did not impose any limits on race-based stops and frisks. Indeed, the NAACP Legal Defense Fund, in its "friend of the court" brief in

Terry v. Ohio, addressed the racial consequences of allowing police to stop and frisk: "The evidence is weighty and uncontradicted that stop and frisk power is employed by the police most frequently against the inhabitants of our inner cities, racial minorities and the underprivileged."[34]

Study after study has shown that *Terry* has indeed fostered race-based policing. Police are far more likely to stop and frisk Black and Latinx than white individuals. In 2013 a lawsuit, *Floyd v. City of New York,* was brought in federal court to challenge the New York Police Department's practices with regard to stops and frisks.[35] The plaintiffs collected detailed evidence concerning police stops in New York between January 2004 and June 2012. During this time, the NYPD conducted over 4.4 million *Terry* stops. In 52 percent of the 4.4 million stops, the person stopped was Black, in 31 percent the person was Hispanic, and in 10 percent the person was white. In 2010 New York City's resident population was roughly 23 percent Black, 29 Hispanic, and 33 white. In 23 percent of the stops of Blacks, and 24 percent of the stops of Hispanics, the officer recorded using force. That figure for whites was 17 percent.

Based on this data, Judge Shira Scheindlin ruled against the city and found that it was engaged in civil rights violations. Mayor Michael Bloomberg aggressively defended the NYPD's stop and frisk policy, including asking the court of appeals to disqualify Judge Scheindlin. But while this was going on, Bloomberg's term ended, and soon after taking office in January 2014, Mayor Bill De Blasio settled the lawsuit and agreed to end the NYPD's use of stop and frisk.

The NYPD in 2004–12 is representative of how the power to stop and frisk is used throughout the country. In one study, Emma Pierson and the Stanford Open Policing Project analyzed data on vehicle stops from twenty-one state patrol agencies and thirty-five city police departments from 2011 to 2018.[36] They found that Black drivers were stopped 43 percent more often than white drivers relative to their share of the population. The more encounters there are with police, the greater the chance that police violence will occur.

Terry v. Ohio is thus directly linked to the fact that Black and Latinx people are far more likely to die at the hands of police than are white individuals.[37]

Why did the Warren Court rule the way it did? Interestingly, in Chief Justice Warren's initial drafts, the opinion was different.[38] In his initial draft, "Warren wrote that the constitutional requirement is probable cause, explicitly rejecting the view that police only need a 'reasonable suspicion.'"[39] Memos and drafts were extensively circulated among the justices, after which Justice Brennan produced a draft, substantially different from the earlier versions, that shifted to "reasonable suspicion" as the test for stops and frisks. Constitutional scholar John Barrett, after reviewing the papers of the justices, concluded: "Warren, the author of *Terry,* actually used much of an opinion that Justice Brennan, who is not identified as an opinion writer in the case, had ghost-written for Warren and persuaded him to use."[40]

Justice Brennan, one of the most liberal ever to serve on the Supreme Court, was the real author of the expansion of police power in *Terry v. Ohio.* Even Justice Marshall, the greatest civil rights lawyer in American history, joined this majority opinion. Only Justice Douglas dissented. We will never know why liberal justices decided to abandon probable cause in favor of the less protective "reasonable suspicion" standard and so to empower police. But, as always, context is enormously important. The period in which *Terry v. Ohio* was decided was extraordinarily tense, with much social unrest.[41] In 1965 a riot erupted in the Watts neighborhood of Los Angeles beginning a series of urban disturbances that would affect almost every major city over the next few years. In the spring of 1967, in reaction to the perception that crime and violence were out of control, President Johnson created a Commission on Law Enforcement and Administration of Justice, chaired by Attorney General Nicholas Katzenbach, to study it and find solutions. That summer saw more riots, in Newark, Detroit, and many other American cities. Anti-Vietnam war protests were by then rife throughout the country, to the point that they were a key factor in President Johnson's decision in March

1968 not to run for reelection. On April 4, Dr. Martin Luther King, Jr., was assassinated, leading to further unrest. Robert F. Kennedy was assassinated in June. Richard Nixon ran for president on a platform of what he called "law and order," aimed explicitly against the Warren Court and its decisions. It was in this year and in this context that the Supreme Court considered and decided *Terry v. Ohio,* and widespread concerns about crime and social order likely affected the justices' thinking.

The Court may also have been reacting to the great criticism of its earlier decision in *Mapp v. Ohio,* as well as its decisions in *Escobedo v. Illinois* and *Miranda v. Arizona.* The justices were repeatedly attacked for handcuffing the police and for being soft on criminals. In light of this criticism, they likely were not willing to take another step to significantly limit law enforcement.

Terry v. Ohio was a pivotal moment in regard to the Court's refusal to impose limits on police, marking the end of the Warren Court era. The police practice that the Court approved was not consistent with the Fourth Amendment and would inevitably be used to the detriment of people of color. Just a year later, the Berger Court would follow, and then the Rehnquist Court and now the Roberts Court. Each successive Court has been less likely to impose controls on police or limit their authority to stop and frisk. Quite the contrary, each subsequent Court has so expanded the police power to stop and frisk that today officers can stop almost anyone at any time. The Court in *Terry,* by giving police this permission, very much empowered race-based policing in the United States.

8

Miranda

Trying to Solve the Problem of Coercion in Police Interrogations

EW DECISIONS OF THE SUPREME COURT HAVE BECOME more embedded in popular culture than *Miranda v. Arizona* in 1966.[1] This decision prescribed warnings that the police must give whenever they question a person who is in custody. These warnings are familiar to anyone who has watched police shows and likely to many who never have done that. Enormously controversial when it was decided, it became a symbol of the Court's perceived leniency toward criminals and handcuffing of the police. Yet in hindsight it is questionable how much it actually accomplished and whether the Court did enough to make a difference.

Prior to *Miranda*, incriminating statements from a suspect would be admitted into evidence so long as they were "voluntary." But determining what was voluntary was often elusive. Torturing someone to get a confession, obviously, makes any statement obtained not voluntary. But what about the myriad ways that police can psychologically pressure a person? Officers might lie to the suspect about the evidence against him or her, or about what witnesses or other suspects have said. They might invoke what is best for the suspect's family members.[2] At some point the length of the interrogation may indicate that the suspect's statements were made involuntarily.[3] And should a suspect's mental condition, including mental illness, matter?[4]

This myriad of factors, and the inherent unpredictability as to how they would be applied, caused many to think that voluntariness was not a sufficient test to protect the privilege against self-incrimination. Many felt that with its focus on the totality of the circumstances, the voluntariness test led to "intolerable uncertainty" as to whether confessions would be admissible.[5] It did not give police guidance as to what was allowed and what was not. Nor did trial judges have a clear rule to apply in deciding whether an incriminating statement should be admitted into evidence.

In 1964, in *Massiah v. Illinois,* the Court held that without the presence of a lawyer, the police may not attempt to deliberately elicit statements from a person who has been indicted.[6] That same year the Court went further and, in *Escobedo v. Illinois,* held that even before there is an indictment, criminal defendants have the right to have an attorney present while police are questioning them in custody.[7]

At about two-thirty a.m. on the night of January 19, 1960, Chicago police officers arrested Danny Escobedo and took him to the police station. Danny's brother-in-law had been fatally shot several hours before. Danny, a twenty-two-year-old Chicano, had no prior criminal record or known contact with the police. He refused to answer police questions and was finally released at about five in the afternoon after his lawyer obtained a state court writ of habeas corpus.

Less than two weeks later, on January 30, Benedict DiGerlando, who was in police custody, told the police that Escobedo had fired the fatal shots. Between eight and nine that evening, Escobedo and his widowed sister were arrested and taken to police headquarters. Police handcuffed Escobedo and told him that DiGerlando had informed the police that he was the one who fired the gun.

Escobedo told the police, "I am sorry, but I would like to have advice from my lawyer."[8] In fact, soon after Escobedo got to the police station, his lawyer, Warren Wolfson, arrived. (Wolfson would go on to become a judge in Chicago and dean of DePaul Law School.) Wolfson, a young criminal defense lawyer, later testified (and it was not contested): "I identified myself to Chief Flynn and asked permission to see my client. He said I could not. I think it was approximately 11:00 o'clock. He said I couldn't see him because they hadn't completed questioning. I had no opportunity to talk to my client that night." Every time Escobedo asked to see his lawyer, the police replied that his lawyer "didn't want to see" him. The Supreme Court noted, "Notwithstanding repeated requests by each, [Escobedo] and his retained lawyer were afforded no opportunity to consult during the course of the entire interrogation."[9]

Escobedo was kept in a standing position for hours while police officers questioned him. An officer told him in Spanish, he later said, that he could go home if he pinned the murder on DiGerlando. Police brought DiGerlando into the interrogation room, and Escobedo said to him, "I didn't shoot Manuel, you did it." Escobedo thus admitted to knowledge of the crime, and as the hours went by, he made additional statements implicating himself in the murder plot.

The Supreme Court, in a 5–4 decision, found that the police had violated Escobedo's right to counsel by questioning him without allowing his attorney to be present. Justice Arthur Goldberg wrote the opinion for the Court, joined by Chief Justice Warren and Justices Black, Douglas, and Brennan. The four more conservative justices on the Court—Clark, Harlan, Stewart, and White—dissented. The Court invoked *Gideon v. Wainwright* and spoke of the importance of counsel. It stressed the dangers of allowing police to interrogate a suspect in secret without the presence of an attorney. Justice Goldberg's majority opinion rejected the concern that the presence of a lawyer would mean that people would stop confessing to crimes: "[N]o system of criminal justice can, or should, survive if it comes to depend for its continued effectiveness on the citizens' abdication through unawareness of their constitutional rights." That is, the success of the criminal justice system in gaining convictions should not depend on people being ignorant of their rights. Justice Golberg explained, "If the exercise of constitutional rights will thwart the effectiveness of a system of law enforcement, then there is something very wrong with that system."[10]

The Court said that Escobedo's Sixth Amendment right to counsel had been unconstitutionally denied. Suspects who are questioned while in custody have a right to a lawyer. If the police refuse a request for an attorney, then any statements gained thereafter must be excluded from being used as evidence.[11]

· · · · · · · · ·

TWO YEARS LATER, in *Miranda v. Arizona,* the Court went even further to protect the privilege against self-incrimination and the right to counsel for those suspected of crimes. On March 13, 1963, in Phoenix, Ernesto Miranda was arrested at his home and taken into custody on suspicion of kidnapping and raping a woman. A police lineup was held at the station, and the victim identified Miranda as her assailant. Miranda was taken to Interrogation Room no. 2 of the detective bureau, where two police officers questioned him. During the interrogation, the officers did not inform Miranda about his Fifth Amendment right against self-incrimination or his Sixth Amendment right to an attorney.

After two hours of questioning, Miranda confessed. He was prosecuted, and the confession was important evidence against him. He was convicted and sentenced to twenty to thirty years in prison. On appeal the conviction and sentence were upheld, and Miranda sought Supreme Court review. The Court took his case and three others, all of which involved individuals who while in police custody had confessed to a crime. None had been informed of their rights, and none had been provided a lawyer.

Miranda's attorney asked the Court to require that attorneys be present during police interrogations. The Court did not go that far, but in its 5–4 decision, it reversed all these convictions. Chief Justice Warren, drawing on his own experience as a prosecutor, wrote for the Court, with the same split among the justices as in *Escobedo.*

Warren began by describing the incommunicado nature of police interrogation and how physical abuse sometimes occurs, but more commonly police exert psychological pressure to induce a confession.

In pages of detail, he described the techniques, outlined in police manuals, that officers use to induce confessions.

Individuals questioned in isolation in police stations feel great pressure to confess, Warren continued. In fact, they may feel much more pressure there than in a courtroom, "where there are often impartial observers to guard against intimidation or trickery."[12] In fact, in-custodial interrogation, he wrote, is inherently coercive: "It is obvious that such an interrogation environment is created for no purpose other than to subjugate the individual to the will of his examiner. This atmosphere carries its own badge of intimidation. To be sure, this is not physical intimidation, but it is equally destructive of human dignity."[13]

Tracing the history of the privilege against self-incrimination, Warren stressed its importance as a protection of individuals and as a limit on police conduct. He affirmed that this privilege undoubtedly applies during police interrogations.

To lessen the coercion inherent to police interrogation, an individual who is questioned while in police custody must be given basic warnings. The suspect must be told that he or she has the right to remain silent, that anything said can be used as evidence against the person, that the person has a right to a lawyer, and if the person cannot afford one, the government will provide an attorney.[14] As in *Escobedo*, the Court stressed the importance of an attorney's presence to protect an individual from police coercion during questioning.

The Court was explicit: if a person invokes the right to remain silent, all questioning must cease. If a person asks for a lawyer, questioning must end until one is provided.[15] An individual may waive these rights, but the burden is on the government to show that there was a knowing and voluntary waiver: "a valid waiver will not be presumed simply from the silence of the accused after warnings are given or simply from the fact that a confession was in fact eventually obtained."[16]

Warren responded directly to the assertion that this requirement would unduly hamper law enforcement. The FBI had warned suspects in this way for years, he noted, and had not been hindered in its interrogations.[17] The need to protect the constitutional rights of individuals was most important, he wrote, observing that the "quality of a nation's civilization can be largely measured by the methods it uses in the enforcement of its criminal law."[18]

The tone of Warren's majority opinion reflects his recognition that this was a major decision to protect the constitutional rights of criminal suspects and to limit police interrogations. As legal scholar Charles Weisselberg has observed: "*Miranda* ... represents a preference for Fifth Amendment values over the interests of law enforcement in obtaining incriminating statements."[19]

Miranda was enormously controversial at the time. Police and politicians sharply criticized it as unduly handcuffing police and making it too difficult for them to obtain confessions. Some feared that it would allow guilty and dangerous people to avoid conviction. Two years after *Miranda,* Congress passed a statute to overrule it by providing that all confessions would be admissible so long as they were voluntary even if no warnings were administered.[20] But the statute was never invoked because every Justice Department thereafter, under both Republican and Democratic presidents, took the position that it was unconstitutional. And indeed, in 2000 the Supreme Court declared this law unconstitutional, stressing that Congress by statute cannot overrule the Court's interpretation of the Constitution.[21]

In reality, contrary to all fears, *Miranda* neither handcuffed police nor kept them from gaining confessions. In the years after *Miranda,* countless studies reached the overwhelming consensus that it had no effect on the ability of police to gain confessions or of prosecutors to gain convictions.[22] Studies in New Haven, Chicago, Los Angeles, and Washington, D.C., all found that *Miranda* had no discernible effect on obtaining confessions.[23] A study in the District of Columbia found that 44 percent of those who received warnings talked to the police, whereas 42 percent who did not receive warnings did so.[24] Legal scholar Stephen Schulhofer found that in its first years *Miranda* had a small effect, but thereafter its effect has been "essentially nil."[25]

A more recent study by scholar Richard Leo also concluded that *Miranda* has had no impact on confessions or convictions.[26]

Why? Why did this decision, which is thought of as one of the most important in history in limiting police and protecting the rights of criminal suspects, make so little difference in police interrogations and in obtaining confessions? First, the prescribed warnings likely do not significantly lessen the coercion inherent during in-custodial police interrogation. The premise of *Miranda* is that being questioned by a police officer while in custody puts pressure on a suspect. But the *Miranda* warnings don't reduce that inherent coercion. Also the assumption that suspects understand the warnings is often likely unfounded. All the studies show that suspects frequently waive their *Miranda* rights.[27] A study in Salt Lake City found that suspects waive their *Miranda* rights in 83.7 percent of interrogations.[28] A national study came to a similar conclusion and found that 81 percent of all suspects waived their rights.[29]

Second, police developed ways to circumvent and undermine *Miranda* warnings. *Miranda* applies only to questioning while the suspect is in custody; if an interrogation occurs before the arrest, no warnings are needed, and the person has no right to counsel if the interrogation occurs before arrest.[30] There is strong evidence that police use precustodial questioning to get around *Miranda*.[31] How police give the warnings, including their disclaimers, and when—such as after "softening up" a suspect—can make a big difference as well.[32] Police often deliver the warnings in a manner and tone that deemphasizes their significance, or they give the warnings "in a way that communicates to the suspect that waiving his rights will result in some immediate or future benefit for him."[33]

Third, police know that even if they intentionally violate *Miranda* and the statements gained are not admissible, the information obtained still can be used in other ways against the suspect. Subsequent Supreme Court decisions allow the statements to be used for other purposes—such as to impeach a criminal defendant at trial[34] or to lead to physical evidence that can be admitted.[35] Police are trained about this and thus are encouraged to question "outside of *Miranda*."[36] Charles Weisselberg, after reviewing police training manuals and police videos, concluded that "officers are now consistently trained in a tactic that allows them to remove a significant category of interrogations from the reach of Miranda."[37]

Miranda's promise to protect suspects' privilege against self-incrimination by lessening coercion in in-custodial police interrogations has not been realized. The general public is not aware of this fact; the popular familiarity with the *Miranda* warnings likely causes people to think they make a difference. In hindsight, if the Court had gone further and required the presence of a lawyer during in-custodial interrogations, it might have made much more of a difference in protecting people from pressure and coercion. But three years after *Miranda*, the Court lost its liberal majority and has never had one since. Subsequent Supreme Courts have chipped away, often in large chunks, at *Miranda* and have shown no indication of expanding its protections of the constitutionally protected privilege against self-incrimination. The Warren Court saw the need to protect the Fifth Amendment's privilege against self-incrimination during police interrogations, but it did far too little to make a real difference in safeguarding this fundamental right.

9

Protecting the Innocent from Wrongful Convictions

Safeguards Against False Eyewitness Identifications

INACCURATE EYEWITNESS IDENTIFICATIONS HAVE LED to many innocent people being convicted for crimes they did not commit. Eyewitness identification of a suspect as the culprit is enormously powerful evidence. Yet countless studies show that eyewitness identifications, especially of people of a race different from the eyewitness's own, are often inaccurate. This is not a new insight. A 1932 study found that among sixty-five cases in which innocent persons were convicted, twenty-nine of the wrongful convictions were the result of an inaccurate eyewitness identification.[1] More than a half-century later, many who had been convicted wrongfully were exonerated by DNA testing; a study of the first two hundred cases found that in nearly 80 percent of those convictions, at least one eyewitness had mistakenly identified the innocent defendant.[2] The Supreme Court has observed that "the annals of criminal law are rife with instances of mistaken identification."[3]

Sometimes the mistake occurs because police use suggestive identification procedures. There are several types of police identification procedures. Lineups, which are familiar to anyone who watches police shows, involve several people standing together, one of whom is the suspect. The witness is asked to identify the person who committed the crime. In photo identification, a witness is shown several photographs and asked to select from that group. In showups, police bring a suspect to a witness (such as in a victim's hospital room) and ask whether he or she is the culprit.

All these procedures can be infected by police suggestiveness. Police can construct a lineup or a photo identification where only one person fits the suspect's description. Or they can give verbal or nonverbal cues as to which person to pick.

Even without suggestiveness, eyewitness identifications are often inaccurate.[4] Witnesses frequently base their identifications on what they saw while under great stress and for a short period of time. People's memories can be flawed. They can change over time.[5]

And extensive empirical research demonstrates that cross-racial identifications—identifying people of other races—are particularly likely to be flawed. Many studies have shown that eyewitnesses are more accurate at identifying perpetrators of their own race than those of a different race. A 2001 meta-analysis that spanned thirty-nine research articles and nearly five thousand participant witnesses concluded that cross-race identifications are 56 percent more likely to be erroneous than same-race identifications.[6]

Despite these problems, juries tend to believe eyewitnesses. One study found that they believe eyewitnesses 80 percent of the time, regardless of the accuracy of the identification.[7] Another concluded, "Jurors appear to over-estimate the accuracy of identifications . . . , do not distinguish accurate from inaccurate eyewitnesses, and are generally insensitive to factors that influence eyewitness accuracy."[8]

Showups, where the witness is shown only one person, are particularly likely to lead to mistaken identifications. One analysis of studies comparing lineups and showups found that showups produce twice as many false identifications as fair lineups.[9] It's easy to understand why: if the witness sees only one person, and there is an understandable desire to catch the criminal, the pressure is great to say he or she is the culprit.

Prior to the Warren Court, the Supreme Court had never imposed any limits on police conduct in identification procedures. But in 1967 in *United States v. Wade,* the Court for the first time provided some protections for criminal suspects subjected to lineups.[10] On September 21, 1964, in Eustace, Texas, a man with a small strip of tape on each side of his face entered a bank and pointed a pistol at the female cashier and the vice-president, the only persons in the bank at the time. The bank employees were forced to fill a pillowcase with money. The man then drove away with an accomplice who had been waiting in a stolen car outside the bank.

On March 23, 1965, an indictment was returned against Billy Joe Wade and two others for conspiring to rob the bank, and against Wade and the accomplice for the robbery itself. Wade was arrested on April 2, and on April 26 an attorney was appointed to represent him. Two weeks later an FBI agent, without notice to Wade's lawyer, arranged to have the two bank employees observe a lineup made up of Wade and five or six other prisoners. It was conducted in a courtroom of the local county courthouse. Each person in the lineup wore strips of tape on his face. Each said "put the money in the bag," the words allegedly uttered by the robber. Both bank employees identified Wade in the lineup as the bank robber.

At trial, the two employees were asked on direct examination if the robber was in the courtroom. Both pointed to Wade. On cross-examination, the prior lineup identification was elicited from both employees. Wade's lawyer objected and said that the lineup had been conducted in violation of the Constitution because he had not been informed or allowed to be present. The lawyer moved to exclude the testimony about the lineup and the resulting identification. The trial court denied this motion, and Wade was convicted.

The Supreme Court, though, found that conducting the lineup without the presence of a lawyer violated Wade's right to counsel. For the first time, the Court expressly acknowledged that police procedures to elicit identifications are "riddled with innumerable dangers."[11] Justice Brennan, writing for the Court, found that police can conduct identification procedures in suggestive ways and that "the dangers for the suspect are particularly grave when the witness' opportunity for observation was insubstantial, and thus his susceptibility to suggestion the greatest."[12] Quite crucially, the Court noted that once a witness has picked the accused out from a lineup, the witness will stick with that identification and repeat it in court even if it is inaccurate.[13] That person becomes the culprit in the witness's mind.

The Court expressed concern that lineups occur in secret, and hence judges and juries have difficulty reconstructing how an identification was done. The witness and the defendant are unlikely to be aware of suggestiveness that occurs. Even if the defendant observes suggestiveness, he or she may not want to take the witness stand, or he or she may not be believed if there is contrary testimony from police officers. At trial, the eyewitness is repeating the earlier identification, however flawed. Besides, when the witness is asked in the courtroom, "Do you see that person here today?", the response almost certainly will be to point to the criminal defendant who is seated next to the criminal defense lawyer. It is a dramatic and powerful moment.

Thus the Court concluded that Wade—and all criminal defendants—are entitled to have their attorney present at lineups that occur *after there has been an indictment*. The Court forcefully stated that there "is grave potential for prejudice, intentional or not, in the pretrial lineup, which may not be capable of reconstruction at trial."[14] The presence of a lawyer at the lineup, by itself, can cause police to avoid suggestive behavior and, at the very least, provide a witness to what occurred. The Court said that the post-indictment lineup is a critical stage of the proceeding and that a criminal defendant has as much right to an attorney there as at the trial itself.

Identifications at post-indictment lineups that are made without counsel being present must be excluded. But interestingly, the Court said that the in-court identification by that witness did not automatically have to be excluded as well. The Court said in-court identifications would be allowed if the government could "establish by clear and convincing evidence" that the identification done in court was "based upon observations of the suspect other than the lineup identification."[15] The Court said this would require that a court consider many factors, such as whether the witness had seen the defendant other than at the lineup, whether there is a discrepancy between any pre-lineup description and the defendant's actual description, whether the witness identified someone else before the lineup, whether there was a failure to identify the defendant on a prior occasion, and whether significant time elapsed between the alleged act and the lineup identification.[16]

The Court in *Wade* thus articulated rules that are followed to this day. A lineup held after an indictment is a critical stage of the proceeding, and the criminal suspect is entitled to have an attorney present. An identification made at a post-indictment lineup without counsel present (unless the suspect waives it) is inadmissible at trial. A subsequent in-court identification by that witness also is inadmissible unless the government can demonstrate with clear and convincing evidence that the in-court identification was based on the observations of the accused independent of the prior lineup identification.

There is much about the Court's decision in *Wade* to cheer. For the first time, the Court expressly recognized the inherent problems with eyewitness identification. For the first time, the Court imposed a constitutional remedy: for post-indictment lineups, a criminal suspect has the right to have his or her lawyer present. The attorney's mere presence might discourage police from engaging in suggestive practices, and the attorney is there to witness what happens.

But by limiting its ruling to post-indictment lineups, the Court gave police an easy way to circumvent it: just conduct the lineup after someone is arrested but before they are indicted. Also, *Wade* did nothing to limit police use of photo identifications, where police show the witness pictures instead of lineups. And allowing prosecutors to use in-court identifications, even after flawed lineups, gave police a further incentive to flout the constitutional limit created by the Court.

Wade could have been an important first step to dealing with the problems of eyewitness identifications that have led to the conviction of so many innocent people. Unfortunately, it was virtually the last step by the Supreme Court. The Burger, Rehnquist, and Roberts Courts almost always refused to add further constitutional limits on identification procedures. In fact, from 1986 until 2020, the Court decided only one case concerning the Constitution and eyewitness identification, and that ruling was in favor of police. This is despite the overwhelming evidence that eyewitness identifications are often done in a suggestive manner, are especially inaccurate when people are identifying those of other races, and far too frequently lead to the conviction of innocent people. Despite study after study showing wrongful convictions because of false identifications, especially of people of color, the justices have done nothing to address the problem since the end of the Warren Court.

10

Rights Need Remedies

ORE THAN ANY OTHER COURT IN HISTORY, THE
Warren Court expanded constitutional rights to constrain police in their searches, their interrogations, and
their identification procedures. But these rights have meaning only if
they can be enforced; unless police face consequences for violations,
the rights are just hollow, unfulfilled promises. There are two basic
remedies against police when they violate the Constitution. One is the
exclusionary rule, which excludes evidence gained as a result of police
misconduct. The Warren Court in *Mapp v. Ohio* took a crucial step
when it applied the exclusionary rule to state and local police.

The other basic remedy is the ability of members of the public to
sue for monetary damages when there are constitutional violations
and to sue for injunctions to prevent future violations. The crucial
statute that allows suits against state and local police when they violate the Constitution is 42 U.S. Code Section 1983, a law adopted
in 1871 in the wake of the Civil War. It is often overlooked that the
Warren Court dramatically changed the interpretation of this statute, which has had enormous consequences in allowing lawsuits for
constitutional violations by police and all who work for state and
local governments.

Following the Civil War and the adoption of the Thirteenth,
Fourteenth, and Fifteenth Amendments, violence against Blacks

was endemic throughout the South. The Senate conducted extensive investigations on this lawlessness, especially focusing on the role of the Ku Klux Klan. A six-hundred-page Senate report detailed the unwillingness or inability of Southern states to control the activities of the Klan.[1] In response, Congress adopted the Civil Rights Act of 1871, Section 1 of which is now embodied in Section 1983. The law, titled "An Act to enforce the Provisions of the Fourteenth Amendment to the Constitution, and for other Purposes," was a direct result of "the campaign of violence and deception in the South, fomented by the Ku Klux Klan, which was denying decent citizens their civil and political rights."[2]

While it was considering the act, Congress held lengthy hearings concerning the uncontrolled violence in the South and the failure of state police and state courts to adequately control the problem. The Supreme Court has frequently summarized this testimony in supporting its conclusion that Section 1983 was meant "to give a broad remedy for violations of federally protected civil rights."[3] It was apparent to Congress that states and state courts could not be trusted to protect Blacks. As the Supreme Court explained, "legislation was passed to afford a federal right in federal courts because, by reason of prejudice, passion, neglect, intolerance, or otherwise," states were likely to violate constitutional rights, and hence a federal forum was needed to enforce the Constitution.[4]

Section 1983 was meant to substantially alter the federal government's relationship to the states.[5] It empowered the federal government, especially the federal courts, to prevent and redress violations of federal rights by state and local government officers and employees. As the Supreme Court declared: "The very purpose of §1983 was to interpose the federal courts between the States and the people, as guardians of the people's federal rights—to protect the people from unconstitutional action under color of state law, whether that action be executive, legislative, or judicial."[6]

Despite the broad aspirations for Section 1983, for decades the law went unused. Between its enactment in 1871 and 1920, only twenty-one cases decided by the federal courts involved Section 1983.[7] Many factors combined to render Section 1983 meaningless during this period. The end of Reconstruction brought a halt to Northern attempts to protect the rights of Blacks in the South. Federal judges in the South were apparently no more willing to stop racism and discrimination than were state judges.[8] Repeatedly during this time, the Supreme Court refused to invalidate discriminatory state laws and, in fact, gave a narrow construction to the federal government's authority to protect civil rights.[9]

Section 1983 was used so infrequently that early in the twentieth century, Justice Oliver Wendell Holmes remarked that he assumed that Congress had not repealed the statute.[10] During the first half of the twentieth century, Section 1983 litigation remained relatively rare. Its most notable use was as a vehicle for invalidating several state laws that disenfranchised Black voters.[11] Still, as recently as 1960, in the entire country, only 287 civil rights suits against state and local governments and their officers were filed in, or removed to, federal court.[12]

Since 1961, however, Section 1983 litigation has grown enormously. In 1977 there were more than twenty thousand such suits; in 1985 the number rose to over 36,000; in 1995 it topped 57,000. Today over sixty thousand suits are filed each year, including prisoner suits.[13] In fact, by the end of the 1960s, commentators were examining possible ways to limit the volume of Section 1983 litigation.[14]

The marked increase in Section 1983 suits can be linked to many factors, but a 1961 Warren Court decision, *Monroe v. Pape*, greatly expanded its scope by permitting suits both for official government actions that violate the Constitution and for unauthorized actions by individual officers in excess or even in violation of state law.[15] The dramatic increase in Section 1983 litigation began, not at all coincidentally, immediately after the *Monroe* decision. Today *all* constitutional litigation against local governments and state and local government officials is brought under Section 1983.[16] If a state or local police officer uses excessive force, the victim sues under Section

1983. If a local government restricts freedom of speech in violation
of the First Amendment, it is sued under Section 1983. If a state legislature or a city council adopts a statute that is discriminatory, the
lawsuit challenging the law is brought under Section 1983.

Section 1983 creates liability against any person who violates the
Constitution or laws of the United States while acting "under color
of any statute, ordinance, regulation, custom, or usage of any state or
territory." This language usually is phrased more simply as a requirement that the plaintiff demonstrate that the defendant acted "under
color of state law."

In defining "under color of state law," the crucial question is
whether Section 1983 applies only to actions taken pursuant to
official government policies or whether suits may also be brought
against unauthorized or even illegal acts by government officials. In
practical terms, if an officer beats a suspect with a nightstick and
seriously injures the person, is the suit precluded because the officer acted without explicit government approval? Before *Monroe v.
Pape* was decided, there was a "long-standing assumption that §1983
reached only misconduct either officially authorized or so widely tolerated as to amount to a 'custom or usage.' "[17]

Monroe v. Pape was the Supreme Court's first occasion to directly
consider the meaning of "under color of law" under Section 1983 and
to address this issue. James Monroe, a resident of Chicago, alleged
that thirteen police officers broke into his home early one morning
and subjected his family to humiliation by making them stand naked
in the living room, then ransacked every room of the house.[18] Monroe was taken to the police station and held for ten hours without
arraignment and without being given the chance to contact an attorney. No charges ever were filed against Monroe. The officers had had
no search warrant and no arrest warrant. Monroe sued the police
officers and the City of Chicago under Section 1983.

A central question before the Supreme Court was whether the
Chicago police officers acted "under color of law," because the conduct obviously was not authorized by the government. The Court

ruled that actions taken by an officer in his or her official capacity
are deemed to occur "under color of law" even if they are not in pur-
suance of any official state policy and even if they violate state law:
"Misuse of power, possessed by virtue of state law and made possible
only because the wrongdoer is clothed with the authority of state law,
is action taken 'under color of' state law."[19]

The Court held that a Section 1983 suit was available even though
adequate state judicial remedies were potentially available. Justice
Douglas, writing for the majority, said that it was irrelevant that the
state had a law that if enforced would provide relief: "The federal
remedy is supplementary to the state remedy, and the latter need not
be first sought and refused before the federal one is invoked. Hence
the fact that Illinois by its constitution and laws outlaws unreasonable searches and seizures is no barrier to the present suit in the federal court."[20]

Section 1983, he explained, was intended to provide a remedy in
situations where states prohibit practices but offer only inadequate
remedies for them, and in instances where state remedies, theoreti-
cally adequate, are unavailable in practice.[21] The Court realized that
a narrow definition of "under color of law"—limiting liability to officials acting pursuant to official policies—would permit state governments to substantially immunize their officers from Section 1983
liability simply by enacting general statutes prohibiting officers from
violating the Constitution or laws of the United States.

Similarly, the Court was unwilling to limit Section 1983 suits only
to instances where it was proven that state remedies are inadequate,
recognizing it often would be difficult or impossible to prove state
court hostility to federal rights. Instead, the Court held that a government officer acts under color of law for all actions taken that violate the Constitution and laws of the United States.

Justice Frankfurter—a consistent conservative voice on the Warren Court—wrote a vehement dissent in *Monroe*.[22] An officer who
acts in excess of his or her authority, or in violation of state law, he
contended, cannot be deemed to act "under color of state law." Jus-

tice Frankfurter would have reserved Section 1983 for instances of official state and local policies or customs that violate federal laws or situations where state remedies are proven to be inadequate. That would have left most victims of police abuses with no remedy.

Monroe v. Pape was thus a huge step toward holding police accountable. After that decision, state and local police officers could be sued for monetary damages for their constitutional violations, such as for illegal searches, and for the use of excessive force. But the decision had one unfortunate limitation: it said that Section 1983 could not be used to sue municipal governments. Congress, the Court noted, had rejected an amendment to Section 1983 that would have made cities liable for acts of violence, such as by the Ku Klux Klan, in their midst. This indicated, said the Court, that Congress did not want to hold local governments liable.[23]

This was a major limitation on suits against police abuses. Liability is essential if cities are to have an incentive to control their police and to hire, train, and supervise officers who will obey the Constitution. Only if local governments have to bear the costs of the misconduct of their officers will they have sufficient reason to take action. Seventeen years after *Monroe*, the Court reversed itself and said that local governments can be sued.[24] But as we will see, the Supreme Court subsequently limited this reversal and thereafter made it increasingly difficult for people to successfully sue a city for the constitutional violations of its police officers.

· · · · · · · · ·

THE ULTIMATE ASSESSMENT of the Warren Court in relation to policing is more complicated and more nuanced than the conventional wisdom has it. To be sure, it imposed more limits on police than any other Court before or after. Unlike any other Court in all of American history, the Warren Court saw the need to protect the constitutional rights of suspects and criminal defendants and thus to limit police conduct. Especially in its rulings to end segregation, such as *Brown v. Board of Education,* the Warren Court also did more to advance racial equality than any Court before or since. Yet the Warren Court also authorized police to engage in stop and frisk, and in many areas it failed to go far enough to allow its decisions to have any real impact. Additionally, many of the limits it placed on police conduct and its protections of the rights of criminal suspects and defendants were subsequently undermined, or even overruled, by the Burger, Rehnquist, and Roberts Courts.

Part IV

RETRENCHMENT

The Burger Court Limits Constitutional Rights

11

"Only the Guilty Have Something to Hide"

Undermining Fourth Amendment Protections

BE SURE TO NEVER DRIVE A CAR WITH A BURNED-out head light or taillight, especially if you're Black or Latinx. A stunning number of arrests begin with police stopping a motorist for that, or at least so the officer testifies. It's what happened to Joseph Alcala, Robert Bustamonte, and Joe Gonzales in January 1967 in Mountain View, California.

That month the proprietor of a car wash in Mountain View discovered that his business office had been broken into and that a check protector and a number of blank checks had been stolen.[1] Later that month at approximately 2:40 a.m., Sunnyvale police officer Joe Rand stopped a Ford car—he had noticed that a headlight and the license plate light were burned out. Alcala and Bustamonte were in the front seat along with Gonzales, the driver. A trio of older men were seated in the rear. All were Latino. The officer asked Gonzales for his license. When Gonzales failed to produce one, Officer Rand asked the other occupants for identification. Only Alcala produced a driver's license, explaining that he had borrowed the car from his brother. The officer told the six men to get out of the car, and they did so peacefully. He issued a traffic citation for the defective lights and for Gonzales's failure to produce a license.

After being joined by another officer, Officer Rand questioned each of the men. A third police car arrived. Rand then asked Alcala if he could search the car. Alcala replied, "Sure, go ahead." Alcala opened the trunk and the glove compartment. He was not advised that he had the right to refuse to consent; nor is there any indication that he had knowledge that he had that right.

The officers found three checks from the car wash wadded up under the left rear seat. Each was signed in the name of the owner of the car wash. Bustamonte, a passenger in the car, was charged with possessing the checks with an intent to defraud.

Bustamonte's lawyer moved to suppress the introduction of the checks as evidence on the ground that police acquired them through an unconstitutional search. They had had no probable cause to search the car; Officer Rand had stopped it for burned-out lights, and he was not going to find any evidence related to that under the seats of the car. The trial court said that was irrelevant because Alcala gave permission for police to search the vehicle. Bustamonte was convicted. The California Court of Appeals affirmed, concluding that Alcala had validly consented to the search and thus waived Fourth Amendment rights.

Bustamonte then went to federal court and filed a writ of habeas corpus, arguing that his conviction violated the Constitution.[2] As is required in such proceedings, he named as the defendant Merle Schneckloth, the warden where he was in prison. The U.S. Court of Appeals for the Ninth Circuit agreed with Bustamonte, explaining that it is the state's burden to prove that a person knows he has a right to refuse consent.[3] To say that a person voluntarily agreed to a search if he didn't realize he could say no is a fiction.

The Supreme Court granted review in *Schneckloth v. Bustamonte*, and the "precise question" was "what must the prosecution prove to demonstrate that a consent was 'voluntarily' given."[4] In a 6–3 decision, the Court reversed the Ninth Circuit and ruled against Bustamonte. Justice Stewart wrote for the Court and was joined by Justice White, both of whom had consistently dissented from the Warren Court's decisions protecting criminal defendants. They were joined by the four Nixon appointees—Chief Justice Burger and Justices Blackmun, Powell, and Rehnquist.

The Court explicitly rejected the argument that the government had to show that the consent to a search had to involve a person's "knowing" waiver of his or her rights. That is, the government need not establish that a person had knowledge of his or her rights in order to have an effective consent.

But why not, especially since the usual test for a waiver of one's rights is whether it is *knowing* as well as voluntary? Justice Stewart, writing for the Court, said candidly that that would make it too hard for police to conduct searches. He said that two competing concerns had to be balanced: law enforcement's need to perform such searches and the desire to prevent coercion. But whenever the Court phrases the inquiry in terms of such balancing, it invariably favors police. Here the Court said: "In situations where the police have some evidence of illicit activity, but lack probable cause to arrest or search, a search authorized by a valid consent may be the only means of obtaining important and reliable evidence."[5]

The Court agreed that the officers had had no probable cause or even reasonable suspicion to search the car; they had had no reason to suspect that it contained evidence of illegal activity. None of the six men had been suspected of anything. The only way they could have searched was with the consent of the driver. Bustamonte claimed that in order for the driver to have waived his Fourth Amendment rights, the prosecutor had to prove that he knew he had the right to refuse consent. The Court explicitly rejected that claim. Proof of knowledge of the right to refuse consent, Justice Stewart wrote, is not "a necessary prerequisite to demonstrating a 'voluntary' consent."[6]

In what would become a theme of the Burger Court's decisions lessening Fourth Amendment protections, Justice Stewart wrote that the way the search was done had nothing to do with the reliability of the evidence. The fact that an illegal search led to the police officer finding the checks under the car's seat did not cast any doubt on the fact that those were the checks that had been stolen. A coerced confession risks that it is false and unreliable. But tangible evidence is not less reliable because it is gained through an illegal search.[7]

Having rejected the idea that "knowledge of a right to refuse is an indispensable element of a valid consent," the Court also said that individuals have no constitutional right to be told that they have the right to refuse consent to a search.[8] As long as suspects give consent voluntarily, even if they have no knowledge of their Fourth Amendment right to refuse, they have waived that right, and any evidence the police gain is admissible.

Schneckloth v. Bustamonte is important on many levels. First, it dramatically empowers police to be able to search. It obviates the need for police to meet all the requirements of the Fourth Amendment, such as the need for probable cause (or at least reasonable suspicion) and the need for a warrant. It is estimated that consent searches comprise over 90 percent of all warrantless searches.[9]

Why do suspects consent so often, even when they have contraband with them? My students are always surprised to read these cases where people are said to voluntarily agree to having their cars searched even when they have drugs or even dead bodies in the trunk. One reason is that people don't know they have the right to refuse when a police officer asks to search. Another reason is that people feel inherently pressured when someone in authority, carrying a gun, makes a request. Under these circumstances, a request feels much more like an order, and the person receiving it is likely to perceive it that way. Experience shows that "most people will feel compelled to allow the police to search, no matter how politely the request is phrased. Such feelings of compulsion are particularly experienced by members of certain racial and cultural groups who fear confrontation with the police."[10]

Doing a better job of letting people know their right to refuse a police request for consent has been shown to make a dramatic difference.[11] Starting in 2012, three cities in North Carolina—Fayetteville, Durham, and Chapel Hill—created policies requiring that police obtain written rather than verbal consent to a search. The number of searches of cars decreased significantly. The reason is simple: "Written consent forms explain to motorists what their rights are, giving some of them the courage to say no. This reduces the incentive for police officers to stop cars as part of a fishing expedition for contraband."[12]

Schneckloth empowers police in another way as well: if police search without a warrant and find evidence, they can lie and say the suspect gave consent. It then becomes the officer's word against the suspect's, and judges are reluctant to exclude evidence that could lead to a guilty person going free. The Mollen Commission, which investigated the New York Police Department in the early 1990s, found that perjury was "so common in certain precincts that it has spawned its own word: 'testilying.'"[13] Former federal appeals court judge Alex Kozinski, a Reagan appointee, observed that it is "an open secret long shared by prosecutors, defense lawyers and judges that perjury is widespread among law enforcement officers."[14] One survey found that "defense attorneys, prosecutors, and judges estimated that police perjury at Fourth Amendment suppression hearings occurs in twenty to fifty percent of the cases."[15] Such perjury no doubt includes lying about consent. One former police chief candidly admitted his belief that police often lie about consent when defendants seek to exclude evidence based on an illegal search: "Hundreds of thousands of police officers swear under oath . . . that the defendant gave consent to a search. This may happen occasionally, but it defies belief that so many drug users are . . . so dumb as to give cops consent to search . . . when they possess drugs."[16]

. . . .

SCHNECKLOTH V. BUSTAMONTE, early in the Burger Court era, reflected the change in the composition of the Supreme Court between 1969 and 1971, when President Nixon appointed four conservative justices: it brought about a major shift in the jurisprudence with regard to the rights of those suspected and accused of crimes. The Warren Court had been concerned that people didn't know their rights and felt inherent pressure when interrogated by police. That was why in *Miranda* it prescribed the famous warnings that must be given to all suspects who are in custody before they are questioned by police. But the Burger Court in *Schneckloth* dismissed that concern. Its priority was to make sure that guilty people got convicted and to make it easy for police to find consent to searches, so that evidence would not be excluded.

The Warren Court recognized that letting people know their rights might interfere with law enforcement but explicitly said that protecting constitutional rights was more important. The Burger Court, in *Schneckloth* and other cases, gave priority to the needs of law enforcement. The Court's definition of consent is a fiction; if a person does not know that he or she has the right to say no, then saying yes to a police search cannot be considered a knowing waiver of one's rights. The Court protected "a broad realm of police conduct not because people in fact feel free to withhold consent, but because it is deemed essential to law enforcement."[17]

That was why the liberal justices who had been part of every major Warren Court ruling in favor of the rights of criminal defendants—Douglas, Brennan, and Marshall—were in dissent in *Schneckloth v. Bustamonte*. The more conservative justices who had dissented in the Warren era—Stewart and White—now were in the majority along with the Nixon appointees. Had this case come before the Warren Court, it would undoubtedly have been decided differently.

· · · · · · · · ·

THE SHIFT IN the Court's ideology was major and sudden. In June 1968 Chief Justice Earl Warren announced his retirement, effective upon the confirmation of his successor. Warren, at seventy-seven, was ready to step down and wanted the chance to travel with his wife. Given the Democratic Senate and the Democratic president, it was expected that a successor would be easily confirmed. But by that point President Johnson was already a lame duck, having announced in March 1968 that he would not seek reelection. Opposition to the

Vietnam War and the strong showing of a challenger for the Democratic nomination, Eugene McCarthy, caused him to withdraw from the race. Also, the Warren Court was very controversial, perhaps especially for its rulings protecting those suspected and accused of crimes, and the process of confirming Warren's successor was sure to become a referendum on it.

Johnson also greatly miscalculated the situation in making his selections. He named Associate Justice Abe Fortas to be the next chief justice and Texas federal judge Homer Thornberry to take Fortas's seat on the Court. Both were widely, and correctly, perceived to be cronies of Johnson. Perhaps no Johnson nominees could have been confirmed that year, but definitely not ones where serious issues were raised.

During his confirmation hearings for chief justice, Fortas was extensively questioned about having received $15,000 for nine speeches he gave at American University. Fortas also received many questions about his close relationship with Johnson. It became clear that Fortas's confirmation was unlikely in 1968, a particularly difficult and tense election year. Fortas's nomination was withdrawn, and Earl Warren remained chief justice. The nomination of Thornberry, who was perceived as having been nominated for his friendship with Johnson and not for his qualifications, was then moot and was withdrawn without a Senate vote.

Not long afterward more serious ethical issues concerning Fortas came to light. In 1966, while he was a Supreme Court associate justice, he had accepted a $20,000 retainer from Wall Street financier Louis Wolfson and signed a contract that would provide him $20,000 a year for the rest of his life.[18] Wolfson was under investigation for securities violations at the time this occurred. When Wolfson was indicted, Fortas returned the money he had received. After being convicted, Wolfson asked Fortas to help secure a pardon from President Johnson, which Fortas refused to do. When all this was revealed, impeachment resolutions were prepared against Fortas. He resigned from the Court, apparently at the urging of Chief Justice Warren.

That meant that President Nixon, immediately upon taking office, would get to make two nominations to the Supreme Court. He had run for president on a campaign of "law and order," and he especially had run against the Warren Court's criminal procedure decisions. Race was a key part of Nixon's appeal on this issue and generally, as he expressed strong opposition to busing and other measures the Warren Court took to end segregation. Nixon was committed to picking justices who would take a very different approach to policing, one that would empower law enforcement and restrict the rights of criminal defendants. He succeeded.

For chief justice, Nixon selected Warren Burger, who had been a judge on the U.S. Court of Appeals for the D.C. Circuit for thirteen years. Burger, who grew up in Minnesota, looked and sounded like a judge sent by central casting, and he was undoubtedly picked because he was a frequent critic of the Warren Court's decisions protecting the rights of suspects and criminal defendants. For example, in a speech, Burger praised European countries that did not accord the privilege against self-incrimination and said, "They go swiftly, efficiently and directly to the question of whether the accused is guilty. No nation on earth goes to such lengths or takes such pains to provide safeguards as we do, once an accused person is called before the bar of justice and until his case is completed."[19] Burger expressed exactly the law and order sentiments, and the antipathy to Warren Court decisions, that Nixon was seeking.

To replace Justice Fortas, Nixon nominated Judge Clement Haynsworth, from South Carolina, who sat on the U.S. Court of Appeals for the Fourth Circuit. Democrats controlled the Senate and opposed Haynsworth because of his perceived hostility to labor. Their efforts succeeded, and Haynsworth was denied confirmation. Senate rejections of presidential nominees to the Court had been common in the nineteenth century—about 20 percent of those picked for the Court were denied confirmation—but such rejections were uncommon in the twentieth century.[20] It had happened only once before, in 1931, when the Senate rejected President Herbert Hoover's pick of John Parker because of his antilabor views.

After Haynsworth's rejection, President Nixon tried again and appointed Judge Harold Carswell, who had recently been elevated to the federal court of appeals. But Carswell's record was much less impressive than Haynsworth's. Evidence surfaced that Carswell, who was from Georgia, supported segregation and opposed women's rights, which was not atypical of Southern judges during this time. At one point, Democratic Senator George McGovern said of Carswell, "I find his record to be distinguished largely by two qualities: racism and mediocrity."[21] Responding to the charge that Carswell was mediocre, Nebraska Republican Senator Roman Hruska infamously responded, "Even if he were mediocre, there are a lot of mediocre judges and people and lawyers. They are entitled to a little representation, aren't they, and a little chance? We can't have all Brandeises, Frankfurters and Cardozos."[22]

Given that defense, the Democrats' defeat of Carswell's nomination was no surprise. Frustrated by the rejection of the nominations of two southerners, Nixon picked federal appeals court judge Harry Blackmun. Like Burger, Blackmun was from Minnesota, and they had known each other since childhood. They were both suitably respectable if bland legal figures, hardly seen as the next Brandeis, Frankfurter, or Cardozo to occupy the bench. Blackmun had been a somewhat obscure, no-nonsense judge on the U.S. Court of Appeals for the Eighth Circuit for a decade when Nixon selected him for the Supreme Court. He was confirmed by a Senate vote of 94–0.

In his initial years on the Court, Blackmun and Burger voted together so often in a conservative direction that they were dubbed the "Minnesota twins." For example, when the Court held in 1971 that *The New York Times* and other newspapers could publish the Pentagon Papers, a history of American involvement in the Vietnam War, they were together in dissent (along with Justice Harlan).[23]

But Blackmun was one of the few justices in history to have had a major change in ideology while on the Court. By the time he retired in 1994, he was a consistent liberal vote.[24] We have no way of knowing why Blackmun shifted his approach so dramatically, but I have heard many who clerked for him speak of his intellectual curiosity, his open-mindedness, and his humility. In the early years of the Burger Court, though, Blackmun voted consistently with the conservative majority to limit the constitutional rights of suspects and criminal defendants.

Two more vacancies on the Court occurred in 1971 when Justices Hugo Black and John Marshall Harlan left the bench. Black, a Franklin Roosevelt appointee, had been in the majority in the Warren Court's decisions to limit police conduct; Harlan, an Eisenhower appointee, had been frequently in dissent. To replace Black, Nixon selected Virginia lawyer Lewis Powell. Powell recently had been president of the American Bar Association, but what likely attracted Nixon's attention was Powell's criticism of mandatory school busing and his sharp attacks on student protests, which he saw as Communist-inspired.[25] In 1971, not long before he went on the Court, Powell wrote a memo for the Chamber of Commerce in which he said, "No thoughtful person can question that the American economic system is under broad attack."[26] Powell especially blamed college students and professors for being engaged in what he called a "frontal assault . . . on our government, our system of justice, and the free enterprise system."[27]

Powell served on the Court from 1972 until 1987 and was thought of as more moderate than William Rehnquist, who went on the bench at the same time, or Antonin Scalia, who joined the Court in 1986. Perhaps this is because Powell was in the majority in protecting abortion rights in *Roe v. Wade*. But especially on criminal justice issues, Powell was a solid vote for police and overall was integral to the Burger Court's dramatic shift from the Warren Court.

Nixon named William Rehnquist to take Harlan's place on the Court. Rehnquist grew up in Milwaukee, attended Stanford Law School, and then settled in Phoenix. He clerked for Justice Robert

Jackson in 1952–53 and was known even then by his fellow clerks for his politically conservative views. For example, as a clerk, Rehnquist wrote a memo to Jackson urging him to reaffirm *Plessy v. Ferguson* and the ability of states to pass laws requiring racial segregation.[28] As a lawyer, Rehnquist was actively involved in Republican politics in Arizona, including the 1964 Barry Goldwater campaign for president. In the early years of the Nixon presidency, Rehnquist became assistant attorney general for the Office of Legal Counsel in the Department of Justice, then was named an associate justice in 1971. He was just forty-seven when he went on the Court and was known for his keen intelligence, his affability, and his unflinching conservativism. In 1986, when Warren Burger stepped down as chief justice, Rehnquist was selected to replace him and remained in that role until his death in September 2005. Rehnquist remained a staunch conservative from the time he went on the Court until he died, though as chief justice he was much less likely than when he was an associate justice to be the sole dissenter in 8–1 decisions. In his thirty-three years on the Court, he was a strong voice for limiting federal power and protecting states' rights—and for constricting the rights of criminal defendants.

For a decade, these four justices—Burger, Blackmun, Powell, and Rehnquist—were often joined by Potter Stewart, an Eisenhower appointee, to create a conservative majority on the Court. It was these five justices, in a 5–4 decision, who held that education is not a fundamental right under the Constitution and that even great disparities in school funding within a metropolitan area are permissible.[29] It was these five justices, again in a 5–4 ruling, that significantly limited the ability of federal courts to remedy school desegregation.[30]

In cases involving criminal procedure, these five justices could count on a sixth vote: Byron White, a Kennedy appointee. White, who grew up in Colorado, is the only justice to have been an All-American college football player and a professional football player. After serving in the navy and graduating from Yale Law School, White clerked on the Court for Chief Justice Fred Vinson. He practiced law in Denver and in 1960 managed John Kennedy's Colorado campaign. As president, Kennedy named White to be a deputy attorney general and then a justice of the Supreme Court.

White, though, was not liberal. It was not that he became more conservative over the years; from his first years on the bench, he was conservative on many issues, especially with regard to criminal law. He dissented in the landmark Warren Court decisions protecting the rights of criminal suspects, such as *Escobedo v. Illinois* and *Miranda v. Arizona*. He and Rehnquist were the only two dissenting votes in *Roe v. Wade*.[31] In 1976 White wrote the opinion for the Court in *Washington v. Davis,* which made it much harder for plaintiffs to prove racial discrimination on the part of the government. It would not suffice to show that a government action had had a significant impact that harmed people of color; now it required proof that the government had acted with the intent to disadvantage a racial minority.[32] White remained on the Court until 1993, when he was replaced by Ruth Bader Ginsburg, who had a markedly different ideology than the football All-American from Colorado.

In 1981 Justice Stewart retired, and President Reagan appointed the first woman ever to serve on the Court. Sandra Day O'Connor, born in El Paso, Texas, grew up on a 198,000-acre cattle ranch near Duncan, Arizona. She attended Stanford University and Stanford Law School, where she served on the law review with, and for a time dated, William Rehnquist. After she graduated from law school, she struggled to find a job, as law firms did not want to hire women. Her first employment after law school was as a volunteer deputy attorney in San Mateo County, California. Many years later, when Attorney General William French Smith interviewed her for consideration for the Supreme Court, she reminded him that after she graduated from Stanford Law School, his law firm had been interested in her only for a secretarial position.

O'Connor settled in Arizona and worked there not only as a lawyer but also as a state legislator and a state appellate judge, experiences that she said very much influenced her views on the law. She is the last justice to have previously served in both capacities. Over the course of her almost twenty-five years on the Supreme Court, she became the "swing justice"—the one most likely to cast the decisive vote in closely divided cases—and was very much thought of in that way until she left the bench in January 2006.[33] But one area where she was a consistent and predictable conservative vote was with regard to policing and the rights of criminal suspects.

In 1975, in another change in the composition of the Court, William Douglas suffered a debilitating stroke and resigned; he was replaced by John Paul Stevens. President Gerald Ford's attorney general, Edward Levi, knew Stevens from their time together in Chicago. Stevens was a Chicago native and, like Levi, attended the University of Chicago Laboratory Schools. Although Stevens was a Republican, like Levi, he was no conservative. Stevens had a reputation for being exceptionally smart—he graduated at the top of his class from Northwestern Law School and then clerked on the Supreme Court for Wiley Rutledge. Stevens practiced law in Chicago and was named to the Seventh Circuit by President Nixon. The Ford presidency was less ideologically defined than was Nixon's or, later, Reagan's, and the nomination of Stevens reflected that. Stevens served on the Court for thirty-five years, until he retired in 2010 at age ninety. In his early years on the Court, he seemed less ideologically defined than most of his Republican-appointed colleagues, but by the end of his tenure, he was a consistently liberal vote.[34] The Court became more conservative over the years he was on the bench, making Stevens seem even more liberal over time.

· · · · · · · · ·

IDEOLOGICALLY, THEN, the Burger Court swung sharply to the right after the liberal Warren Court, and it paved the way for the even more conservative Courts that followed. For seventeen years, from 1969 until Chief Justice Burger's retirement in 1986, the Court had a solid conservative majority to rule in favor of police and against the constitutional rights of suspects and criminal defendants. This was evident in its decisions about search and seizure, the privilege against self-incrimination, and police identification procedures. It had a more mixed record about remedies for police misconduct, narrowing the availability of the exclusionary rule but expanding the ability to bring civil suits. Issues of race hovered in the background: usually unspoken, they are so often present in cases about policing. But the Burger Court, in many of its decisions, seemed unaware that race even existed, and it consistently seemed unconcerned about its decisions' racial implications for policing.

Schneckloth v. Bustamante was representative of the Burger Court's approach to the Fourth Amendment. Unlike the Warren Court, the Burger Court started with the premise that Fourth Amendment violations committed by police in the course of collecting evidence did not undermine the reliability of the evidence they collected. Based on this premise, the Burger Court significantly limited the application of the exclusionary rule, so that evidence would not be suppressed even though it was obtained by unconstitutional means. And the premise affected other important doctrines as well.

One decision attracted little media attention but dramatically changed the ability of federal courts to enforce the Constitution. In *Stone v. Powell* in 1976, the Burger Court held that Fourth Amendment claims could not be presented to a federal court on a writ of habeas corpus as long as the criminal defendant had the chance to litigate them while being prosecuted in state court.[35] The Constitution, in Article I, Section 9, says that "The Privilege of the Writ of Habeas Corpus shall not be suspended, unless when in Cases of Rebellion or Invasion the public Safety may require it." *Habeas corpus* is a legal petition that a person can file in court if he or she claims to be illegally detained or imprisoned by the government. It existed in English law long before the United States existed and was called the "Great Writ" because of its importance in protecting freedom. Congress, in the Judiciary Act of 1789, permitted federal prisoners to bring habeas corpus petitions in federal court, and in 1867 it authorized state prisoners to do so as well.

The usual rule is that once a matter has been litigated in one court, it cannot be relitigated in another except on a direct appeal from the trial court to the appellate court. So if a matter is litigated in state court, the losing party can appeal to the state appellate courts, but the losing party cannot seek to relitigate the same issue in a federal district court or that of another state.

Habeas corpus is a crucial exception to that usual rule. In *Brown v. Allen,* decided in 1953, the Supreme Court, in an opinion by Justice Frankfurter, held that a constitutional claim may be raised on habeas even though it had been raised, fully litigated, and decided in state court.[36] Justice Frankfurter observed that "even the highest State courts" had failed to give adequate protection to federal constitutional rights.[37] The Court explained that habeas corpus exists to remedy state court disregard of violations of defendants' rights. Therefore the Court established that a state prisoner should have the chance to have a hearing in federal court on his or her federal constitutional claims. In fact, the Court so valued the importance of reaching correct decisions on the rights of criminal defendants that it held that a prisoner convicted by a federal court could also raise issues on habeas that had been presented and decided at trial. The Court concluded that availability of habeas corpus rests "fundamentally upon a recognition that adequate protection of constitutional rights . . . requires the continuing availability of a mechanism for relief."[38] Habeas corpus is vitally important in enforcing constitutional rights.

In over thirty-nine states, state court judges face some form of election. In some states, judges run in partisan elections for fixed terms, just like other elected officials. In other states, judges face retention elections, where voters vote yes or no as to whether a judge should remain on the bench. Many studies have shown that state judges, knowing that they must run for reelection, may be less inclined to enforce the Constitution than federal judges, who have life tenure.

For example, state supreme court justices who face electoral review are much less likely to overturn death sentences than are those who have life tenure.[39]

In *Schneckloth v. Bustamonte*, Justice Powell wrote a separate opinion, joined by Chief Justice Burger and Justice Rehnquist, urging the Court to end the ability of criminal defendants to argue on habeas corpus that they had been subjected to an illegal search or arrest. Justice Powell said a "state prisoner's Fourth Amendment claims—claims which rarely bear on innocence—should be confined solely to the question of whether the petitioner was provided a fair opportunity to raise and have adjudicated the question in state courts."[40] Justice Powell said that habeas corpus should be available only when there is a claim that an innocent person was convicted, but that is not what Fourth Amendment claims are usually about; they most often concern whether police illegally searched or arrested someone.[41]

Three years later Justice Powell's approach was adopted by a majority of the Court, reflecting how much its ideology had changed in a short time. In *Stone v. Powell* in 1976, the Court concluded that Fourth Amendment claims that had been raised and decided in state courts could not be heard in federal habeas corpus review.[42] Despite the legalistic nature of the Court's language in the case, the decision was of great significance, presaging an era of continuing erosion of the rights of criminal defendants. The Court stated that "where the State has provided an opportunity for full and fair litigation of a Fourth Amendment claim, a state prisoner may not be granted federal habeas corpus relief on the ground that the evidence obtained in an unconstitutional search or seizure was introduced at his trial."[43] Even though President Nixon had been forced to resign in disgrace only two years earlier, his conservative, law and order Court remained firmly in place.

What precipitated this historic decision was a murder resulting from a fracas between two men. At about midnight on February 17, 1968, Lloyd Powell—no relation to Justice Lewis Powell—and three other men entered the Bonanza Liquor Store in San Bernardino, California. Powell and Gerald Parsons, the store manager, got involved in an altercation over the theft of a bottle of wine. In the scuffle that followed, Powell shot and killed Parsons's wife.

Ten hours later an officer of the Henderson, Nevada, Police Department arrested Powell for violation of the Henderson vagrancy ordinance. Powell was searched incident to the arrest, and the officer discovered a .38-caliber revolver with six expended cartridges in the cylinder. He was extradited to California and tried for second-degree murder in California state court. Powell argued that the arrest and search violated the Fourth Amendment and moved to suppress the evidence. The trial court rejected this, and Powell was convicted of murder. In October 1969 the California Court of Appeal affirmed the conviction. The court of appeal did not rule on the legality of the arrest or search, concluding that there was sufficient other evidence that even if a constitutional violation had occurred, it was "harmless error."

Powell filed a petition for a writ of habeas corpus in federal court, arguing that the officer's testimony concerning the .38-caliber revolver should have been excluded as the fruit of an illegal search. His arrest had been unlawful, he argued, because the Henderson vagrancy ordinance was unconstitutionally vague and the arresting officer lacked probable cause to believe that he had been violating it. The federal district court ruled against Powell, but the U.S. Court of Appeals for the Ninth Circuit reversed. It concluded that the arrest had been illegal, that the resultant search also was impermissible, and that it wasn't harmless error.

The Supreme Court, in a 6–3 decision, reversed and concluded that Fourth Amendment claims cannot be raised in federal court on habeas corpus so long as there was an adequate chance to present them in state court. The Court emphasized that Fourth Amendment claims do not relate to the accuracy of the fact-finding process, and the exclusionary rule as a remedy for Fourth Amendment violations exists to deter illegal police practices. The Court concluded that deterrence would be increased marginally, if at all, by allowing exclusionary rule claims to be raised on habeas corpus.[44] Moreover, the Court stressed the costs of the exclusionary rule in permitting guilty defendants to go free and in undermining respect for the criminal justice system.[45]

The Court also rejected the assertion that state judges would be less vigilant than federal court judges in upholding the Fourth Amendment. Whereas the Court in *Brown v. Allen* had explicitly noted frequent state court disregard of the Constitution, Justice Powell, writing for the majority in *Stone,* said that the Court was "unwilling to assume that there now exists a general lack of appropriate sensitivity to constitutional rights in the trial and appellate courts of the several States." The Court said there is no "intrinsic reason" why the fact that someone is a federal judge rather than a state judge "should make him more competent or conscientious or learned" with respect to Fourth Amendment claims.[46] But if this is so, there is never a need to allow issues to be heard in federal court on habeas corpus once they were ruled on in state court; indeed, there is no need for habeas corpus in federal courts at all.

The Fourth Amendment is the only constitutional claim that cannot be raised on habeas corpus. Many aspects of the Court's *Stone* decision are troubling.[47] First, there is a separation of powers problem: the Court exceeded its proper judicial role in deciding that certain constitutional claims could not be heard on habeas corpus review. Federal statutes make habeas corpus available for *any* denial of a constitutional right.[48] The Court should not have decided on its own that certain claims of constitutional violations cannot be raised on habeas corpus. Certainly there is no indication that Congress intended for Fourth Amendment claims to be treated differently from other constitutional issues. Congress has enacted statutes to limit habeas corpus and could have done so with regard to Fourth Amendment claims.[49] The conservative justices, who profess a need for fidelity to statutory language, ignored it here to deny the ability of those convicted in state court to have their claims heard on habeas corpus.

Second, *Stone* wrongly assumes parity between federal and state courts in the protection of constitutional rights. In fact, the very existence of habeas corpus for state prisoners is based on the availability of federal courts to hear constitutional claims. It was not coincidental that in 1867 Congress, seeing how southern states were treating the newly freed slaves, passed the statute allowing state prisoners to raise their constitutional claims in federal court. Almost a century later, *Brown v. Allen* in 1953 was based on the premise that federal courts are uniquely situated to effectively vindicate constitutional claims, justifying relitigation of constitutional issues on habeas corpus.[50] A presumption that federal and state courts are equally able and willing to enforce the Constitution would have broad implications. If state courts were the same as federal courts in their protection of constitutional rights, there would seem to be little justification for ever allowing relitigation in federal courts for cases that had had a full and fair hearing in state courts. But so far, even after almost a half-century, the Court has not extended *Stone v. Powell* beyond the Fourth Amendment. This powerfully reflects that *Stone v. Powell* was based on the Burger Court's hostility to the Fourth Amendment and the exclusionary rule and not on some more general principle with regard to state courts.

Finally, the *Stone* decision's assumption that habeas corpus review of exclusionary rule claims would serve little purpose is unfounded. The Court emphasized that the exclusionary rule does not bear on the actual guilt or innocence of the petitioner. In fact, in another decision, a plurality of the Court stated that the "central reason for habeas corpus [was to afford] a means . . . of redressing an *unjust* incarceration."[51] Although a primary purpose of individual liberties is to prevent the conviction of innocent persons, rights also are enforced as a way of deterring unlawful police practices and of protecting individual privacy and dignity from government infringement. The exclusionary rule additionally exists to keep the judicial system from being tainted by convictions resulting from constitutional violations committed by police. Justice Brennan stated this view forcefully in his dissent in *Stone*: "[P]rocedural safeguards . . . are not admonitions to be tolerated only to the extent they serve functional purposes that ensure that the 'guilty' are punished and the 'innocent' freed."[52] Under this view, habeas corpus exists to ensure that no person is in custody in violation of the Constitution. Without it, police could illegally break into someone's house to gather evidence, and if the state court wrongly allowed it to be used against the defendant, there would be nothing the federal court could do.

· · · · · · · · · ·

WITH *STONE V. POWELL*, the Burger Court took a major step to lessen enforcement of the Fourth Amendment and thereby empower law enforcement, establishing a pattern that over subsequent decades has greatly expanded the power of police to search people and gather information about them. Another step was the development of the "third-party doctrine." When a person shares information with a third party, the Court would find, there is no reasonable expectation of privacy, and therefore no Fourth Amendment protection, for that information.

The key initial case was *United States v. Miller* in 1976, the same year as *Stone v. Powell*.[53] On December 18, 1972, a deputy sheriff from Houston County, Georgia, based on an informant's tip, stopped a van-type truck. The truck contained distillery apparatus and raw material for distilling alcohol. On January 9, 1973, a fire broke out in a Kathleen, Georgia, warehouse rented to Mitchell Miller. During the blaze, firemen and sheriff department officials discovered a 7,500-gallon-capacity distillery, 175 gallons of non-tax-paid whiskey, and related paraphernalia. The informant's tip, the discovery of the distillery apparatus in the truck, and the findings at the fire led police to conclude that they had found an illegal business in making and selling whiskey.

Two weeks later, agents from the Treasury Department's Alcohol, Tobacco and Firearms Bureau presented grand jury subpoenas, which had been issued in blank by the clerk of the district court, to the presidents of two banks where Miller maintained his accounts. The subpoenas required the two bank presidents to appear in court on January 24, 1973, and to produce "all records of accounts, i.e., savings, checking, loan or otherwise, in the name of Mr. Mitch Miller . . . or Mitch Miller Associates."

The bank presidents ordered their employees to make the records immediately available and to provide copies of any documents the agents desired. The agents were given detailed copies of Miller's bank records, including all checks, deposit slips, two financial statements, and three monthly statements. The bank presidents were then told that it would not be necessary for them to appear in person before the grand jury. Miller was never told that all his financial documents had been provided to the federal agents.

Miller was indicted and moved to suppress the evidence gained from the banks. The district court denied this motion, but the U.S. Court of Appeals for the Fifth Circuit reversed and concluded that the Fourth Amendment had been violated. No warrant had been issued for these records. The court was understandably concerned that people regard their financial records as private and believed that a judge should have to approve a warrant before they can be obtained.

The Supreme Court, in a 7–2 decision, reversed the Fifth Circuit decision and ruled against Miller. The Court quoted *Katz* that "what a person knowingly exposes to the public . . . is not a subject of Fourth Amendment protection."[54] Miller, in making his financial transactions, had shared the financial information with the bank, the Court said, and thus he could claim no reasonable expectation of privacy and no protection under the Fourth Amendment. Justice Powell, again writing for the Court, declared that "the Fourth Amendment does not prohibit the obtaining of information revealed to a third party . . . , even if the information is revealed on the assumption that it will be used only for a limited purpose and the confidence placed in the third party will not be betrayed."[55]

The implications of *Miller*, in expanding police power to gather information about an individual without needing to comply with the requirements of the Fourth Amendment, are vast. *Miller* says that when police obtain information that a person has shared with a third party, it is not a search. Therefore, the requirements for probable cause and a warrant—the key protections of privacy under the Fourth Amendment—do not apply or need to be met. Justice Brennan, in his dissenting opinion, lamented, "To permit a police officer access to these records merely upon his request, without any judicial control as to relevancy or other traditional requirements of legal process, and to allow the evidence to be used in any subsequent criminal prosecution against a defendant, opens the door to a vast and unlimited range of very real abuses of police power."[56] Any information we share with a third party, no matter how private—what we tell a doctor, or a suicide prevention hotline, or an accountant—is not protected by the Fourth Amendment and can be obtained by police without needing a warrant based on probable cause.

Three years later the Court took this a step further when, in *Smith v. Maryland,* it held that police can obtain a list of phone numbers that a person calls, or receives calls from, without needing to get a warrant or have probable cause.[57] People know, the Court said, that they are sharing the information with the phone company, which records it and uses it in calculating phone bills (or at least it did at that time, when there were additional charges for toll and long-distance calls). The Court was skeptical that "people in general entertain any actual expectation of privacy in the numbers they dial."[58] Moreover, "[a]lthough subjective expectations cannot be scientifically gauged, it is too much to believe" that telephone users have a subjective expectation of privacy for the numbers they call or receive calls from.[59] The U.S. Court of Appeals for the Ninth Circuit later applied this notion to say that government can monitor the email addresses a person sends to or receives from, or a list of the websites a person visits, without needing a warrant or probable cause.[60]

The courts seriously underestimate how much police can learn from phone numbers, email addresses, and websites. Information that a person has called a suicide hotline reveals something private, as would the phone records of a couple having an affair, or of a confidential source in communication with a journalist. An enormous amount can be learned about a person from the websites they visit. Today a Web search is likely the first thing most people do when they are having unusual health symptoms or receive a medical diagnosis. Sometimes much can be learned about a person's sexual orientation from knowing what websites are visited.

In 2018, in *Carpenter v. United States*, the Supreme Court did not overrule or narrow the third-party doctrine, but it refused to extend it to cover stored cellular location information.[61] Commentators criticized the third-party doctrine strongly: Wayne LaFave, a preeminent expert on the Fourth Amendment, said it was "dead wrong"[62] and Justice Sonia Sotomayor has said it makes no sense in our digital world.[63] Yet it remains the law to this day that because of these Burger Court decisions, police can obtain our financial records or our phone records or an enormous amount of other information about us without needing a warrant.

· · · · · · · · ·

IN TERMS OF our daily lives, the Burger Court also lessened our protections from police by creating and expanding exceptions to situations where police need to get a warrant to conduct a search. For example, it expanded the automobile exception to the Fourth Amendment. Almost all of us have cars, and many of us keep personal things in them, but the Burger Court created a path that has led, in subsequent decades, to police basically being able to stop any car any time and search it.[64] The automobile exception provides that police may search a car without a warrant when they have probable cause that it may contain contraband or evidence of illegal activity. The requirement that they get a warrant—that is, prior approval of a judge—doesn't exist, and if they stop and search a car illegally, they can make up a basis for probable cause, confident that the evidence is unlikely to be excluded.

The automobile exception to the warrant requirement, in fact, long preceded the Burger Court. *Carroll v. United States,* in 1925, involved a search of a car without a warrant, for bootleg liquor.[65] The Court, in an opinion written by Chief Justice Taft, explained that the mobility of cars justified allowing police to search them without needing a warrant because the "vehicle can be quickly moved out of the locality or jurisdiction in which the warrant must be sought."[66]

In 1970 the Burger Court invoked this decision and significantly expanded the automobile exception in *Chambers v. Maroney.*[67] On the night of May 20, 1963, in North Braddock, Pennsylvania, two men robbed a Gulf service station. Each of them carried and displayed a gun. They took the money from the cash register. Two teen-agers had earlier noticed a blue compact station wagon circling the block near the Gulf station; then they saw the station wagon speed away from a parking lot also near the station. About the same time, they learned that the station had been robbed and called the police.

The police officers arrived quickly and were told that there had been four men in the station wagon that sped away. The gas station attendant told police that one of the men was wearing a trench coat and another a green sweater. The officers broadcast a description of the car and the two men over the police radio. Within an hour, about two miles from the Gulf station, police stopped a light blue compact station wagon answering the description and carrying four men. Frank Chambers, one of the men in the car, was wearing a green sweater. The occupants were arrested, and the car was driven to the police station.

While the men were in custody and the car was parked at the station, the officers thoroughly searched the car. They found, concealed in a compartment under the dashboard, two .38-caliber revolvers and cards bearing the name of Raymond Havicon, the attendant at a Boron service station in McKeesport, Pennsylvania, who had been robbed at gunpoint a week earlier.

Police, however, did not have a warrant to search the car. They certainly could have gotten one. They had probable cause, and they had time to get a warrant; the car was parked and the suspects were

in custody. But in *Chambers*, the Supreme Court invoked the automobile exception to the Fourth Amendment and said "automobiles
and other conveyances may be searched without a warrant in circumstances that would not justify the search without a warrant of
a house or an office" if officers have probable cause to believe that
the car contains articles that they are entitled to seize.[68] Police could
have searched the car at the time of the arrest without a warrant, the
Court reasoned, so they had no need for one when the search was at
the stationhouse.

This reasoning, though, ignores the importance of the warrant
requirement and greatly expands the ability of police to search cars.
The Fourth Amendment requires warrants for searches so that a neu-
tral official, a judge, can determine whether there is probable cause.
It is one thing to allow police to search a car when it might be moved
before a warrant can be obtained, but it is something very different
to allow it to be searched when it is parked and obviously not going
anywhere because its owner is in police custody.

In subsequent cases, the Court shifted the rationale for dispensing with the warrant requirement. Instead of emphasizing the car's
mobility, it ruled that people have a lower expectation of privacy
with motor vehicles, and that cars are regulated by the government.
In *Cady v. Dombrowski* in 1973, an off-duty Chicago police officer,
Dombrowski, was arrested for driving while intoxicated.[69] His car
was towed to a police lot. The arresting officer thought Dombrowski's service revolver still might be in the car, so he went and searched
the vehicle. In the course of the search, the officer found evidence
that tied Dombrowski to a murder. The evidence turned out to be
crucial and led to Dombrowski's conviction.

The Supreme Court, invoking the automobile exception, concluded 5–4 that the search of the car without a warrant did not
violate the Fourth Amendment and that the evidence gained was
therefore admissible. The Court noted that original basis for the
automobile exception had been the "mobile nature" of vehicles,[70] and
it acknowledged that the exception had nonetheless been applied in

cases where mobility was "remote, if not nonexistent."[71] It now gave a different explanation for the automobile exception: "the extensive regulation of motor vehicles and traffic."[72]

A year later, in *Cardwell v. Lewis*, the Court gave yet another rationale for dispensing with warrants when it came to searches of automobiles: "One has a lesser expectation of privacy in a motor vehicle because its function is transportation and it seldom serves as one's residence or as the repository for personal effects. A car has little capacity for escaping public scrutiny. It travels public thorough-fares where its occupants and contents are in plain view."[73]

The Court went on to apply this rationale to allow police to search a parked motor home, even when it was a person's residence and the repository for personal effects. In *California v. Carney* in 1985, police received a tip that a man was using his motor home as a place to exchange drugs for sex.[74] The motor home was parked in a city lot, and it would have been easy for police to get a warrant. But the officers searched the motor home without a warrant and found drugs. The Court said the warrantless search did not violate the Fourth Amendment because the motor home was "obviously readily mobile by the turn of an ignition key."[75] But the motor home had been parked, and the police had watched it for almost two hours. During that time they could easily have obtained a warrant.

The Court has held that when police conduct a warrantless search of a vehicle, they may search all containers within it that might contain evidence of a crime or contraband.[76] They may search even containers belonging to passengers who are not suspected of criminal activity.[77] Once a purse or a backpack or a briefcase is placed inside a car, police can open it and search it without any need for a warrant if they have probable cause that the car contains contraband or evidence of a crime.[78]

Case by case, the Court expanded the rationale for and the scope of the automobile exception to the warrant requirement. It ultimately concluded that the law provides little protection for the privacy of the contents of a car because the government regulates cars and because people do not expect privacy for what is in their cars. These assumptions, which underlie the broadened automobile exception to the warrant requirement, are highly questionable. The Court's statement that a car "seldom serves as one's residence or as the repository for personal effects" is untrue. Some people, like those in *California v. Carney,* live in motor homes; some people who are homeless have a car and nowhere else to sleep. Many people keep documents and possessions of all sorts in their cars. It is true that cars are regulated, but so are homes by building codes and businesses by myriad rules. Moreover, the issue is not a choice between forbidding searches and permitting warrantless searches; the issue is whether warrants should be required. It is hard to see why police would need a warrantless search for a parked car or why all the containers within a car should be searchable without a warrant.[79] In all these cases, police likely had enough information to gain a warrant but apparently didn't want to go to the effort to get one. But once police were given the broad power to search cars without warrants, it was inevitably used in instances where no judge would have approved a warrant for a search.

· · · · · · · · ·

THE BOTTOM LINE is that in ways large and small, the Burger Court made it easier for police to search and has limited the rights of criminal suspects. During its seventeen years, it approached the Fourth Amendment from a very different perspective than that of the Warren Court. The Burger Court's majority emphasized the interests of law enforcement, not the privacy of individuals. Its view was that if people are innocent, they have nothing to hide; and if they are guilty, the evidence of their crime should be admissible in court no matter how it was gained. Although none of the decisions were explicit about race, everything we know about policing tells us that expanding the power to search will be felt most in communities of color. In the decades after the Burger Court, the Rehnquist and Roberts Courts built upon these decisions and went much further in empowering police and in lessening the protections of the Fourth Amendment.

12

Hollowing Out
Miranda

T HE WARREN COURT DECIDED *MIRANDA V. ARIZONA*
in 1966, just three years before the beginning of the Burger
Court. For the Burger Court, the decision was like an
unwanted child. The dissenters from *Miranda*—Justices Harlan,
Stewart, and White—now had colleagues who shared their view and
thus a strong majority that disagreed with that decision. The Burger
Court did not abandon or overrule *Miranda*, but it used every opportunity to chip away at and to limit its application. Never again did
the Court speak of the coercion inherent in police interrogations in
custody. Never did it recognize a racial dimension to interrogations,
especially when a person of color was surrounded and questioned by
white officers. Never did the Court acknowledge that suspects are
sometimes pressured or even tricked into making false confessions,
as when police lie to them about the evidence and tell them how
much easier it would be if only they admitted to the crime. Not once
in its seventeen years did the Burger Court do anything to strengthen
the privilege against self-incrimination.

The Burger Court was explicit that *Miranda*'s protections applied
only during police interrogations of persons in custody. It therefore
narrowed what constituted an "interrogation" and what constituted "custody," to limit the time when police had to comply with
Miranda.[1] Most of all, the Court gave police the ability to easily

undermine *Miranda,* such as by allowing them to deviate from and even negate the required warnings, which were key to *Miranda*'s effort to protect people from police coercion. In *California v. Prysock* in 1981, the Court held, 6–3, that statements that a juvenile had given to police were admissible even though he was never told— as *Miranda* clearly requires—that he would be provided a free attorney if he could not afford one.[2] The Court said that it had "never indicated that the 'rigidity' of *Miranda* extends to the precise formulation of the warnings given a criminal defendant." No "talismanic incantation," the Court said, "was required to satisfy its strictures."[3]

But in that case, the police failure lay not in minor changes in the wording of the warnings; rather, the officers had completely omitted to give the suspect the crucial information that the government would provide a lawyer if he wanted one and could not afford it. The point of the *Miranda* warnings is that most people really don't know they have these rights and that the presence of a lawyer can make all the difference in police questioning. By characterizing *Miranda* warnings in this way, the Court encouraged police to deviate from them in ways that undermine their purpose.

The implications of *California v. Prysock* became evident in the Court's 1989 decision in *Duckworth v. Eagan.*[4] Late on May 16, 1982, Gary Lee Eagan contacted a Chicago police officer he knew to report that he had seen the naked body of a dead woman lying on a Lake Michigan beach. Eagan took several Chicago police officers to the beach, where they found that the woman was actually alive and was crying for help. When she saw Eagan, she exclaimed: "Why did you stab me? Why did you stab me?" Eagan told the officers that he had been with the woman earlier that night, and that they had been attacked on the lakefront by several men who abducted the woman in a van.

The next morning, after realizing that the crime had been committed in Indiana, the Chicago police turned the investigation over to the Hammond, Indiana, Police Department. Eagan repeated to the Hammond police officers his story that he had been attacked on the lakefront and that the woman had been abducted by several men. He steadfastly denied that he had stabbed her. At about eleven a.m., Hammond police questioned Eagan. Before doing so, they read him a waiver form, entitled "Voluntary Appearance; Advice of Rights," and asked him to sign it. The form provided:

> Before we ask you any questions, you must understand your rights. You have the right to remain silent. Anything you say can be used against you in court. You have a right to talk to a lawyer for advice before we ask you any questions, and to have him with you during questioning. You have this right to the advice and presence of a lawyer even if you cannot afford to hire one. *We have no way of giving you a lawyer, but one will be appointed for you, if you wish, if and when you go to court.*

It is astounding that the police's printed form was flatly wrong as to the law. It said the police had no way of providing a lawyer during interrogations, even though the Supreme Court had held that one was required. It said the suspect would get a lawyer "if and when" he or she went to court, but suspects have the right to a lawyer during questioning at the police station, as the Court held in *Escobedo* and in *Miranda*.

Eagan signed the form and repeated his story. He was then placed in the "lockup" at the Hammond police headquarters. Some twenty-nine hours later, at about four p.m. on May 18, the police again questioned him. He confessed to stabbing the woman. Eagan's lawyer later moved to exclude his confession on the ground that the police had violated *Miranda* by given him false information as to his rights. The Supreme Court, relying on *California v. Prysock*, brushed aside this concern, saying, "We have never insisted that *Miranda* warnings be given in the exact form described in that decision."[5] In other words, even though the Hammond police improperly administered the *Miranda* warnings and gave Eagan false information about his rights, the Court found no constitutional violation. It thereby encouraged police to disregard the Court's prescription in *Miranda* and to give their own version of the warnings, which could be incomplete and even inaccurate.

The Burger Court's ambivalence, to put it generously, toward *Miranda* is reflected in the exceptions that it carved. By allowing prosecutors to use statements gained in violation of the *Miranda* requirements, the Court encouraged police to circumvent, indeed to ignore *Miranda*.[6] In 1971, early in the Burger Court era, the justices held in *Harris v. New York* that a statement obtained without complying with *Miranda* could be used to impeach a criminal defendant who took the witness stand.[7] In other words, if police question a suspect in violation of *Miranda*—such as by not reading the warnings, or not providing counsel, or continuing to question after the suspect asserts the right to remain silent—any statement they gain cannot be used as evidence against that person. But if the criminal defendant takes the witness stand at trial, a statement so gained can be used to contradict his testimony. Then, of course, the jury hears the incriminating statement, and it will have an impact on the jurors as they decide whether to convict.

The experience of Viven Harris shows exactly how police do this. Harris was arrested for selling heroin to undercover police officers. After his arrest, police questioned him without giving him *Miranda* warnings, and Harris made incriminating admissions. But even the prosecutor conceded that these admissions could not be used as evidence against him. Harris took the witness stand at his trial and denied the crime. The prosecutor then sought to use Harris's incriminating statements against him to impeach his credibility. The judge allowed it, and Harris was convicted. The Supreme Court agreed and was untroubled that the jury had heard statements gained by police in violation of the Constitution.

Justice Brennan wrote for the four dissenting justices and lamented that the Court had allowed impermissibly obtained statements to come into evidence at all. The privilege against self-incrimination, he explained, is based on "the respect a government . . . must accord to the dignity and integrity of its citizens" and that this is undermined when the jury can hear statements gained when the police violate the requirements of *Miranda v. Arizona.* He expressed his outrage that the Court was so undermining *Miranda,* calling it "monstrous that courts should aid or abet the law-breaking police officer."[8]

When police know that statements they obtain unconstitutionally can be admitted as evidence and used for impeachment purposes, then they have an incentive to ignore *Miranda* altogether. They know that incriminating statements, even when obtained in violation of *Miranda,* are potentially of great value to the prosecution. The statements may keep defendants from taking the witness stand, since such statements could well be used to impeach them, or to pressure them to plead guilty. And if a defendant doesn't plead guilty and takes the witness stand, the incriminating statement could be introduced in court and used against him or her.

This possibility is not hypothetical. Charles Weisselberg carefully reviewed police training manuals and training bulletins in California and found that they instructed police in "questioning outside *Miranda.*" Police were trained to deliberately violate the Constitution because, as the manuals explained, incriminating statements could still be used to impeach a defendant's credibility if he testified.[9] Weisselberg concluded: "There can be no doubt that the practice of questioning 'outside *Miranda*' has spread throughout California. The training materials were distributed statewide" and in other states as well.[10] The Burger Court gave police an incentive to ignore *Miranda,* and police often have done so.[11] The Burger Court left the crucial protection created by the Warren Court, the right to remain silent, in tatters.

The Burger Court did not expressly overrule *Miranda,* though unquestionably a majority of its justices disagreed with its holding. Instead, it undermined *Miranda* at every opportunity. It never questioned the central premise of *Miranda,* that in-custodial police interrogation is inherently coercive. Nor did it offer any alternative to the remedy provided by *Miranda.* But a majority of its justices believed that *Miranda* limited police too much in their ability to gain confessions, and they did not want to keep juries from hearing the admissions, even when police violated the law to get them. They reduced *Miranda* to little more than a formality. Police still have to give some form of warnings in order for incriminating statements to be admissible, but even if police don't do that, prosecutors have other ways to use the admissions. Police got the message loud and clear that they could ignore *Miranda* and that prosecutors would benefit from their unconstitutional acts.

13

Refusing to Check Police Eyewitness Identification Procedures

"BETTER THAT TEN GUILTY PERSONS ESCAPE, THAN that one innocent suffer" is a deeply revered adage in criminal law.[1] Everyone, liberals and conservatives alike, agrees that in criminal justice systems, procedural safeguards must protect innocent people from being convicted. But wrongful convictions do take place, and one of the most frequent causes is inaccurate eyewitness identifications. Moreover, cross-racial identifications—where a person identifies someone of a different race—are particularly likely to be inaccurate. Unfortunately, the Supreme Court never has acknowledged this fact, and in the last half-century, it has never overturned a conviction based on how the identification was done, even when police used very suggestive identification procedures.

In 1967, in *United States v. Wade,* the Warren Court acknowledged that many innocent people have been wrongly convicted because of faulty identifications.[2] It held that a person represented by counsel has the right to have that attorney present at a post-indictment identification. This should have been the first step in dealing with the problem, and the Court should then have expanded the right to counsel to other identification procedures and should have created further safeguards to protect innocent people from being wrongly identified and convicted. It never happened. Actually *Wade,* decided over a half-century ago, was the last time the Court imposed any limits on police in conducting identifications.

In fact, the Burger Court lessened the constitutional protections against false eyewitness identifications, in two ways: it limited the right to counsel to post-indictment lineups, and it allowed even identifications following very suggestive police procedures to be admitted as evidence as long as they are "reliable." And without exception, the Burger Court found every identification to be reliable and thus a sufficient basis for a conviction. Despite countless cases where it was later learned that innocent people were convicted because of false identifications and a mountain of social science evidence documenting the problems with eyewitness identifications, the Court has done nothing to address the problem.

Early in the Burger Court era, the justices had the chance to extend *Wade*'s requirement to have attorneys present at lineups occurring before indictment and also at photo identification procedures. At these events, attorneys are important in deterring police from being suggestive to the witness about who to pick and in ensuring that the identification procedure is done properly. But in both instances— for pre-indictment lineups and for photo identifications—the Court declined to require that counsel be present. This gives police an easy way to circumvent *Wade* and conduct identifications without the presence of an attorney.

In *Kirby v. Illinois* in 1972, the Burger Court made it clear that it would treat *Wade* as an anomaly, declining to extend it to lineups taking place before indictments.[3] On February 21, 1968, in Chicago, Willie Shard reported to police that on the previous day on a street, two men had robbed him of a wallet containing, among other things, traveler's checks and a Social Security card. On February 22 two officers stopped Thomas Kirby and Ralph Bean on West Madison Street and asked the men for identification. Kirby produced a wallet that contained three traveler's checks and a Social Security card, all bearing the name of Willie Shard. Papers with Shard's name were also found in Bean's possession. When asked to explain his possession of Shard's property, Kirby told the officers that he had won them in a crap game. The officers arrested Kirby and Bean and took them to a police station.

Only after arriving at the station, and checking the records there, did the arresting officers learn of the Shard robbery. Police went to Shard's place of employment, picked him up, and brought him to the station. As soon as Shard entered the room where Kirby and Bean were seated at a table, he positively identified them as the men who had robbed him two days earlier. No lawyer was present, and neither of the suspects had been advised of any right to the presence of counsel.

Six weeks later Kirby and Bean were indicted for the robbery of Willie Shard. Kirby then was appointed a lawyer. The attorney moved to suppress Shard's identification of Kirby as having been done in a manner that violated the Constitution. The trial court denied this motion, and Kirby was convicted.

At the Supreme Court, Kirby's lawyer argued that his client should have had the opportunity for a lawyer to be present at the identification procedure. In a 6–3 decision, the Court rejected this argument, stressing that *Wade* had created a right to an attorney only at a *post*-indictment identification procedure; Shard had identified Kirby before there was an indictment. At the very least, the Court gave police an easy way to circumvent the requirements of *Wade*: conduct the identification before the indictment. But all the concerns that *Wade* expressed as to why identification procedures can lead to mistaken identifications and convictions of innocent people apply just as much to pre-indictment identifications as to post-indictment identifications. All the reasons *Wade* gave as to why counsel can make a difference in identification procedures apply just as much to pre-indictment identifications. The line that the Court drew in *Kirby* is simply unjustifiable. As Professor Joshua Dressler has noted, the "risks inherent in lineups and other identification procedure are as substantial before formal charges are brought as they are after. If defense counsel is needed at a post-indictment lineup, he also is needed at a pre-indictment identification procedure."[4] And once a witness has identified someone, that witness is very likely to repeat that identification throughout the proceedings.

A year after *Kirby,* in *United States v. Ash,* the Court again limited the protections of *Wade.*[5] The issue was whether a criminal defendant has the right to have counsel present when police, after indictment, show a witness a set of photographs. After all, the suggestiveness that rightly was of great concern to the Court in *Wade* could occur in a photo identification as well. A police officer might subtly tap on one of the pictures or give other nonverbal cues as to which individual is the suspect. The Court in *Wade* stressed the importance of an attorney being present at identifications, because the lawyer is "more sensitive to, and aware of, suggestive influences than the accused himself, and [is] better able to reconstruct the events at trial."[6]

Ash, like *Wade,* concerned identification procedures after a person has been indicted. But *Ash* was decided by the Burger Court, not by the Warren Court, and that made all the difference. On the morning of August 26, 1965, a man with a stocking mask entered a bank in Washington, D.C., and waved a pistol. He ordered an employee to hang up the telephone and instructed all others present not to move. Seconds later a second man, also wearing a stocking mask, entered the bank, scooped money from the tellers' drawers into a bag, and left. The gunman followed, and both men escaped through an alley. The robbery lasted three or four minutes.

A government informer, Clarence McFarland, told authorities that he had discussed the robbery with Charles J. Ash, Jr. Acting on this information, on February 3, 1966—five months after the robbery—an FBI agent showed each of four witnesses black and white mugshots of five Black males, including Ash, all of generally the same age, height, and weight, but "[n]one of the witnesses was able to make a 'positive' identification of Ash."[7] At this time Ash was not in custody and had not been charged. On April 1, 1966, an indictment was returned, charging Ash and a co-defendant, John L. Bailey, on five counts related to the bank robbery.

Trial was set for May 1968, almost three years after the crime. In preparing for trial, the prosecutor used a photographic display to determine whether the witnesses he planned to call would be able to make in-court identifications. Shortly before the trial, an FBI agent and the prosecutor showed five color photographs to the four witnesses who previously had tentatively identified the black and white photograph of Ash, even though none were sure of their identification. Three of the witnesses selected the photo of Ash, but one was unable to make any selection. None of the witnesses selected the photo of Bailey that was also in the group.

Ash's lawyer objected and moved to exclude the witnesses from testifying on the ground that the photo identification was done without an attorney present. The trial judge denied the motion. At trial, the three witnesses who had been inside the bank identified Ash as the gunman, but they were unwilling to state that they were certain of their identifications. None of them made an in-court identification of Bailey. The fourth witness, who had been in a car outside the bank and had seen the fleeing robbers after they removed their masks, made positive in-court identifications of both Ash and Bailey. Bailey's counsel then sought to impeach this in-court identification by calling the FBI agent who had shown the color photographs to the witnesses immediately before trial. Bailey's counsel demonstrated that the witness who had identified Bailey in court had failed to identify a color photograph of Bailey. During the course of the examination, Bailey's counsel also brought out the fact that this witness had selected another man as one of the robbers.

The jury convicted Ash on all counts. It was unable to reach a verdict on the charges against Bailey, and his motion for acquittal was granted.

The issue before the Supreme Court was whether Ash's right to counsel was violated by the photo identification conducted without his lawyer being present. The Court, in a 6–3 decision, ruled against Ash. Justice Blackmun wrote for the Court, while Brennan, Douglas, and Marshall—all of whom had been in the majority in *Wade* and had voted to expand constitutional rights during the Warren Court—dissented. This was early in Blackmun's tenure on the Court, before he transformed into one of its more liberal justices. The Court said the right to counsel exists to advise the accused. Because the suspect has no right to be present at a photo identification, there is no right to have the lawyer present:[8] "We hold, then, that the Sixth Amendment does not grant the right to counsel at photographic displays conducted by the Government for the purpose of allowing a witness to attempt an identification of the offender."[9]

Justice Brennan, writing for the dissent, said that the decision marked "simply another step towards the complete evisceration of the fundamental constitutional principles established by this Court."[10] All the concerns raised about police suggestiveness and false identifications for lineups are also at issue for photo identifications. But the accused is not present for a photo identification, so no one from the defense can witness police officers' actions there. And as with a lineup, once a witness makes an identification, he or she is very likely to stick with it even if it is incorrect.

Kirby and *Ash* must be understood as the shift from the Warren Court, which was focused on protecting the constitutional rights of criminal defendants, to the Burger Court, which was much more concerned with ensuring that police and prosecutors could convict criminals. Having rejected criminal suspects' right to counsel at pre-indictment lineups and post-indictment photo identifications, did the Burger Court offer them any protection at all when it came to identifications?

· · · · · · · · ·

THE WARREN COURT said that unduly suggestive identification procedures violate due process and that identifications resulting from them have to be excluded.[11] As a principle this makes great sense, but the later Courts have consistently refused to bar even very suggestive identifications from being admitted as evidence. Only once in all of American history has the Court found an identification to be so suggestive as to violate due process, and that was in 1969 at the end of the Warren Court, in an opinion by Justice Abe Fortas.[12] Since then, the Court has developed a series of legal doctrines that make it extremely difficult for a suspect to successfully challenge an identification as unconstitutionally suggestive.

First, the Court has held that even highly suggestive procedures do not violate due process, and that if the identifications are deemed necessary, they are admissible as evidence.

This actually stems from a decision of the Warren Court. In 1961, Dr. Behrendt was stabbed to death, and his wife was injured in the same attack. Police brought the alleged assailant, Theodore Stovall, along with five police officers and two assistant district attorneys, to Mrs. Behrendt's hospital room. Stovall was handcuffed and was the only Black person in the room. Mrs. Behrendt said that he was the man who had killed her husband and stabbed her. At trial, she and the officers testified that she had identified Stovall in the hospital room, and she also made an in-court identification of Stovall in the courtroom. Stovall was convicted of murder and sentenced to death.

In *Stovall v. Denno* in 1967, the Warren Court recognized that this type of identification, where the victim is shown only one person, is the most prone to error. The Court observed, "The practice of showing suspects singly to persons for the purpose of identification, and not as part of a lineup, has been widely condemned."[13]

Nonetheless, the Court found no violation of due process, saying that the in-hospital identification had been "imperative": "Faced with the responsibility of identifying the attacker, with the need for immediate action and with the knowledge that [the victim] could not visit the jail, the police followed the only feasible procedure and took Stovall to the hospital room."[14]

I have never understood this conclusion. The Court did not deny the inherent suggestiveness of what the police did, but said it had been necessary. This is tantamount to saying that because it is necessary for police to find someone to accuse of a crime, it doesn't matter whether they have the right person. It wasn't necessary to bring Stovall to the hospital room by himself, though, because there were many alternatives. Stovall had been indicted and had been appointed a lawyer, so at the very least, they could have had his attorney there. The police could have done a lineup in the hospital room, where the victim would have had the chance to see Stovall next to a few other African American men of similar height and weight. They could have shown her several photographs, including Stovall and other men who were similar in appearance.

As it was, the Court established a principle that even very suggestive identification procedures are acceptable and don't violate due process as long as they are subsequently deemed necessary. This principle reflects the view that the Constitution should not constrain police identifications and that courts should simply trust witnesses not to make mistakes. The problem is that eyewitness identifications are indeed prone to error and often lead to innocent people being convicted.

The second legal doctrine making it difficult for suspects to challenge identification procedures as unconstitutionally suggestive is that the Court has been willing to allow even very suggestive identifications if it concludes that they are sufficiently reliable. For example, in *Neil v. Biggers* in 1972, the Court refused to find a violation of due process in a very troubling police identification procedure.[15]

In 1965 in Tennessee, a woman was raped. Over a seven-month period, she viewed suspects in her home or at the police station, some in lineups and others in showups, and she was shown between thirty and forty photographs. At one point, she told the police officer that a man pictured in one photograph had features similar to those of her assailant, but she identified none of the suspects.

About eight months after the rape, the police called the victim to the station to view Archie Biggers, an African American man who was being detained on another charge. The police had two detectives walk him in front of the victim. At her request, the police directed

Biggers to say "Shut up or I'll kill you." She identified Biggers as the rapist. Biggers was convicted in state court and sentenced to twenty years in prison.

In *Neil v. Biggers*, the Supreme Court acknowledged that the police could have waited until they found other men to be in a lineup with Biggers and done the identification that way. Nor did the police make a claim of time urgency since this was already eight months after the assault. But the Court said that even if an identification procedure is "unnecessarily suggestive," it is admissible in court so long as it is "reliable." The victim was "sure" of her identification and said she would never forget what her assailant looked like. The Court said that since she was a "reliable" witness, the identification was admissible.[16]

But social science research shows that the certainty of an identification has no relationship to its reliability.[17] People are often completely wrong in their identifications but still profess certainty. Moreover, courts have every incentive to want to convict someone of a heinous crime and are reluctant to throw out critical, often decisive evidence, by saying that the identification was not reliable.

In *Manson v. Brathwaite* in 1977, an identification had been the only evidence brought against the defendant. The Supreme Court conceded that the identification was unnecessarily suggestive but still found no violation of due process.[18]

In 1970 in Hartford, Connecticut, an undercover police officer, Jimmy Glover, had purchased heroin from a man in the doorway of an apartment. Another officer, based on Glover's description, obtained a picture of Nowell Brathwaite from the Department of Motor Vehicles and showed it to Glover. Glover identified Brathwaite as the man from whom he had purchased the drugs. As the Court noted, the "sole evidence tying Brathwaite to the possession and sale of the heroin consisted in his identifications by the police undercover agent, Jimmy Glover."[19]

No one—not even the prosecutor—denied that this identification procedure was unnecessarily suggestive. The Court noted that the government "acknowledges that the procedure in the instant case was suggestive (because only one photograph was used) and unnecessary (because there was no emergency or exigent circumstance)."[20] But the Court said there had been no violation of due process because the identification was reliable, and "reliability is the linchpin in determining the admissibility of identification testimony."[21] It pointed to all the reasons why it found Glover's testimony reliable and affirmed the conviction. The Court's conclusion is deeply troubling: the results of unnecessary, very suggestive identifications are admissible as evidence.

Not once since the start of the Burger Court in 1969 has the Supreme Court found any identification to be unreliable. Not once has it expressed the slightest concern about cross-racial identifications. Many "studies document a significant difference in the ability of white American subjects to recognize white and black faces. The impairment in ability to recognize black faces is substantial."[22] This phenomenon is not newly discovered. Forty years ago federal appeals court judge David Bazelon lamented that the criminal justice system had neglected the rate of cross-racial misidentification because it primarily affects minorities.[23]

Lower courts and police have gotten the message from the Supreme Court that identifications are rarely excluded from being used as evidence. What explains the Supreme Court's failure to acknowledge, let alone deal with, the problem of eyewitness identifications? The justices likely minimize the chances that an eyewitness will identify the wrong person, ignoring all the studies showing that identifications are often wrong yet are powerful for juries. The Court trusts police to arrest and prosecute the right person and is willing to presume that the person is guilty. Even if police sometimes make mistakes, the Court assumes, witnesses generally are accurate, and if they are not, cross-examining them at trial is adequate to protect the innocent. I fear that the Court's unstated assumption is that it is more important to convict somebody, even the wrong person, than to leave a crime unsolved.

14

Eroding Remedies for Police Misconduct

I F POLICE FACE NO CONSEQUENCES FOR VIOLATING A person's constitutional rights, those rights might just as well not exist. I learned from interviewing many police officers that they are acutely aware of whether the law imposes any sanctions on them for impermissible conduct, and if so, what those sanctions might be. Unless they experience possibly significant consequences for unconstitutional behavior, police know that they can violate the Constitution with impunity. The Burger Court greatly lessened the likelihood of any adverse consequences for police misconduct.

There are two possible remedies for police misconduct. One is the exclusion of evidence. But the Burger Court was very skeptical, it is fair to say hostile, to the exclusionary rule—which prevents prosecutors from using evidence gained from police violating the Constitution—and looked for ways to narrow its application. The other possible remedy is civil lawsuits brought against the officers or their departments. Here the story is more complicated. It was the Burger Court, in 1983, that decided *City of Los Angeles v. Lyons* and made it extremely difficult, and often impossible, for members of the public to sue for an injunction to stop unconstitutional police behavior. But it also was the Burger Court that expanded people's ability to sue officers and cities for monetary damages for police misconduct. Unfortunately, the Rehnquist and Roberts Courts, which followed the Burger Court, significantly undercut these civil remedies and have made it even more difficult for our society to hold police and those who employ them accountable.

In no area was the shift from the Warren Court to the Burger Court clearer than in the justices' attitude toward the exclusionary rule. The Warren Court believed that police would be less likely to violate the Constitution, such as by carrying out illegal searches, if they knew that the fruits of their misconduct could not be used as evidence against a criminal defendant. This view was embodied in *Mapp v. Ohio,* the 1961 decision that applied the exclusionary rule to the states.

But *Mapp* was a 5–4 decision and has always been controversial. Conservatives regard the exclusionary rule as undesirable because it keeps crucial evidence from being heard and allows guilty people to go free. This view is problematic for several reasons. Without the exclusionary rule, the only other means to deter police from violating the Constitution is civil suits, but the Supreme Court has made such suits extremely difficult, even impossible. Hence, without the exclusionary rule, police know that they can violate the Fourth Amendment with impunity. The conservative view is also problematic because, as the Supreme Court itself said in creating the exclusionary rule and applying it to the states, courts are tainted when people are convicted based on evidence obtained in violation of the Constitution. The integrity of the judiciary demands that it not imprison or execute people based on evidence gained from constitutional violations.

But the Burger Court, with its conservative majority, looked for every occasion to cut back on the exclusionary rule and lessen its application. For example, in *Stone v. Powell* (discussed earlier), the Court held that those convicted in state court could not raise claims in federal court on habeas corpus that that they are being held in violation of the Constitution on the ground that evidence should have been excluded because the police violated the Fourth Amendment. A person convicted in state court can raise any constitutional right in federal court via a habeas corpus petition, except for the Fourth Amendment's protection against illegal searches and arrests.

Within its first few years, the Burger Court created a number of new exceptions to the exclusionary rule. It did not eliminate the exclusionary rule, though Justices Burger and Rehnquist said that they wanted to. Instead, it lessened its applicability. And the greater the exceptions to the exclusionary rule, the more police in 1970s America gained incentives to violate the Fourth Amendment, knowing that illegally seized evidence might now be used against a criminal defendant.

In the early 1980s, the Burger Court mirrored the politics of the very conservative president, Ronald Reagan. In *Segura v. United States* in 1984, for example, it held that evidence does not have to be excluded if there is an independent source for the information, *even if the independent source involves a police violation of the Fourth Amendment*. Police, in February 1981, had illegally entered Andres Segura's apartment in New York City without a warrant.[1] No one was home, and the officers walked around the apartment. In a bedroom, they saw evidence of drug dealing. At that point, they decided to get a warrant to search the apartment and seize the evidence. At least two agents remained in the apartment—through a night and almost all the next day—while the other officers went to get a warrant. Police had entered the apartment at about eleven p.m. on Saturday evening, but the warrant application was not presented to the magistrate until five p.m. on Sunday. The officers would blame it on an "administrative delay." The warrant was issued, and at approximately six p.m., some nineteen hours after the agents' initial entry into the apartment, the search was performed. The officers seized the evidence of drugs and drug dealing that they had first seen the previous evening.

The defendant moved to exclude the evidence on the ground that the police had violated the Fourth Amendment: they had entered the apartment without a warrant and then stayed there for almost a day. The Court, in a 5–4 decision, rejected the application of the exclusionary rule. "The exclusionary rule," the majority opinion, written by Chief Justice Burger, concluded, "has no application [where] the Government learned of the evidence from an independent source."[2] But what could they have possibly deemed the "independent source" allowing introduction of the evidence? The police searching the apartment once they got a warrant were themselves the "independent source." The Court held that the evidence was admissible even though the officers illegally entered the apartment without a warrant and stayed there for over nineteen hours before the warrant was obtained, and even though all the evidence seized had been seen by the police before they obtained the warrant.

This decision gave broad authorization to police to violate the Fourth Amendment, as soon became clear in a subsequent case, *Murray v. United States* in 1988, near the end of Reagan's second term.[3] In 1983 in Boston, federal law enforcement agents, based on information received from informants, were watching Michael Murray and James Carter. At about 1:45 p.m. on April 6, they observed Murray drive a truck, and Carter drive a green camper, into a warehouse in South Boston. About twenty minutes later, the two men drove the vehicles back out. The agents saw that inside the warehouse there was a tractor-trailer rig bearing a long, dark container.

Several agents converged on the warehouse and forced entry. Inside they observed in plain view numerous burlap-wrapped bales that were later found to contain marijuana. They left without disturbing the bales, kept the warehouse under surveillance, and did not reenter it until they had a search warrant. In applying for the warrant, the agents did not mention their prior illegal entry. When the warrant was issued—at 10:40 p.m., approximately eight hours after the initial entry—the agents immediately reentered the warehouse and seized 270 bales of marijuana and notebooks listing customers for whom the bales were destined. This took place in the midst of the war on drugs, when law enforcement gave much greater attention to illegal drugs, including marijuana, and traffickers suffered vastly larger criminal penalties.

The defendants' lawyer moved to exclude the evidence because the police officers, by entering the warehouse without a warrant, had clearly violated the Fourth Amendment. The Supreme Court, in an opinion written by Justice Antonin Scalia, disagreed, saying once more that there had been an independent source for the evidence. But again, what was the independent source? The Court held that the police saw the evidence when they entered with the warrant, and that that was sufficient basis for the evidence to be admissible, notwithstanding the earlier violation of the Fourth Amendment.[4]

This decision means that the police can enter a home or a business illegally, and if they see contraband or evidence of illegal activity, they can then go to a magistrate for a warrant. The police don't have to tell the judge about their illegal entry. They just need to invent some reason why they have probable cause for the warrant. The officers then can go back and reenter and seize the evidence. As Justice Marshall lamented, this decision "emasculates the Warrant Clause and undermines the deterrence function of the exclusionary rule."[5] The police now had an incentive to violate the Fourth Amendment and search without a warrant, knowing that if they later went back with one, the evidence would be admissible.

· · · · · · · · · ·

THE BURGER COURT created another important exception to the exclusionary rule by allowing the admission of evidence if the police reasonably relied on an invalid warrant to conduct a search or seizure. *United States v. Leon*, the key case, was very controversial when it was decided in 1984. For the first time ever, the Court recognized a good faith exception to the exclusionary rule and paved the way for a much broader exception later. Ultimately the fundamental disagreement in *Leon* between the majority and the dissent was over the desirability of having an exclusionary rule in the first place.[6]

In 1981 in Burbank, California, police got a search warrant from a judge based on an affidavit from a police officer; unknown to them, the affidavit was based on an unreliable informant. Relying on the warrant, the police searched a house and found drugs. A court later found that the affidavit had been insufficient to provide probable cause for a warrant; the judge said that there just hadn't been enough evidence to allow the police to search. That the search violated the Fourth Amendment was undisputed—it had been done without probable cause. But the Supreme Court ruled that the evidence was nonetheless admissible at trial.

Justice White, who had dissented in so many Warren Court decisions protecting those accused of crimes, wrote the majority opinion and expressed great skepticism about the desirability of the exclusionary rule. After twenty years on the Court, he was now part of the conservative majority. The exclusionary rule was not part of the Fourth Amendment, he noted; nothing in the amendment's language required or even suggested this remedy. The application of the exclusionary rule, he wrote, should be determined "by weighing the costs and benefits of preventing the use in the prosecution's case in chief of inherently trustworthy tangible evidence."[7]

Justice White stressed the "substantial social costs exacted by the exclusionary rule." The rule impedes "the truth-finding functions of judge and jury," he lamented, and means that "some guilty defendants may go free or receive reduced sentences as a result of favorable plea bargains."[8] The costs of the exclusionary rule, balanced against its benefits, he wrote, justify a good faith exception. Compared to the "substantial costs of exclusion," he saw only "marginal or nonexistent benefits [from] suppressing evidence."[9]

Justice White's reasoning was an argument, not for creating a narrow exception to the exclusionary rule, but for eliminating it altogether. He was explicit that convicting people, even on the basis of illegally obtained evidence, is more important than enforcing Fourth Amendment protections.

Justice Brennan dissented, powerfully declaring, "In case after case, I have witnessed the Court's gradual but determined strangulation of the [exclusionary] rule. It now appears that the Court's victory over the Fourth Amendment is complete."[10] Brennan saw this case as the "pièce de resistance" of the Burger Court's fifteen-year assault on the exclusionary rule. Having dissented in case after case, his frustration with the decisions was clearly apparent. If the application of the exclusionary rule depended on the Supreme Court weighing its costs and its benefits, conservative justices were always likely to say that the costs of letting potentially guilty people go free outweighed the benefits of deterring police misconduct; that was why their goal was not to modify but to eliminate the exclusionary rule. In one importance sense, Justice Brennan was wrong: *Leon* was not the "pièce de resistance" and did not mark the end of the exclusionary rule. Rather, in later years the Court went much further in limiting the exclusionary rule and Fourth Amendment protections that are supposed to limit the police.

· · · · · · · · ·

IF THE BURGER COURT was unabashedly hostile to the exclusionary rule, it had a more mixed record on the other possible remedy for police misconduct, civil suits against officers and police departments. In some areas, the Court was very restrictive of people's ability to sue cities. In *City of Los Angeles* in 1983, it largely closed the door on civil suits for injunctive relief to reform the police—a crucial restriction on the power of the federal courts that continues to this day. To be sure, the Burger Court also expanded the ability of citizens to sue federal officers for monetary damages for violating the Constitution. But at the same time it significantly expanded the immunity of government officers from being held liable. It greatly enlarged people's ability to sue cities, which is key for holding police accountable, but it also imposed restrictions on such suits that over time have made it increasingly difficult to succeed in such litigation.

Actually, even before *City of Los Angeles v. Lyons* imposed restrictions on injunctive relief against police departments, another troubling Burger Court decision had already limited the ability of federal courts to deal with police misconduct. *Rizzo v. Goode* in 1976 involved two class action suits that had been brought against the City of Philadelphia and its police department alleging a pervasive pattern of illegal and unconstitutional mistreatment by police officers, especially directed at Blacks.[11] The plaintiffs sought an injunction to order the city to improve its handling of citizens' complaints and to cease violating citizens' rights. The Philadelphia Police Department had engaged in racially discriminatory and harassing policing: it illegally stopped people based on race, carried out searches without warrants or probable cause, and exercised excessive force especially at people of color. Philadelphia was notorious for its racist, aggressive policing, which Frank Rizzo, its police commissioner and then mayor, vocally defended.

In the *Rizzo* case, the federal district court held a twenty-one-day hearing and heard 250 witnesses. The "amount of evidence" that Philadelphia police had committed racial discrimination and constitutional violations was "staggering," as the Supreme Court would later say.[12] The federal district court found a "pattern of frequent police violations" of the rights of African Americans and of protesters. It ordered city officials to implement a program for dealing with complaints against police that satisfied minimal constitutional standards. The U.S. Court of Appeals for the Third Circuit upheld this decision.

But the Supreme Court reversed and ruled in favor of the City of Philadelphia. Presaging what it would decide in *Lyons* seven year later, it said that past wrongs were not a basis for an injunction against police.[13] The Court in *Rizzo* went even further and said that federal court relief against police departments was limited by principles of states' rights and federalism. Earlier, the Court had limited the ability of federal courts to issue injunctions against state courts to keep them from violating the Constitution.[14] The Court said the same concerns kept federal courts from issuing injunctions to cities and their police departments. "Principles of federalism," the Court said, "likewise have applicability where injunctive relief is sought, not against the judicial branch of the state government, but against those in charge of an executive branch of an agency of state or local governments such as petitioners here."[15]

This proposition is astounding and radical. Even when a federal court finds pervasive constitutional violations, particularly directed at people of color by a city police department, that federal court is limited in providing a remedy because of principles of states' rights and federalism.

In fact, there is no reason why concern about states' rights ever should limit the ability of the federal courts to provide remedies for constitutional violations. Throughout the 1950s and '60s, southern states tried to defend segregation by invoking states' rights. The Court properly rejected such claims, and it should have done so in *Rizzo v. Goode* as well, another case about racial discrimination. Federalism should not provide state and local governments with the power to ignore the Constitution in any area, least of all in policing. *Rizzo v. Goode*, followed a short time later by *City of Los Angeles v. Lyons*, eliminated the power of federal courts to remedy proven patterns of racist, unconstitutional policing. These cases attracted relatively little public attention because they were about federal court jurisdiction, but they remain the law to this day, and for decades they have dramatically limited the ability of judges to prevent unconstitutional police conduct, even when, as in *Rizzo*, the evidence of racism and police abuse is "staggering."

· · · · · · · · ·

WHEN POLICE VIOLATE the Constitution, the other type of relief that can be sought in a lawsuit is monetary damages. The threat of such liability can deter police misconduct and, at the very least, provide compensation to those who have been injured by it. Although the Burger Court interpreted constitutional protections for those accused of crimes very restrictively and greatly narrowed the exclusionary rule, in some ways it expanded people's ability to sue officers and the cities that employ them for monetary damages.

As explained in Chapter 10, if a state or local police officer violates the Constitution, the officer can be sued under 42 U.S. Code Section 1983. But no federal statute authorizes federal courts to hear suits or give relief against federal officers who violate the U.S. Constitution. Although Section 1983 authorizes suits against state and local officers, it has no application to the federal government or its officers. Nor are suits against federal officers authorized by any analogous federal statute.

In its landmark 1971 decision *Bivens v. Six Unknown Federal Narcotics Agents,* the Supreme Court ruled that federal officers who violate constitutional rights can be sued for monetary damages directly under the Constitution.[16] Such lawsuits, known as "*Bivens* suits," are an essential way to enforce the Constitution and hold federal officers liable, especially since the U.S. government has sovereign immunity and generally cannot be sued for monetary damages. But over the last forty years, the Supreme Court has dramatically backed away from the *Bivens* decision and made it increasingly difficult for members of the public to sue federal officers, even those who commit egregious constitutional violations.

The Supreme Court, though, was clearly correct when it held in *Bivens* that the plaintiff could sue to seek monetary damages from individual federal officers for their alleged violation of his rights under the Fourth Amendment. Before this decision, plaintiffs could not sue federal officers for monetary remedies in federal court no matter how egregious the constitutional violations or how severe the injuries. Victims could pursue claims only under state tort law, which almost always had to be litigated in state courts, and they did not often succeed. If a federal law enforcement officer used excessive force and seriously injured or killed someone in violation of the Constitution, there was *no* ability for people to sue that officer in federal court for monetary damages.

The plaintiff, Webster Bivens, a Brooklyn resident, alleged that he had been subjected to an illegal and humiliating search by agents of the Federal Bureau of Narcotics and sought monetary damages as compensation. On the morning of November 26, 1965, narcotics agents had entered his apartment and arrested him for alleged narcotics violations. The agents manacled him in front of his wife and children and threatened to arrest the entire family. They searched every part of the apartment. They took Bivens to the federal courthouse in Brooklyn, where he was interrogated, booked, and required to remove his clothes and be inspected. Ultimately, the charges against him were dismissed.

Bivens sued, saying that he had suffered great humiliation, embarrassment, and mental suffering as a result of the agents' unlawful conduct that clearly violated the Fourth Amendment. Bivens sought $15,000 damages from each officer. The district court dismissed the case, saying that the law provided no basis for relief, and the U.S. Court of Appeals for the Second Circuit affirmed, holding "that the Fourth Amendment does not provide a basis for a federal cause of action for damages arising out of an unreasonable search and seizure."[17] Bivens's only remedy against the federal officers, according to the Second Circuit, was under state tort law in state court, to the extent that state law even allowed relief.

The U.S. Supreme Court reversed this ruling, holding that Bivens did not need to rely on a federal statute to sue but could sue for damages based on the Fourth Amendment alone. The majority opinion, written by Justice Brennan, emphasized that individuals whose constitutional rights have been violated should not have to resort to state remedies, which might be inadequate or hostile to the federal constitutional interest.[18] The Fourth Amendment, Brennan wrote, limits what federal police can do and must be seen as authorizing a remedy for people like Bivens. Furthermore, the judiciary has the authority and the duty to provide remedies to ensure the necessary relief for violations of federal rights.[19]

In an important and often-cited concurring opinion, Justice Harlan explained that the federal courts have long-standing remedies for violations of federal law.[20] Furthermore, he explained, it is essential that federal courts be able to provide such relief: "it is apparent that some form of damages is the only possible remedy for someone in Bivens' alleged position. . . . For people in Bivens' shoes it is damages or nothing."[21] Harlan rejected the argument that the Court violates separation of powers when it creates such a cause of action and remedy. In his view, the Court is responsible for upholding and enforcing the Bill of Rights and thus need not wait for the legislature in order to act.[22]

Chief Justice Burger and Justices Black and Blackmun dissented, each writing a separate opinion contending that separation of powers meant that Congress, not the Court, should create a cause of action for damages against federal officers.[23] Chief Justice Burger also used his dissent to mount a lengthy attack on the exclusionary rule and to urge its complete elimination. It should be abolished, he wrote, because its costs in releasing guilty criminals outweigh its benefits in deterring police misconduct. The exclusionary rule was an "experiment," he wrote, and "we should be prepared to discontinue what the experience of over half a century has shown neither deters errant officers nor affords a remedy to the totally innocent victims of official misconduct."[24] Burger, who had come onto the Court just two years earlier, could not have shown more clearly how much he differed in judicial philosophy from his predecessor, Earl Warren, whose Court had expanded the use of the exclusionary rule as a remedy for police violations of the Constitution.

Bivens is a vital decision in ensuring enforcement of the Constitution. It is the judiciary's role to provide a remedy for violations of rights. Courts traditionally have fashioned remedies in the absence of legislative action, including the exclusionary rule for Fourth and Fifth Amendment violations and damage remedies under federal statutes. Moreover, as Justice Harlan argued, rights under federal law and the Constitution should not depend on the vagaries of state law but must be safeguarded and enforced by federal courts. Damage remedies are essential, both to compensate those whose rights have been violated and to provide a deterrent against future violations.

For the first decade after the decision, the Court expanded citizens' ability to file *Bivens* suits.[25] But beginning in the 1980s, *every* Supreme Court decision about *Bivens* suits has narrowed their availability.[26] As the Court has become steadily more conservative over the last few decades, it has become ever more hostile to *Bivens* suits. The dissenters' views in *Bivens* have triumphed today, as the Court's majority now makes exactly their arguments. In a recent case, *Ziglar v. Abbasi,* the Court said that it had "made clear that expanding the *Bivens* remedy is now a 'disfavored' judicial activity" and that it would hesitate to extend *Bivens* to new contexts.[27] In 2020 Justice Clarence Thomas, joined by Justice Neil Gorsuch, urged "discarding the *Bivens* doctrine altogether."[28]

· · · · · · · · ·

ALTHOUGH *BIVENS* is to be applauded for providing a needed remedy for police misconduct, the Burger Court also created a new limit, which would grow into a huge obstacle, to suing police: the development of immunity law to protect those sued for constitutional violations. The subsequent Rehnquist and especially the Roberts Courts have greatly expanded immunity so as to make it very difficult to successfully sue police officers for monetary damages for their constitutional violations, including for the use of excessive force.

Under the terms of Section 1983, any state or local official who violates the Constitution can be sued for an injunction or for money. It does not mention any defenses; it is written in seemingly absolute language. But in a series of cases beginning in the Burger Court era, the Court has ruled that government officials who are sued for monetary damages—whether they are federal officers sued under *Bivens* or state or local officers sued under Section 1983—have an immunity defense. Step by step it has found that many in the criminal justice system—judges, prosecutors, and police officers as witnesses—are absolutely immune from being sued. And it has done so in a deliberate way that keeps courts from remedying serious civil rights violations.

For example, the Burger Court held that judges have absolute immunity to suits for monetary damages for their judicial acts.[29] Absolute immunity exists even when there are charges that the judge acted maliciously; it exists "however erroneous the act may have been, and however injurious in its consequences it may have proved to the plaintiff."[30]

In *Stump v. Sparkman* in 1980, an Indiana state court judge was sued for issuing an order to sterilize a fifteen-year-old girl.[31] The girl's mother went to the judge in his chambers and asked him to sign an order approving a tubal ligation for her daughter. The mother said the girl was mentally deficient (although she attended public school and was promoted each year with her class) and that she was staying out overnight with older men. The mother said that sterilizing the girl would "prevent unfortunate circumstances."

Although the judge lacked any statutory authority to issue such an order, he did so. The girl was told that her appendix was being taken out, when actually she was surgically sterilized. She learned the true nature of the operation later, when she was married and unable to conceive a child. She then sued, among others, the judge who approved the operation.

A compelling case can be made that the judge was acting without jurisdiction. Under Indiana law, the judge had no authority to hear such a case or issue such an order. No case was filed with the court; there were no pleadings and no docket number was assigned. The matter was handled without either the girl or any representative for her present or allowed to respond.

Forced sterilization has a tragic history in the United States; it is estimated that over sixty thousand people were subjected to it as part of the eugenics movement.[32] Decades earlier the Supreme Court had held that the right to procreate is a fundamental constitutional right.[33] Nonetheless, in *Stump* the Court found that the judge had absolute immunity to the suit for monetary damages. *Stump* is a very disturbing decision because the judge was accorded absolute immunity even after he had acted without any legal authority, not even the barest rudiments of due process, and inflicted great harm.

Immunity from civil suits was not limited to judges: the Burger Court also found that prosecutors have absolute immunity for their prosecutorial acts, no matter how egregious they are or how much harm they inflict. In *Imbler v. Pachtman* in 1976, a prosecutor had been sued for damages for knowingly using perjured testimony that resulted in an innocent person's conviction and incarceration for nine years.[34] The Court accorded him absolute immunity, concluding that anything less risked "harassment by unfounded litigation [that] would cause a deflection of the prosecutor's energies from his public duties, and the possibility that he would shade his decisions instead of exercising the independence of judgment required by his public trust."[35] But this means prosecutors cannot be sued, no matter how serious their constitutional violations and no matter how severe the injury that they caused others to suffer. In another case, the Court found that prosecutors were protected by absolute immunity when their misconduct—in this case, not revealing crucial information that they were constitutionally required to disclose—led to an innocent person spending over twenty-three years in prison.[36]

Surely the Court could protect discretion of prosecutors without going so far as to extend absolute immunity to them. Would prosecutorial liability for intentional use of known perjured testimony really chill discretion in an undesirable way? Quite the contrary, isn't that exactly the type of prosecutorial conduct that should be chilled?

The Burger Court also found that police officers have absolute immunity when they testify as witnesses, even when they commit perjury and even when their perjured testimony results in the conviction of an innocent person. In general, police officers have only qualified, good-faith immunity to suits against them, pursuant to Section 1983.[37] But in *Briscoe v. LaHue* in 1983, the Court concluded that police officers who commit perjury can never be sued for monetary damages, even when the testimony leads to an innocent person being convicted and imprisoned.[38] Officers should be able to testify as witnesses without worrying about possible civil litigation, the Court contended, arguing that if absolute immunity did not exist, officers would be sued frequently. Allowing officers to be sued for their testimony as witnesses "might undermine not only their contribution to the judicial process but also the effective performance of their other public duties."[39] Police officers, like all other witnesses, can be criminally prosecuted for perjury, the Court said, which provided an adequate deterrent to perjury. But an innocent person who suffers greatly from a police officer committing perjury has no ability to sue and can get no remedy for the misconduct that led to their false imprisonment. Many studies have shown that police lying is a serious problem and can inflict great harm on innocent people.[40] Nonetheless, the Court accorded police complete immunity from liability for such wrongful conduct.

. . . .

IN ADDITION TO judicial officials, the Burger Court has also found that some other government officials have absolute immunity and cannot be sued at all, no matter how malicious or egregious their constitutional violations. Legislators have absolute immunity for their legislative acts, as does the president for acts taken in carrying out the presidency.

All other government officers—and this includes all police (except for their testimony in court)—have "qualified immunity," a doctrine that has become very important in limiting the ability of the public to bring lawsuits to recover damages against police. For a victim to sue a police officer—say, for use of excessive force or an illegal search or an unconstitutional stop—success depends on overcoming the officer's claim to qualified immunity, which requires proving that the officer violated clearly established law that every reasonable officer should know.

The Court first attempted to define qualified immunity in *Scheuer v. Rhodes* in 1974.[41] The doctrine's relatively recent origin may seem surprising, but it was not until 1961 in *Monroe v. Pape* that the Court significantly opened the door to suing state and local police officers, and not until 1971, in *Bivens v Six Unknown Federal Narcotics*

Agents, that it allowed suits against federal law enforcement officers. Soon after the Court permitted these suits against police, qualified immunity developed as a defense. In the years since those cases, the Court has made qualified immunity an ever greater barrier to holding police accountable for their actions.

Scheuer v. Rhodes arose out of a traumatic event that inflamed a generation of college students. On May 4, 1970, the Ohio National Guard killed four students who had been participating in an anti–Vietnam War demonstration at Kent State University. College campuses across the country protested, and demonstrators shut many of them down. The folk-rock group Crosby, Stills, Nash, and Young powerfully sang of "Four Dead in Ohio." Litigation on behalf of three of the students who were killed was commenced against the governor of Ohio and several state officials. The complaint alleged that the defendants "intentionally, recklessly, willfully and wantonly" deployed the National Guard and instructed them to act illegally.

The Supreme Court ruled that the governor was not protected by absolute immunity, but could claim qualified immunity: "the existence of reasonable grounds for the belief formed at the time and in light of all the circumstances, coupled with good-faith belief, . . . affords a basis for qualified immunity of executive officers."[42] The *Scheuer* test for qualified immunity thus contained both an objective component (was the act reasonable?) and a subjective component (did this officer believe in good faith that it was reasonable?). The Court, following what seemed to be common sense, was saying that to meet the standard for qualified immunity, a police officer had to have acted reasonably under the circumstances and in good faith, without malice or the desire to harm. Under *Scheuer*'s approach, a plaintiff could refute the second component, the officer's good faith, and recover monetary damages *either* by demonstrating that a reasonable officer would have found the action impermissible *or* by showing that this particular officer knew his or her action was unreasonable. The Court rejected a purely subjective standard, equating bad faith solely with malice or intent, because it might encourage perjury and would not set a high enough standard for officer conduct. On the other hand, it also rejected a purely objective standard, excluding liability based on the officer's actual state of mind, because of a desire to deter and punish those who knowingly act in a wrongful manner.

Over the next decade, conservatives argued that this test made it too easy for people to sue government officials, including police, and urged the Court to change the legal standard to make such suits more difficult.[43] As the Court became more conservative, such as with the appointment of Justice Sandra Day O'Connor in 1981, these calls found a receptive audience. In *Harlow v. Fitzgerald* in 1982, the Burger Court substantially reformulated the test for determining whether an officer acted in good faith and eliminated the ability to hold an officer liable because he or she acted maliciously or in bad faith.[44] In other words, the Court eliminated the subjective prong of the test. The fact that an officer knew that his or her conduct was wrongful was not enough to overcome qualified immunity.

In 1968 A. Ernest Fitzgerald, an air force analyst, testified before Congress about cost overruns in building the C-5 transport plane. President Nixon was furious at him for embarrassing the government and ordered him fired. Fitzgerald sued the president, saying that his firing violated his rights to freedom of speech and to petition government for redress of grievances. In *Nixon v. Fitzgerald* in 1972, the Supreme Court found President Nixon to be completely immune from suit, but it accorded the executive officials who had carried out his order to fire Fitzgerald only qualified immunity.[45] However, the Court held, whether a government official acted intentionally to violate the Constitution, or even maliciously, was irrelevant; the only question is whether the official violated clearly established law. The test that the Court articulated has since then been used in thousands, likely tens of thousands of cases, in evaluating whether government officers can be sued: "government officials performing discretionary functions gener-ally are shielded from liability for civil damages insofar as their conduct does not violate clearly established statutory or constitutional rights of which a reasonable person would have known."[46]

The Court said that the subjective element—allowing recovery upon proof of malice—was too disruptive of government operations: it was too easy for plaintiffs to allege malice in the hope of finding evidence during discovery. Such discovery was time-consuming for officers, and additionally, cases almost always would have to be tried before a jury so that it could decide whether the officer acted with malice. The justices lamented the inefficiency of this and wanted instead a legal standard that courts could usually apply without needing a trial. Focusing solely on whether the officer violated clearly established law that every reasonable officer should know, the Court said, would accomplish this.

So a police officer who uses a taser and inflicts great harm, or perhaps even kills someone, can be held liable only if the victim (or the victim's estate) can show that such use of the taser was already clearly established to be unconstitutional. Evidence that the officer acted with intent to harm the victim, even with malicious intent, is irrelevant as to whether liability will be allowed.

The effect of the Court's decision in *Harlow v. Fitzgerald* is to allow unscrupulous officers to engage in malicious conduct unless clearly established law forbids that specific behavior. If an officer knowingly violated someone's rights, even intentionally, that was no longer enough to hold the officer liable. Simply put, the Burger Court was more concerned with protecting officers from the additional costs of defending meritless suits than with ensuring that injured individuals receive compensation for the wrongs they have suffered. Today, in the twenty-first century, qualified immunity has become a major obstacle to successfully suing police for constitutional violations, including for excessive use of force.

· · · · · · · · ·

FOR ALL THE Burger Court did to empower the police, it also took one important step to increase the accountability of law enforcement:

it made it easier for people to sue local governments, such as cities and counties, for constitutional violations. This step is important because so much policing is done at the local level. Although the federal and state governments rarely can be sued because they are protected by sovereign immunity,[47] the Supreme Court has held that local governments—cities and counties—do not have sovereign immunity.[48]

Unfortunately, in 1961, in *Monroe v. Pape,* the Supreme Court held that municipal governments may not be sued under Section 1983.[49] It pointed to a proposed amendment that Congress had rejected in 1871, when Section 1983 was adopted: the Sherman Amendment would have created municipal liability for acts of violence occurring within a county's or town's borders.[50] The Court in *Monroe* said that this shows that Congress did not want cities to be held liable. But this argument is seriously flawed, and academics and judges widely criticized it. That Congress in 1871 did not want cities to be held liable for acts of violence by private citizens, especially by the Ku Klux Klan, does not show that Congress wanted cities to avoid liability for the wrongful acts of their own officers and employees.

In *Monell v. Department of Social Services* in 1978, the Court responded to the criticisms of its decision in *Monroe* and overruled its limitation on municipal liability.[51] *Monell* involved a suit brought by female employees of the New York City Department of Social Services and Board of Education challenging a policy that required pregnant teachers to take unpaid leaves of absence. The Court again reviewed the legislative history of Section 1983 and this time concluded that Congress had never intended to preclude municipal liability. Justice Brennan, an unabashed liberal, was able to pull together a majority for a surprising result to advance civil rights.

Writing for the majority, Brennan stated that in its 1871 rejection of the Sherman Amendment, Congress intended not to protect municipalities and other local governments from liability for their own violations of the Fourteenth Amendment but rather to prevent them from being held liable for the wrongful acts of others.[52] "Congress *did* intend local government units to be included among those persons to whom §1983 applies," he wrote.[53] But then he imposed a substantial limitation on such liability: municipal governments might be sued only for their own unconstitutional or illegal policies, not for the acts of their employees. Brennan likely had to make this concession to gain the support of a majority of the justices. The Court ruled that "a local government may not be sued under §1983 for an injury inflicted solely by its employees or agents."[54] A city can be sued only when a police officer or city employee inflicts injury pursuant to an official municipal policy.

Monell was wrong in holding that local governments can be held liable only when their own policies violate the Constitution.[55] If members of the public were able to sue cities when their officials violated the Constitution, cities would have a reason to act to prevent violations of rights, and at the very least, it would require them to provide compensation to those injured. But in *Monell,* the Court concluded that although allowing a city to be held liable for the conduct of its employees would serve deterrence and risk-spreading, the defeat of the Sherman Amendment was evidence that Congress rejected these goals. But Congress, in rejecting the Sherman Amendment, had refused only to create an affirmative duty for cities to keep the peace by making them monetarily liable for the actions of *private citizens.* Nothing in its rejection supports giving local governments immunity when their employees, such as police officers, violate the Constitution.

In holding that a local government can be held liable only if its own policies violate the Constitution, not on the grounds that its employees acted unconstitutionally, the Court has developed legal rules for local government that are different from rules in almost all other areas of law. A private employer is always liable if its employees injure someone while they are performing their duties. This principle, termed *respondeat superior,* means that employers are liable for harms inflicted by their employees who were acting within the scope of their duties. If a UPS driver gets into a car accident while on the job and is at fault, UPS is liable to those injured in the accident. This principle ensures that the victim gets compensation and gives the employer an incentive to do all it can to prevent harm. But the Supreme Court has been emphatic that local governments cannot be held responsible on this basis—only if their own policies violate the Constitution.

In a subsequent case, Justice Stephen Breyer, in a dissenting opinion joined by Justices Stevens and Ginsburg, sharply criticized *Monell* and declared that the "case for reexamination is a strong one."[56] Neither the language of Section 1983 nor its legislative history, Breyer argued, supports *Monell*'s preclusion of municipal liability for the conduct of its employees.[57] Unfortunately, the Supreme Court has never had a majority interested in reexamining *Monell*; quite the contrary, in the years that followed, the Court greatly compounded the problem by making it very difficult to prove the existence of a municipal policy. No city ever will have an officially stated policy that its police officers should use excessive force, even if the culture in the police department condones it. No city ever will have a policy that approves of racial profiling or racial discrimination in exercising the power to stop and frisk. Yet absent such express policies, the Court has created obstacles to proving municipal liability that are often insurmountable and thus effectively preclude suits against cities based on police misconduct.

· · · · · · · · · ·

THE BURGER COURT constituted a strong reaction against its predecessor, the Warren Court. Where many Warren Court decisions had protected criminal suspects and defendants, their dissenters became the majority under the Burger Court. Meanwhile the justices who were in the Warren Court majority—Justices Brennan, Marshall, and Douglas—now found themselves frequently in dissent. These champions of individual rights, who saw the need to control the police, found themselves powerless to do anything but dissent in the face of a conservative majority. A solid majority of the justices perceived a need to empower the police and to restrict the rights of those suspected or accused of crimes. In case after case, the Burger Court did just that. And it did so in the midst of the war on drugs, which dramatically increased policing and incarceration, especially of people of color.

But the Burger Court was also a transition between the liberal Warren Court and the even more conservative Rehnquist and Roberts Courts that followed it. As the Supreme Court became increasingly conservative in the following decades, it built on Burger Court precedents to greatly lessen constitutional restrictions on police and to go much further in making it difficult for American society to hold the police accountable.

Part V

EMPOWERING POLICE

The Rehnquist and Roberts Courts

Los Angeles police do a traffic stop and search of men they suspect of being gang members, January 1988. *(Photo by Getty Images/ Bob Riha, Jr.)*

15

The Police Can
Stop Anyone,
at Any Time,
and Search Them

S OMETIMES SUPREME COURT JUSTICES APPEAR TO BE
indifferent to the real-world effects of their decisions. That certainly seems to be true for its ruling that allows police to use
evidence that results from illegal stops of individuals. *Utah v. Strieff*
in 2016 gives police an incentive to violate the Fourth Amendment
knowing that the fruits of an illegal stop still will be admissible as
evidence.[1]

The case began, as they so often do, with an anonymous tip. In
2006 police in South Salt Lake City, Utah, received information from
an unknown source that drug dealing was occurring in a certain
house. Narcotics detective Douglas Fackrell investigated the tip.
Over the course of about a week, Officer Fackrell conducted inter-
mittent surveillance of the house. As he was watching the house, he
saw Edward Strieff briefly enter and then leave. Strieff walked to a
nearby convenience store. There Fackrell stopped him.

Fackrell asked Strieff what he was doing there and requested his
identification. Strieff produced his Utah identification card. Fackrell
relayed Strieff's information to a police dispatcher, who reported that
Strieff had an outstanding arrest warrant for a traffic violation. Fackrell then arrested Strieff pursuant to that warrant. He searched Strieff

incident to the arrest—as police are allowed to search anyone they arrest for any reason under the law of the Fourth Amendment—and discovered a Baggie of methamphetamine and drug paraphernalia.

No one disputed that the police stop of Strieff was illegal and in violation of the Fourth Amendment. According to the 1968 decision *Terry v. Ohio*, police may stop a person only if they have "reasonable suspicion" that the person has committed, is committing, or is about to commit a crime. In *Strieff,* even the prosecutors conceded, both in the trial court and on appeal, that Fackrell had not had reasonable suspicion to justify stopping Strieff; briefly entering and leaving a house does not provide a legal basis for a police stop. Nor does an anonymous, unverified tip provide sufficient grounds for the police stopping a person.

The issue before the Supreme Court was whether the evidence— the drugs found on Strieff—had to be excluded from the trial because they were obtained as the direct result of the police officer's violating the Fourth Amendment and illegally stopping Strieff. The Court had long established that prosecutors cannot use the products of police violations as evidence because they are "the fruit of the poisonous tree."[2] Otherwise, police would have too great an incentive to violate the law, especially given their general immunity from civil lawsuits. Strieff's attorney moved to exclude the evidence as the result of an illegal search. The Utah Supreme Court, not known as one of the more liberal state courts, unanimously ruled in Strieff's favor and concluded that the violation of the Fourth Amendment necessitated excluding the evidence.

But the State of Utah took the case to the Supreme Court, and in a 5–3 decision (it was the year of Justice Scalia's death), it reversed the Utah court and held that the evidence was admissible against Strieff, notwithstanding that it had been obtained as a result of the police officer violating his Fourth Amendment rights. Justice Thomas, who for decades has sided with the police virtually without exception, wrote in the opinion that once the police officer discovered the existence of an outstanding warrant for Strieff, the resulting search as part of his arrest became permissible. The outstanding warrant for Strieff's arrest, he said, was a critical intervening circumstance that was independent of the illegal stop: its discovery broke the causal chain between the unconstitutional stop and the search. The stop's unlawfulness was irrelevant; the evidence gained, the illegal drugs, could be admitted against Strieff in court to gain his conviction.

This ruling greatly incentivizes police to illegally stop individuals, knowing that if an outstanding arrest warrant surfaces, they can search, and anything they find will be admissible as evidence. Outstanding warrants are surprisingly common. For example, if a person with a traffic ticket misses a fine payment or a court appearance, a warrant is issued. The Department of Justice found that in Ferguson, Missouri—a city of 21,000 people that is almost 70 percent Black—some 16,000 had outstanding warrants against them. Justice Sotomayor noted in her dissent that the states and the federal government maintain databases with over 7.8 million outstanding warrants, the vast majority of which appear to be for minor offenses.[3]

Given the prevalence of warrants and the permissiveness of the Court in *Strieff,* this ruling significantly expanded police power and eroded citizen rights. Justice Sotomayor wrote in a strong dissent: "This case allows the police to stop you on the street, demand your identification, and check it for outstanding traffic warrants—even if you are doing nothing wrong. If the officer discovers a warrant for a fine you forgot to pay, courts will now excuse his illegal stop and will admit into evidence anything he happens to find by searching you after arresting you on the warrant."[4]

As a woman of color who grew up in a housing project, Justice Sotomayor spoke eloquently: "[T]his case tells everyone, white and black, guilty and innocent, that an officer can verify your legal status at any time. It says that your body is subject to invasion while courts excuse the violation of your rights. It implies that you are not a citizen of a democracy but the subject of a carceral state, just waiting to be cataloged." Given the reality of policing in the United States, people of color would be the most affected by this decision. Justice Sotomayor concluded her opinion, which no other justice joined: "It is no secret that people of color are disproportionate victims of this type of scrutiny. For generations, black and brown parents have given their children 'the talk'—instructing them never to run down the street; always keep your hands where they can be seen; do not even think of talking back to a stranger—all out of fear of how an officer with a gun will react to them."[5]

The Supreme Court first held more than a century ago that evidence gained as a result of constitutional violations by the police must be excluded from use against a criminal defendant. Ending illegal and abusive police stops means making sure that the police cannot benefit from their constitutional violations. The Court's decision in *Utah v. Streiff* does just the opposite, and egregiously so: it gives police an incentive to violate the Fourth Amendment and engage in illegal stops of individuals.

· · · · · · · · · ·

SEVERAL MONTHS AFTER the Court issued its decision in *Strieff,* and well before the 2020 George Floyd murder catalyzed protests against the police in cities across the world, I met with the inspector general of the police department in a major city and his staff. He had asked to meet with me because of my work on policing and my writing on this case. He and his staff expressed great concern that the officers in their department, having learned of the Court's ruling, were engaging in illegal stops of individuals, knowing that they could then check for an outstanding warrant. If there was none, they would let the person leave. If there was an outstanding warrant, no matter how trivial the offense, they would arrest the person and do a search incident to the arrest. If they found contraband, they knew it could be used against the person. If they found nothing, they would usually let the person go, unless the warrant was for a serious matter.

Their question was what could be done about this. My answer was that the city's police commission, or perhaps its city council, would have to limit what police can do in their jurisdiction. Or the state supreme court could find that such evidence should be excluded under state law; states can provide more protection than the U.S. Constitution affords. Also, police departments can discipline officers for illegal stops, even if the evidence is admissible. But the reality is that these things will rarely happen. The Supreme Court has created a significant incentive for police to engage in unconstitutional stops without reasonable suspicion. And everything we know about policing in the United States leaves no doubt that people of color are most likely to be subjected to such stops.

Utah v. Strieff was one of many cases during the Rehnquist and Roberts Courts—from 1986 to the present—that empowered and encouraged police to violate the Constitution. One might surmise that after the Burger Court, little more remained that the Supreme Court could do to weaken the constitutional limits on the police and to further eviscerate remedies for misconduct. But that surmise would be incorrect. Over the last few decades, the Supreme Court has built on the Burger Court's jurisprudence and gone much further to limit the constitutional rights of those suspected and accused of crimes. The Rehnquist Court started in 1986, when Chief Justice Warren Burger retired, and President Reagan nominated then associate justice William Rehnquist to replace him as chief. At the same time, Reagan nominated conservative federal appeals court judge Antonin Scalia to take Rehnquist's seat. Scalia, who had been a University of Chicago law professor and then a judge on the U.S. Court of Appeals for the D.C. Circuit, was an outspoken conservative and a favorite of the emerging Federalist Society. He was an entertaining speaker and did nothing to hide his conservative politics.

Civil rights leaders consciously chose to try to block Rehnquist's confirmation and to allow Scalia to go through unopposed. No one doubted that Scalia would be as conservative on the Supreme Court as he had been on the federal court of appeals. But civil rights leaders sensed that they had a realistic chance to block only one of the nominees, and Rehnquist seemed the more vulnerable. In 1971, when he was nominated to be an associate justice, a memo had surfaced that

Rehnquist wrote as a law clerk to Justice Robert Jackson in the early
1950s, when the Court was considering *Brown v. Board of Education*.[6] Rehnquist urged Justice Jackson to reaffirm the invidious 1896
decision in *Plessy v. Ferguson*,[7] which held that laws requiring separation of the races are constitutional. When questioned about this at
his confirmation hearings, Rehnquist said that Justice Jackson had
asked him to present the arguments for this position.

Now in 1986 civil rights leaders seeking to block him were ready
to show that Rehnquist had not told the truth at the earlier confirmation hearings and that he had been expressing his own views in
favor of upholding segregation. They had testimony from Jackson's
secretary, Jackson's biographer, and other law clerks. The memo had
clearly been written in Rehnquist's voice. His opponents also had
evidence that Rehnquist had engaged in minority voter suppression
efforts when he was a lawyer in Arizona. And fifteen years' worth
of his opinions as a justice left no doubt as to his very conservative
judicial philosophy.

Nonetheless, the Senate confirmed Rehnquist by a vote of 65–33,
which to that point was the most votes ever cast against a justice
who was confirmed. (Later forty-eight votes would be cast against
the confirmations of Clarence Thomas, Brett Kavanaugh, and Amy
Coney Barrett.) Antonin Scalia was the beneficiary of the Rehnquist
fight; he slid through with little scrutiny and was confirmed without
a negative vote.

A year later another vacancy opened on the Court when Justice
Powell announced his retirement. Powell had been a staunchly pro-
business and pro-police justice, but he was perceived as relatively
moderate, perhaps because he voted with the majority in *Roe v.
Wade* to protect a woman's right to an abortion. To replace Powell, President Reagan nominated conservative federal appeals court
judge Robert Bork. Although he had impeccable qualifications, having been a Yale law professor, U.S. solicitor general, and a federal
judge, Bork was opposed because of his very conservative judicial
ideology. He was seen as a sure vote to overrule *Roe* and limit civil

rights protections. After an intense battle, the Senate rejected Bork's nomination, with fifty-eight senators voting against him. President Reagan then said he would nominate federal appeals court judge Douglas Ginsburg, but Ginsburg withdrew when reports emerged that he had used marijuana with students while a Harvard Law professor. Having been frustrated twice, President Reagan picked federal appeals court judge Anthony Kennedy to replace Justice Powell. Kennedy was easily confirmed.

Kennedy had been a lawyer, mostly a lobbyist in Sacramento, California, and a teacher of constitutional law at McGeorge Law School. He was involved in Republican politics in California, and Governor Reagan had recommended him for a judicial appointment to President Gerald Ford. Kennedy, thirty-eight at the time, was confirmed and served twelve years as a judge on the U.S. Court of Appeals for the Ninth Circuit. Then President Reagan picked him for the Supreme Court. It has been widely rumored that Attorney General Ed Meese reassured President Reagan as to Kennedy's conservativism and his willingness to overrule *Roe v. Wade*.

In some areas of law, such as gay rights and abortion, Kennedy bitterly disappointed conservatives and voted with the liberal justices.[8] But as to criminal procedure issues, he did not disappoint the right; Kennedy was a consistent vote for police throughout his thirty years on the Court, retiring in 2018. After Justice O'Connor retired in 2006, Kennedy became the "swing" justice on the Court, so much so that many referred to it as the "Kennedy Court," and lawyers wrote their briefs and planned their arguments to appeal to him. In one case I argued, I later quipped that my brief was a shameless attempt to pander to Justice Kennedy; if I could have, I would have put a picture of Anthony Kennedy on the front of my brief.

Rehnquist, Scalia, and Kennedy were joined by two holdovers from the Burger Court to provide a solid majority in favor of law enforcement. Justice White, a nominee of President Kennedy, was very conservative on policing issues, writing the lead dissent in *Miranda v. Arizona*.[9] And Justice Sandra Day O'Connor, named by President Reagan, also regularly voted in favor of the police and against the rights of criminal suspects and defendants throughout her time on the Court.

These five justices were frequently the majority in cases that restricted constitutional rights and lessened judicial limits on the police. But the Court then became even more conservative. In 1990 the liberal lion Justice William Brennan was replaced by David Souter, appointed by President George H. W. Bush. Although Souter had served as chief justice of the New Hampshire Supreme Court, his opinions gave little indication of his judicial philosophy. Everyone scrutinized his rulings, but the only insight gleaned from them, as legal scholar Burt Neuborne remarked, was that the New Hampshire court had a very boring docket. In time Souter would prove to be one of the more liberal justices, though not nearly as progressive as Brennan, the justice he replaced. Some suggested that Souter changed while on the Court, but in truth no one knew what to expect from him when he became a justice.

Most important in terms of the Court's becoming more conservative, in 1991, Justice Thurgood Marshall retired, and President Bush appointed federal appeals court judge Clarence Thomas to replace him. Ideologically, including on police issues, Justice Thomas could not be more different than Justice Marshall. Rarely, over the decades, has Thomas voted in favor of constitutional limits on the police. No justice since 1937, and perhaps none in history, has been more conservative than Justice Thomas.

In 1993 Justice White was replaced by liberal court of appeals judge Ruth Bader Ginsburg. As a law professor, Ginsburg had founded the ACLU's Women's Rights Project and argued path-breaking cases about gender equality before the Supreme Court itself. President Jimmy Carter had named her to the federal court of appeals in D.C., and President Bill Clinton elevated her to the Supreme Court. In time she became a cultural hero—"the notorious RBG"—in a way unlike any other justice in history. Although her appointment significantly changed the ideology of this Court seat, five justices could still be counted on to rule in favor of police: Rehnquist, O'Connor, Scalia, Kennedy, and Thomas. And as the Court became more conservative, she took on the role of passionate dissenter, especially in cases involving sex discrimination and reproductive autonomy.

A year later, in 1994, Justice Blackmun was replaced by court of appeals judge Stephen Breyer, a former Harvard law professor, aide to Senator Edward Kennedy, and a federal court of appeals judge. Although Breyer is often perceived as a liberal, he has been much less so with regard to policing and especially the Fourth Amendment. For instance, *Utah v. Strieff* was a 5–3 decision (Justice Scalia had died and there were only eight justices), and it was Breyer who cast the fifth vote for the police, joining Chief Justice Roberts and Justices Kennedy, Thomas, and Alito.[10]

This was the Rehnquist Court, and from 1994 to 2005 these were the justices. In 2005 Rehnquist died of thyroid cancer, and his former law clerk, John Roberts, was nominated by President George W. Bush and confirmed to be chief justice. Roberts had been a renowned Supreme Court advocate—in private practice and as deputy solicitor general—before Bush named him to the U.S. Court of Appeals for the D.C. Circuit. In every way, Roberts had the résumé and the appearance of a Supreme Court justice; if Central Casting were choosing someone to be chief justice, it couldn't have done better than Roberts. A graduate of Harvard College and Harvard Law School, Roberts had clerked for famous judges, worked in the Reagan and first Bush Justice Departments, and had been a partner at a big Washington law firm. He was known to be conservative, but he had not taken positions on particularly controversial issues or shown himself to be especially far right wing.

Actually, Roberts was initially named to replace O'Connor as an associate justice, but then was named to be chief justice when Rehnquist died. President Bush then initially nominated Harriet Miers, his White House counsel, to take O'Connor's place on the Court, but strong Republican opposition to her nomination developed, and she withdrew from consideration. Bush then nominated conservative federal court of appeals judge Samuel Alito to replace O'Connor. Alito, who had worked in the Reagan White House and had been U.S. attorney for New Jersey, was a very conservative judge on the U.S. Court of Appeals for the Third Circuit. In January 2006, I testified against his confirmation before the Senate Judiciary Committee, based on his judicial record, which was consistently hostile to individual rights.

But the Senate confirmed Alito, with the result that the Court retained a conservative majority: Roberts, Scalia, Kennedy, Thomas, and Alito. Overall Chief Justice Roberts has been conservative, and although he has sometimes disappointed conservatives,[11] he generally has not done so in criminal procedure cases.[12] Justice Alito, by contrast, never has disappointed conservatives; in virtually all the cases where the Court has been ideologically divided, he has voted with the conservative justices and has forcefully advocated very conservative positions.

Since 2005, vacancies have opened and new justices have been appointed, but the majority has remained solidly conservative, particularly on issues concerning the police and criminal justice. In 2009 Sonia Sotomayor replaced David Souter, and in 2010 Elena Kagan replaced John Paul Stevens. Sotomayor had been a state prosecutor and a lawyer in a firm before becoming a federal district court and then a federal appeals court judge. As in her dissent in *Strieff*, Sotomayor, the first Latina to be a justice, has been a powerful voice on the Court in speaking of the problems of race in society generally and with regard to policing.[13] More than most justices, she has become part of popular culture, speaking in many venues when her autobiography was published and even appearing on *Sesame Street*.

Kagan, for her part, had spent most of her career as an academic, as a law professor at University of Chicago and Harvard and then as dean at Harvard Law School, with time in the Clinton White House. President Barack Obama named her to be U.S. solicitor general in 2009 and then to the Supreme Court a year later. Although both Sotomayor and Kagan have often voted for greater limits on the police—

both, for example, dissented in *Utah v. Strieff*—they have usually done so only in dissent.

Finally, and most recently, President Donald Trump made three picks to the high Court: Judge Neil Gorsuch took the seat that had been occupied by Justice Scalia, and Judge Brett Kavanaugh replaced the justice he had clerked for, Anthony Kennedy. Gorsuch had worked in the Justice Department in the George W. Bush administration and then spent a decade as a conservative judge on the U.S. Court of Appeals for the Tenth Circuit, which is headquartered in Denver. President Trump was able to make this pick because Senate Republicans refused to hold hearings or a vote on President Obama's nomination of Chief Judge Merrick Garland to replace Justice Scalia.

Kavanaugh had worked with Kenneth Starr on the Whitewater investigation that led to President Clinton's impeachment for lying about having sex with intern Monica Lewinsky. Later Kavanaugh worked in the Bush administration, then was named to the U.S. Court of Appeals for the D.C. Circuit. After Trump nominated him, an intense confirmation fight ensued, including allegations of a sexual assault by Kavanaugh while in high school. The Senate confirmed him by a 50–48 vote.[14] So far Gorsuch and Kavanaugh have both been consistent votes in favor of police in cases involving the constitutional rights of criminal suspects and defendants.

In September 2020, Justice Ruth Bader Ginsburg died at age eighty-seven, and to replace her, President Trump nominated Judge Amy Coney Barrett. All her writings as a law professor and her opinions as a judge indicate that Barrett likely will be a very conservative justice; it is hard to imagine Justice Ginsburg being replaced by anyone more ideologically different.

· · · · · · · · ·

THE BOTTOM LINE is that the Roberts Court, like the Rehnquist Court that preceded it, has always had at least five justices who in almost every criminal procedure case have voted in favor of police.

This means we may consider these two eras of the Supreme Court together. Both Courts have shared the same approach to policing and to the constitutional provisions that protect those suspected and accused of crimes. They have lessened the Fourth Amendment limits on the ability of police to stop and search individuals, significantly decreased the protections of the privilege against self-incrimination, and allowed the fruits of suggestive identifications to be used in court. Perhaps most important, the Rehnquist and Roberts Courts have both restricted the remedies available for police violations of the Constitution. Although they have never said so explicitly, their decisions reflect a majority that presumes that suspects are guilty and that sides with the ability of police to do what they perceive as needed to protect public safety. In the period from 1986 to today, spanning the two Courts, I cannot think of a single instance where a majority opinion expressed concern about the role of race in policing in the United States.

Perhaps the most dramatic change with regard to policing during the Rehnquist and Roberts Courts is how easy they have made it for the police to stop virtually anyone at any time. And police inevitably use this power most against individuals of color. No single decision was more responsible for expanding police power to stop individuals with impunity than *Whren v. United States* in 1996.[15]

On the night of June 10, 1993, in the District of Columbia, plain-clothes vice squad officers of the Metropolitan Police Department were patrolling what the Court would call a "high drug area" in an unmarked car. The officers' suspicions were aroused, the Court said, when they passed a dark Pathfinder truck with temporary license plates and youthful occupants waiting at a stop sign. The driver was looking down into the lap of the passenger at his right. What made the police officers suspicious? The "truck remained stopped at the intersection for what seemed an unusually long time—more than 20 seconds," the Court would say. For those, like me, who have a terri-ble sense of direction, it is common to remain at a stop sign for that long, to try to read a map or, more recently, to look at a GPS.

The unmarked police car made a U-turn to follow the truck. The truck turned right without signaling. The police pulled up to the car, and the officers directed it to stop. The officers then looked into the car and saw two plastic bags of what appeared to be crack cocaine. The defendants were charged with drug possession. Their attorney moved to have the evidence excluded, arguing that the officers' ground for stopping the car—"to give the driver a warning concerning traffic violations"—was pretextual. And undercover officers in D.C. were not allowed to enforce traffic laws. The purpose of the stop had obviously been to look for drugs, but the police had had no reasonable suspicion, let alone probable cause, to justify a stop for that kind of crime. They had stopped the car for a minor traffic violation patently as an excuse to search for drugs.

The Court recognized in *Whren,* as it had to, that "[t]emporary detention of individuals during the stop of an automobile by the police, even if only for a brief period and for a limited purpose, constitutes a 'seizure' of 'persons'" under the Fourth Amendment.[16] The Constitution clearly requires, the Court said, that an automobile stop must be reasonable under the circumstances. What makes it reasonable? "[T]he decision to stop an automobile is reasonable where the police have probable cause to believe that a traffic violation has occurred."[17] In this case, the Court said, there was probable cause for the stop: the police observed the car break a traffic law by turning without a signal.

In response to objections that this traffic stop had clearly been a pretext, and that the officers had neither the authority to enforce traffic laws nor interest in doing so, the Court said that does not matter. The actual motivation of the officers is irrelevant.[18] As long as an officer has probable cause, or even reasonable suspicion, that a traffic law has been violated, he or she may stop the vehicle.

Practically speaking, the *Whren* ruling empowers police to stop anyone at any time. If officers follow any car long enough, they will observe the driver changing lanes or making a turn without a signal, or exceeding the speed limit by a mile or two per hour, or—and this is the easiest for police—not stopping long enough, or stopping too long, at a stop sign. That the officer's actual motivation for the stop had nothing to do with traffic enforcement is irrelevant for Fourth Amendment purposes.

Once police pull the car over, they can order the driver and the passenger out of the car.[19] They can then search the passenger area of the car, including all containers within it.[20] This is to protect the officers, the Court explained, to ensure that the car contains no weapon that an individual might reach for.

But the power of the police goes even further: the officer can, if he or she wishes, formally arrest the person who was stopped for the traffic infraction. The Supreme Court has held that a person can be arrested and taken into custody for even minor traffic violations. In *Atwater v. Lago Vista* in 2001, the Court held that police did not violate the Fourth Amendment when they arrested a mother, and took her to the stationhouse for booking, for not having her children in seat belts—an infraction under Texas law.[21] The Court has said that even if state law expressly forbids arrests for traffic violations, such an arrest still does not violate the Fourth Amendment.[22]

Once a person is arrested, he or she can be searched incident to the arrest. If police find nothing, the person can be given a traffic ticket and allowed to go. Anything police obtain that is evidence of a crime can be used against the person. Also, once police arrest a person, they can impound the car and search the entire vehicle.[23]

Whren, then, opened the door to the police being able to stop any vehicle if they observe even the most trivial of traffic offenses, and once stopped, the police gain broad powers to search and arrest. Not by coincidence, the driver and the passenger in *Whren* were Black. The Court's description of the neighborhood a "high drug area" was a euphemism for a neighborhood in which the residents were predominantly people of color. And the Court was explicit that in evaluating the constitutionality of the stop under the Fourth Amendment, race was irrelevant.[24]

Surprisingly, the *Whren* decision was unanimous. That the liberal justices John Paul Stevens and Ruth Bader Ginsburg went along with it has always baffled me; I wonder if they somehow missed the implications of the Scalia opinion they were joining. In the quarter-century since the *Whren* decision, the Court has reaffirmed that the officers' subjective motivation is irrelevant in evaluating whether a stop or an arrest is lawful under the Fourth Amendment. As long as the officer can articulate reasonable suspicion for making a stop, even if it had nothing to do with the real reason for the stop, he or she has not violated the Fourth Amendment. In *Davenpeck v. Alford* in 2004, the Court expressly reaffirmed *Whren*: "Our cases make clear that an arresting officer's state of mind . . . is irrelevant to the existence of probable cause. . . . Subjective intent . . . is simply no basis for invalidating an arrest."[25] As long as the officer can claim to have pulled the car over for changing lanes without a signal, or for making a rolling stop at a stop sign, or for slightly exceeding the speed limit, that officer has not violated the Fourth Amendment even if the real basis for suspicion was subjective—the officer's dislike of the race of the driver or a desire to search the car for drugs or other evidence of crime.

In 2018 Justice Ginsburg, in an opinion joined by no other justice, said that it may be time to reexamine *Whren* because it "sets the balance too heavily in favor of police unaccountability to the detriment of Fourth Amendment protection."[26] No one else, not even Justice Sotomayor, joined this call, and certainly a majority of justices on the increasingly conservative Court are not so inclined.

· · · · · · · · · ·

ALTHOUGH *WHREN* essentially provides police with carte blanche authority to stop almost anyone at almost any time, it must be seen as a larger pattern of the Supreme Court making it very easy for police to stop cars, especially those driven by people of color. In *Navarette v. California* in 2014, the Court ruled that an anonymous tip that a person is driving erratically is a sufficient basis for a police stop.[27] The usual rule is that in order for an anonymous tip to be the basis for a police stop, it must have some corroboration,[28] but in this case the Court held that no such corroboration is required to pull a vehicle over.

On August 23, 2008, in Mendocino County, California, an anonymous call to 911 had said that a car was driving erratically and had run the caller off the road. The 911 dispatch team recoded the call as: " 'Showing southbound Highway 1 at mile marker 88, Silver Ford 150 pickup. Plate of 8-David-94925. Ran the reporting party off the roadway and was last seen approximately five [minutes] ago.' " Within fifteen minutes, police officers located the pickup truck that had allegedly been driving erratically, and they followed it for five minutes. They did not observe anything awry; the driver violated no traffic laws and was not driving erratically during this time. Nonetheless, the officers pulled the truck over solely because of the anonymous 911 call. When they approached the truck, they later said, they smelled marijuana, and a search of the truck bed revealed thirty pounds of it.

They arrested the driver, Lorenzo Prado Navarette, and the passenger, José Prado Navarette. The two men moved to suppress the evidence from being used against them, arguing that the traffic stop violated the Fourth Amendment because the officers had lacked reasonable suspicion of criminal activity. The California Superior Court ruled against their suppression motion, and they were convicted and sentenced to jail.

In its 5–4 decision, the Supreme Court rejected the defendants' Fourth Amendment arguments. This was one of several Fourth Amendment cases, including *Utah v. Strieff*, in which Justice Breyer provided the crucial fifth vote in favor of police. Justice Thomas wrote the opinion for the Court, joined by Chief Justice Roberts and Justices Kennedy, Breyer, and Alito. Justice Scalia, who usually was very much on the side of the police, wrote a vehement dissent, which was joined by Justices Ginsburg, Sotomayor, and Kagan.

Justice Thomas, writing for the majority, said that it was a "close case," but the "totality of the circumstances" had made it permissible for the police to stop the vehicle.[29] The tip had evidently come from an eyewitness to the reckless driving, and the officers' corroboration of the truck's description, location, and direction established that it had been reliable enough to justify a traffic stop. The caller had reported driving that was sufficiently dangerous, the Court felt, to merit an investigative stop without waiting for the officers to observe additional reckless driving.

Justice Scalia, in dissent, said that the case established a new rule: "So long as the caller identifies where the car is, anonymous claims of a single instance of possibly careless or reckless driving, called in to 911, will support a traffic stop."[30] But that makes it too easy for someone to subject another person to a police stop by calling 911 and making an anonymous report of erratic driving. If someone doesn't like the bumper sticker on a car, he or she need only make a 911 call describing the vehicle and saying that it was driving erratically. And even if the car was behaving erratically at one moment, there are many other possible explanations besides driver intoxication. The driver may have sneezed or swerved to avoid an animal in the road.

The Court could have provided an alternative simply by requiring that police themselves observe erratic driving or a traffic violation before they pull over a vehicle. This would not have restricted the police from stopping cars where that was appropriate, but it would have prevented an anonymous call by itself from becoming the basis for a stop. Combating drunk driving is certainly critically important, but requiring police to have more than an anonymous tip of erratic driving would not impede law enforcement.

Being pulled over by the police always is upsetting, even if one has done nothing wrong. Police can order individuals out of the car and then search the passenger area. Sometimes such stops escalate into police use of force. An anonymous tip by itself should not be sufficient to trigger such a chain of events. Unfortunately, the majority of the justices did not see it that way, and as a result, we all have less freedom from police stops when we are driving.

The Court even has said that a combination of purely innocent factors is enough for the police to stop a vehicle. In 1998 in a remote area of southeastern Arizona, police stopped Ralph Arvizu while he was driving.[31] Unlike the case of *Whren,* where the police observed a traffic violation, albeit a minor one of turning without a signal, and unlike the case of *Navarette,* where a car had been seen driving erratically, in *Arvizu* police did not observe the driver breaking any law or doing anything dangerous. But Arvizu was in an area where human and narcotics smuggling were known to occur, police later said, and he was driving a minivan, which is often used in those crimes. The officer said the driver was suspicious because he "appeared stiff and his posture very rigid," and he did not look at the officer or give the "border patrol agents a friendly wave."[32] The officer said children were sitting in the backseat with their knees appearing high, then began to wave at the officer in "an abnormal pattern."[33]

That's it. Not one of these things—driving on a remote road, driving a minivan, not waving at the police officers, or children having their knees up and waving strangely—is evidence of any crime. Anyone who has children can attest that sometimes they sit with their knees up and wave and make funny faces at other cars. But based on these factors alone, the officer pulled Arvizu's minivan over, searched it, and found a large amount of marijuana.

The Supreme Court unanimously ruled that this combination of innocent events had been sufficient to justify stopping the car. The opinion written by Chief Justice Rehnquist held that under "[t]he totality of the circumstances," the officer "had reasonable suspicion to believe that respondent was engaged in illegal activity."[34] A set of purely innocuous factors that made the officer suspicious was enough for the Court to hold that the stop had been consistent with the Fourth Amendment. "Totality of the circumstances" is so amorphous as a legal test as to allow a court to find almost anything to be enough to justify a stop and to allow the evidence gained to be used against the defendant.

· · · · · · · · ·

THE ABILITY OF the police to stop virtually anyone at any time goes beyond those in cars.[35] Under the standard set by the Supreme Court, the police need to be able to articulate mere "reasonable suspicion" for a stop, and the Court has made it quite easy for them to do so.

William Wardlow, a young Black man, was walking down the street in Chicago when he saw four unmarked police cars driving in what appeared to be caravan fashion.[36] Wardlow reversed course and began walking in the other direction. Based solely on this behavior, a police officer in one of the cars did a U-turn and drove up to Wardlow. He stopped Wardlow and frisked him. Performing a frisk requires reasonable suspicion, and the officer later said that he "immediately conducted a protective patdown search for weapons because in his experience it was common for there to be weapons in the near vicinity of narcotics transactions."[37] During the frisk, the officer squeezed the bag Wardlow was carrying and felt a heavy, hard object similar in shape to a gun. The officer opened the bag and discovered a .38–caliber handgun with five live rounds of ammunition. He arrested Wardlow for illegal possession of the gun.

What had Wardlow done to create "reasonable suspicion"? He was in what the Court said was "an area known for heavy narcotics trafficking."[38] That is another way of saying, it was a predominantly Black neighborhood. And he walked the other direction after seeing police cars. But there are many reasons why people might choose to change course in a walk and even why seeing police might cause a person to walk in another direction. In light of the history of police violence in many cities, it might be prudent for someone, especially a young Black man, to avoid the police. Perhaps the person had had a bad experience with a police officer before or had friends whose experience had cautioned him to avoid the police when possible. All

Wardlow did was walk the other way to avoid police. Certainly, that behavior should not be seen as sufficiently incriminating to justify reasonable suspicion for a stop under the Fourth Amendment.

But that's not how the Supreme Court saw it. In an opinion written by Chief Justice Rehnquist, the Court ruled against Wardlow and upheld the reasonableness of the stop: "officers are not required to ignore the relevant characteristics of a location in determining whether the circumstances are sufficiently suspicious to warrant further investigation."[39] This gives police the ability to act differently depending on the neighborhood. I live in the Oakland Hills, a fairly affluent racially integrated neighborhood in Oakland, California. But I am just a few miles from West Oakland, an almost exclusively Black area and one that is more economically disadvantaged. Chief Justice Rehnquist and the Court have told the police that they have more authority to stop people in the latter area. That is an open invitation to race-based policing, and police use it just that way.

The other basis for stopping Wardlow had been that on seeing the four unmarked cars, he changed the course of his walking. "[I]t was not merely respondent's presence in an area of heavy narcotics trafficking that aroused the officers' suspicion," the chief justice wrote, "but his unprovoked flight upon noticing the police. Our cases have also recognized that nervous, evasive behavior is a pertinent factor in determining reasonable suspicion."[40] After so many police killings of unarmed Black men and other instances of excessive force, is it irrational for a Black man to feel nervous and want to avoid the police?

The Court has made it easy for an officer to manufacture a basis for stopping anyone, at any time, especially a person of color in a predominantly minority neighborhood. As explained earlier, police often lie in court to justify their actions, including their stops and frisks. The Mollen Commission, named after Judge Milton Mollen who led the investigation into corruption in the New York City Police Department in the early 1990s, reported that it occurs frequently: "Officers reported a litany of manufactured tales. For example, when officers unlawfully stop and search a vehicle because they believe it contains drugs or guns, officers will falsely claim in police reports and under oath that the car ran a red light (or committed some other traffic violation) and that they subsequently saw contraband in the car in plain view."[41] The Mollen Commission detailed other ways that police routinely lie: "To justify unlawfully entering an apartment where officers believe narcotics or cash can be found, they pretend to have information from an unidentified civilian informant or claim they saw the drugs in plain view after responding to the premises on a radio run. To arrest people they suspect are guilty of dealing drugs, they falsely assert that the defendants had drugs in their possession when, in fact, the drugs were found elsewhere where the officers had no lawful right to be."[42]

Of course, the Supreme Court did not create the problem of police officers who are willing to lie after the fact to justify their actions. But by allowing stops based on reasonable suspicion, and by greatly expanding the definition of what constitutes reasonable suspicion, the Court has made it easy for police to lie and justify virtually any stop. Once police have stopped a person, they need reasonable suspicion for a frisk. For that, though, all an officer has to say is that he or she saw a bulge that might have been a weapon.

. . . .

THE REHNQUIST and Roberts Courts have allowed officers, especially in communities of color, to presume that anyone is guilty and to stop anyone at almost any time. People who look like me or my children are unlikely to be stopped. But those who look like Michael Brown or Eric Garner or George Floyd or Daniel Prude are likely to have a very different story.

The Supreme Court has held that excessive police force is a seizure of a person and thus a violation of the Fourth Amendment.[43] In *Graham v. Connor* in 1989, the Court said that excessive force "claims are properly analyzed under the Fourth Amendment's 'objective reasonableness' standard."[44] But one will search almost in vain for cases where the Court has applied this decision and condemned police use of force as excessive, even when the force is deadly. Studies of the application of this standard in the lower federal courts demonstrate how difficult it is for victims of police abuse to bring lawsuits to recover damages under this legal rule.[45]

When I teach criminal procedure and the detailed rules of the Fourth Amendment, I often have the sense that as a constraint on the police, it is ever more a myth. Of course, police and prosecutors go to courts for warrants all the time, knowing that many judges will simply rubber-stamp them. But the police also know how easy it is for them, even without a warrant, to stop anyone whenever they want and subject the person at least to a frisk and often to a full search. And study after study shows that it is people of color who, by far, bear the brunt of this procedure. Some police stops turn violent and even deadly, as they did for Walter Scott and Eric Garner and George Floyd. They can all be traced in a straight line back to the Supreme Court decisions that have relaxed the requirements of the Fourth Amendment and empowered the police.

16

You Don't Really Have the Right to Remain Silent

POLICE ARE STILL REQUIRED TO GIVE SOMEONE IN custody the famous warnings from *Miranda v. Arizona* before questioning them, but ever since the Warren Court, the justices have taken every opportunity to weaken the privilege against self-incrimination. Perhaps because *Miranda* warnings are deeply embedded in popular culture, the justices have not been willing to overrule that decision. The reality is that the Burger Court significantly undercut the Warren Court's protection of the privilege against self-incrimination, and the Rehnquist and especially the Roberts Courts have gone much further in lessening constitutional protections for this fundamental right.

Interestingly, the Supreme Court had a chance to completely eliminate the requirement for *Miranda* warnings and chose not to do it. In *Dickerson v. United States* in 2000, Chief Justice Rehnquist, writing for the 7–2 majority, declared: "We do not think there is such justification for overruling *Miranda. Miranda* has become embedded in routine police practice to the point where the warnings have become part of our national culture."[1]

The procedural context of this case was unusual. Congress, in the Omnibus Crime Control and Safe Streets Act of 1968, sought to overturn *Miranda* by statute.[2] Section 3501 of the law provided that confessions would be admissible in federal court as long as they were voluntary, even if *Miranda* warnings were not properly given: "In any criminal prosecution brought by the United States or by the District of Columbia, a confession . . . shall be admissible in evidence if it is voluntarily given." This legislation passed the Senate 72–4 and the House 369–17. This reflects how controversial the *Miranda* decision initially was and how much it was perceived at the time as unduly hampering the police. Even liberals in Congress felt the need to go along with a law whose stated goal was to overrule *Miranda* and restore the law to what it was before 1966. Adopted soon after the *Miranda* decision, Congress was responding to strong political pressure to get tough on crime.

Every Justice Department, starting in 1968, refused to invoke this statute. They all took the position that Section 3501 is unconstitutional in that Congress impermissibly sought to overrule a Supreme Court decision that interpreted the Constitution.[3] Congress has no power to override a Supreme Court ruling on a constitutional issue. Although federal prosecutors have an obvious desire to have confessions used as evidence against criminal defendants, for over thirty years—during Republican and Democratic administrations alike—Justice Department attorneys did not use the statute.

Nor was Section 3501 invoked in the prosecution of Charles Thomas Dickerson. Dickerson, who was arrested and indicted for bank robbery in 1997, made incriminating statements to federal agents, but the U.S. District Court suppressed the confession on the grounds that *Miranda* warnings had not been properly administered. The government appealed, solely on the issue of whether there had been a violation of *Miranda*. In its brief to the U.S. Court of Appeals for the Fourth Circuit, the government declared: "[W]e are not making an argument based on Section 3501 in this appeal."[4] The Washington Legal Foundation, a conservative public interest group, filed a friend of the court brief in the Fourth Circuit urging the court to raise Section 3501 on its own. A very conservative panel of judges on that court accepted this invitation, invoked the statute, and held the confession admissible because it had been voluntary even though *Miranda* warnings had not been properly administered.

The Supreme Court reversed the Fourth Circuit and held that Section 3501 is unconstitutional. It explained that *Miranda v. Arizona* is "constitutionally based" and states a "constitutional rule." Because *Miranda* warnings were deemed a constitutional requirement, Congress could not eliminate them by statute. Therefore Section 3501 was unconstitutional because "Congress may not legislatively supersede our decisions interpreting and applying the Constitution."[5]

Why didn't the conservative majority on the Rehnquist Court effectively overrule *Miranda* when it could have, or allow Congress to do so? Justice Scalia would have done so, as he wrote in his scathing dissent in *Dickerson:* "Today's judgment converts Miranda from a milestone of judicial overreaching into the very Cheops' Pyramid (or perhaps the Sphinx would be a better analogue) of judicial arrogance."[6]

In part, the Supreme Court decided the way it did to protect its own power. If the Court had decided that *Miranda* was not constitutionally required, as the federal court of appeals had concluded, that might have opened the door for Congress to eliminate other judicially created remedies in constitutional cases. If Congress could overrule the Court's command that confessions be excluded from evidence if they were obtained without proper administration of *Miranda* warnings, then it could also overturn judicial orders in other cases, such as orders for busing in school desegregation litigation or suits for damages against federal officers.

Another reason for the Court's decision in *Dickerson* was that *Miranda,* it turned out, did not actually limit the police or keep them from gaining confessions as had been feared. The overwhelming consensus of countless studies is that *Miranda* has had no effect on the ability of police to gain confessions and of prosecutors to gain convictions. Legal scholar Stephen Schulhofer has concluded that the long-term effect of *Miranda* in decreasing confessions is "essentially nil."[7] *Miranda* warnings don't appreciably decrease the coercion of in-custodial police interrogation, and police have developed techniques for undermining the warnings and circumventing the decision.

In fact, many in law enforcement had come to regard *Miranda* as helpful to the police. It is easy to see why. Justice Souter once explained that "giving the warnings and getting a waiver has generally produced a virtual ticket of admissibility."[8] As long as the police administer the warnings properly, there is a strong presumption of voluntariness and admissibility of any confession. The Supreme Court has noted that it is extremely rare for a confession to be deemed involuntary once the *Miranda* warnings are properly given.[9]

The alternative to *Miranda,* created by Section 3501, is that confessions would be admissible so long as they were voluntary. But the line between "voluntary" and "involuntary" is inherently uncertain and provides police with less guidance than their knowing that if they properly administer the *Miranda* warnings, the confession will most likely be admissible at trial. Thus the Court's choice to keep *Miranda*—with even conservative Chief Justice Rehnquist writing the majority—was based on the sense that it helped police much more than it hindered them.

But having preserved *Miranda,* the Court in reality has undercut and weakened it at every opportunity. One of the most important instances was in 2010, in *Berghuis v. Thompkins,* where the Roberts Court took a major step to lessening the Constitution's protection against self-incrimination.[10] Among the Miranda warnings that police are required to give a suspect is the warning that he or she has the right to remain silent.

The *Berghuis* case involved Van Chester Thompkins, who in January 2000 was arrested by Michigan police on suspicion of having committed murder outside a shopping mall. The officers took him to the stationhouse, gave him his *Miranda* warnings, and asked him to sign a statement that he understood them. He refused. There is a factual dispute as to whether he indicated his understanding orally.

Police then questioned Thompkins for two hours and forty-five minutes. During this time he remained almost entirely silent. Occasionally he would answer a question with a single word or a nod. Almost three hours into the interrogation, the officer asked Thompkins, "Do you believe in God?" Thompkins said, "Yes." The officer then asked Thompkins whether he prays to God, and once more he said, "Yes." The officer then asked, "Do you pray to God for shooting that boy down?" Thompkins again said, "Yes."

At trial, this statement—actually three one-word answers—was admitted against Thompkins and was the crucial evidence in gaining his conviction. He was sentenced to life in prison without the possibility of parole.

The issue that came before the Supreme Court was whether Thompkins's using these short answers had violated his privilege against self-incrimination, especially after he had remained silent for almost three hours. In a 5–4 decision, the Court ruled against Thompkins and found that there had been no infringement of his Fifth Amendment rights. Justice Kennedy wrote for the majority, joined by Chief Justice Roberts and Justices Scalia, Thomas, and Alito.

The Court concluded that a suspect's silence is not sufficient to invoke the right to remain silent. Rather, the Court said, the suspect must make an "unambiguous" invocation of this right. Earlier, the Court had held that a suspect must invoke the right to counsel under *Miranda* in a clear and unambiguous manner;[11] in *Berghuis,* the Court ruled that the same is true of the right to remain silent. Simply put, a person is not protected by the right to remain silent unless he or she knows to say and actually says something as explicit as "I wish to assert my right to remain silent."

By answering those three questions from the police, the Court said, Thompkins had validly waived his right to remain silent. A person's waiver of this right, the Court said, need not be explicit: "An implicit waiver of the 'right to remain silent' is sufficient to admit a suspect's statement into evidence."[12] In other words, even almost three hours of silence in the face of persistent police questioning was not enough to trigger the right to remain silent, and answering three questions with one-word answers constituted a waiver. The Court thus upheld Thompkins's conviction.

Justice Sotomayor wrote a blistering dissent, joined by Justices Stevens, Ginsburg, and Breyer. She accused the majority of turning *Miranda* on its head and lamented the irony that silence is not sufficient to invoke the right to remain silent. It is impossible, she said, to reconcile the Court's decision in *Berghuis v. Thompkins* with *Miranda v. Arizona.* In *Miranda,* the Court had said that when police interrogate a suspect without an attorney being present, "a heavy burden rests on the government to demonstrate that the defendant knowingly and intelligently waived his privilege against self-incrimination."[13] But in *Berghuis,* the Court said the government need not show a knowing and intelligent waiver in order to find a suspect's statements admissible.

In *Miranda,* furthermore, the Warren Court had said that "lengthy interrogation or incommunicado incarceration before a statement is made is strong evidence that the accused did not waive his rights."[14] It also said that statements made after long police questioning had to be assumed to be the product of coercion. But the Roberts Court in *Berghuis* held that there is no violation of the privilege against self-incrimination even when statements follow hours of silence in the face of police questioning.

Nor is it consistent with the right to remain silent to hold that silence itself is insufficient and that a criminal suspect must specifically say that he or she is invoking the privilege against self-incrimination, must explicitly say, "I am invoking my right to remain silent." The Court presumes that someone being arrested will understand the technical difference between merely remaining silent and saying they wish to remain silent, but that is ludicrous. The vast majority of people arrested in this country are not trained in criminal law and would have no idea that they need to utter magic words in order to have their right to remain silent. Probably only criminal defense lawyers and law students who have studied criminal procedure know this. Since *Berghuis*, police have been able keep questioning a silent suspect for hours and hours until they finally obtain an incriminating answer.

Miranda created a strong presumption that confessions were inadmissible if police obtained them after questioning unless the suspect explicitly waived the Fifth Amendment privilege against self-incrimination. In sharp contrast, *Berghuis* creates a strong presumption that confessions are admissible if obtained after questioning unless the suspect has explicitly invoked the right to remain silent. This really does turn *Miranda* on its head.

· · · · · · · · ·

THE WARREN COURT had decided *Miranda* based on its great concern that subjecting suspects to in-custody police interrogation is inherently coercive. The Rehnquist Court explained in 1993 that *Miranda* reflects our society's "preference for an accusatorial rather than an inquisitorial system of criminal justice" and a "fear that self-incriminating statements will be elicited by inhumane treatments and abuses." It is based on a realization that while the "privilege is sometimes a shelter to the guilty, [it] is often a protection of the innocent."[15] But in *Berghuis* the Roberts Court came down on the side of the police and against the rights of criminal suspects. It almost always does.

The Roberts Court has undercut *Miranda* in other ways as well, especially in ruling that tangible evidence may be used against a criminal defendant, even if the police learned of it only through an interrogation that was done in violation of *Miranda*. In *United States v. Patane* in 2004, the Court held that police failure to give a criminal suspect the required *Miranda* warnings does not require suppression of physical evidence learned as a result of the questioning.[16] Imagine an officer deliberately violates the requirements of *Miranda* in interrogating a suspect while in custody and that the person, while being questioned, says things that lead to their finding tangible evidence. *Patane* says that the evidence is admissible, even though the statements would have to be excluded. This ruling provides police with yet another incentive to disregard *Miranda*.

No Supreme Court decision ever has questioned the Warren Court's conclusion in *Miranda* that custodial police interrogation is inherently coercive. The Warren Court thought the solution was to require that police provide warnings to suspects before questioning, and that these would lessen the coercion. But we now know that *Miranda* warnings do not succeed; suspects often do not understand them, and just reading the warnings does not lessen coercion. Besides, police have found ways to undermine the warnings and even to benefit from ignoring them.

One would hope that the Supreme Court would have looked for other ways to protect citizens' privilege against self-incrimination, which is enshrined in the Fifth Amendment. Unfortunately, the justices have done just the opposite: they have preserved the requirements prescribed in *Miranda* but subverted both its effectiveness and the privilege against self-incrimination at every opportunity.

17

Ignoring the Problem of False Eyewitness Identifications

I F I WERE FORCED TO LIMIT MYSELF TO MAKING ONLY one criticism of the Supreme Court in its failure to protect those suspected and accused of crimes, it would be its total refusal to deal with the problem of false eyewitness identifications. Justice Sotomayor wrote in 2012 that the "empirical evidence demonstrates that eyewitness misidentification is the single greatest cause of wrongful convictions in this country."[1] She observed: "Researchers have found that a staggering 76 percent of the first 250 convictions overturned due to DNA evidence since 1989 involved eyewitness misidentification. Study after study demonstrates that eyewitness recollections are highly susceptible to distortion by postevent information or social cues; that jurors routinely overestimate the accuracy of eyewitness identifications; that jurors place the greatest weight on eyewitness confidence in assessing identifications even though confidence is a poor gauge of accuracy; and that suggestiveness can stem from sources beyond police-orchestrated procedures."[2] And as we have seen, many studies document that eyewitness identifications are most fallible when people are identifying those of a different race.

So it is surprising that the Supreme Court, in the entire Rehnquist and Roberts eras, spanning from 1986 through today, has decided only one case concerning eyewitness identifications, and in that decision it sided with the police. I always have wondered why. Is it that the justices are ignorant of the mountain of research done by social psychologists on the flaws of eyewitness identifications? Are they unaware that the Innocence Project has so often proved that individuals were wrongly convicted because of mistaken identifications? Or do they possess an uncritical faith that police will not conduct suggestive identifications, that witnesses will be accurate in their identifications, and that cross-examinations at trial will reveal any problems? Or are they merely reluctant to overturn convictions for fear of letting guilty people go free?

The Supreme Court's single case dealing with eyewitness identifications since 1986 was *Perry v. New Hampshire* in 2012.[3] At about three a.m. on August 15, 2008, in Nashua, New Hampshire, Joffre Ullon called police to report that an African American male was trying to break into cars parked in the lot of Ullon's apartment building. Officer Nicole Clay responded to the call. She saw Barion Perry standing between two cars. Perry, who was holding two car stereo amplifiers in his hands, walked toward Officer Clay. She asked Perry where the amplifiers came from. He responded, "[I] found them on the ground."

Ullon's wife, Nubia Blandon, woke her neighbor, Alex Clavijo, and told him she had just seen someone break into his car. Clavijo immediately went downstairs to the parking lot to look at his car. He observed that one of the rear windows had been shattered. Then on further inspection, he discovered that the speakers and amplifiers from his car stereo were missing.

By this time, another officer had arrived at the scene. Officer Clay asked Perry to stay in the parking lot with that officer, while she and Clavijo went to talk to Blandon. Clay and Clavijo then entered the apartment building and took the stairs to the fourth floor, where Blandon's and Clavijo's apartments were located. They met Blandon in the hallway just outside the open door to her apartment.

Asked to describe what she had seen, Blandon stated that, around two-thirty a.m., she saw from her kitchen window a tall African American man "roaming" the parking lot and looking into cars. She said the man circled Clavijo's car, opened the trunk, and removed a large box. Clay asked Blandon for a more specific description of the man. Blandon pointed to her kitchen window and said that the person she saw breaking into Clavijo's car was standing in the parking lot, next to the police officer. She pointed to Perry, whom the police then arrested.

About a month later, the police showed Blandon a photographic array that included a picture of Perry and asked her to point out the man who had broken into Clavijo's car. Blandon was unable to identify Perry. In light of this, Perry's attorney argued that admitting the eyewitness identification against him violated due process. At the very least, a judge should need to prescreen identifications before the jury hears them to ensure their reliability.

But the Supreme Court, in an 8–1 decision, rejected these arguments and ruled against Perry. Justice Ginsburg wrote the opinion for the Court; only Justice Sotomayor dissented. The police did not create the suggestive situation for the eyewitness identification, Justice Ginsburg wrote; unless police are responsible for the suggestiveness, they have not violated due process and the identification is admissible as evidence: "the potential unreliability of a type of evidence does not alone render its introduction at the defendant's trial fundamentally unfair."[4] The ability to cross-examine the witness at trial is a sufficient safeguard, she held, but offered no evidence to support that cross-examination actually succeeds in exposing wrongful identifications.

It is puzzling that Justice Ginsburg would have taken such a formalistic approach and said that eyewitness identifications were admissible in court, no matter how suggestive the circumstances, unless the police were responsible for the suggestiveness. Perhaps it was because the Court had earlier ruled that even the fruits of suggestive identification procedures are admissible as long as the court deems the resulting identification to be "reliable."[5]

Justice Sotomayor, in her solo dissent, said that there is no basis for limiting due process protections to situations where the police create the suggestive identification. Suggestive identification procedures violate due process, she said, regardless of "the source of suggestiveness": " '[i]t is the likelihood of misidentification which violates a defendant's right to due process.' "[6] An identification that results from suggestive circumstances, whether they were created intentionally or inadvertently, is equally likely to misidentify the perpetrator and to be powerful to the jury. And the defendant is no more or less prejudiced at trial or equipped to challenge the identification through cross-examination.

The evidence is overwhelming that faulty eyewitness identifications lead to the convictions of innocent people. Yet the Court's deciding only one case about the subject in almost thirty-five years, and siding with the police, sends a strong message to police and judges: there is little constitutional limit on what police can do in obtaining eyewitness identifications. Prosecutors can then introduce them into evidence at trial, where inevitably they have a powerful effect on the jury. Innocent people will continue to be wrongly convicted on the basis of mistaken identifications, and the Supreme Court either doesn't see it or doesn't care.

18

The Vanishing Remedies for Police Misconduct

THE REHNQUIST AND ROBERTS COURTS HAVE MADE it very difficult for judges to find that a police officer has engaged in an illegal search or arrest in violation of the Fourth Amendment, or infringed the privilege against self-incrimination, or violated due process with an unduly suggestive police identification procedure. But even worse, when they do find a violation, the Court has dramatically lessened the remedies available. Rights are meaningless without remedies. Police know when they can act with impunity since their actions will have no consequences.

As explained earlier, there are two major remedies for police misconduct: excluding evidence illegally obtained, and bringing civil suits against either the officers or the government that employs them. The Rehnquist and Roberts Courts have significantly narrowed both remedies.

As for the exclusionary rule, the conservative justices on the Roberts Court have substantially eroded it as a remedy for illegal police conduct. In 2006 in *Hudson v. Michigan,* four justices—Roberts, Scalia, Thomas, and Alito—called for the complete elimination of the exclusionary rule.[1] This decision, just one year into Roberts's tenure as chief justice, conveyed a clear message as to how his Court felt about this crucial remedy for police violations of the Fourth Amendment.

For many years, the Supreme Court had held that police usually must knock and announce their presence before entering a residence.[2] The purpose is to protect the people inside the home and also the officers, since an unannounced entry often can lead to violence when those inside have no idea who has entered. This is what led to the death of Breonna Taylor in Louisville in 2020, as police, executing a warrant, allegedly did not knock or announce their presence. Her boyfriend, not knowing who was coming in, fired a shot. (His gun was licensed.) The police fired back and bullets struck and killed Taylor.

In *Hudson,* all the justices, and all the judges hearing the case in the lower courts, agreed that police had violated the requirement for knocking and announcing. The question was whether the evidence they gained had to be suppressed.

The Supreme Court ruled 5–4 that when police violate the Fourth Amendment's requirement for "knock and announce," the exclusionary rule does not apply. In fact, Justice Scalia's majority opinion called into question the very existence of the exclusionary rule. He referred to it as a "last resort." He did not explain what he meant by that, but he seems clearly to have been implying that excluding evidence should be avoided as much as possible, and ideally entirely. The exclusionary rule, Justice Scalia stressed, "generates substantial social costs, which sometimes include setting the guilty free and the dangerous at large."[3] The exclusionary rule was unnecessary, he argued, because civil suits against police were available as a remedy, and police forces were increasingly professionalized. As we will see, this claim is disingenuous because Justice Scalia played a key role in limiting civil liability for police misconduct and consistently voted to restrict people's ability to sue police officers for use of excessive force and other constitutional violations.

Justice Scalia's arguments were not about making an exception to the Fourth Amendment in knock-and-announce cases. They were arguments that conservatives had been making for decades against the very existence of the exclusionary rule. They were arguments that the dissenters in *Mapp v. Ohio* had made, in the case where the Supreme Court had applied the exclusionary rule to the states, and they were the arguments that Chief Justice Warren Burger had made in 1971, shortly after coming on to the Court, in calling for the complete elimination of the exclusionary rule.[4]

Since the 2006 *Hudson* decision, police have had virtually no reason ever to meet the Fourth Amendment's requirements for knocking and announcing before entering a dwelling. They know they will likely face no consequences for violating this rule.

Justice Scalia mentioned the possible alternative remedy of bringing civil suits against police officers, but in the vast majority of instances where the police violate the knock-and-announce requirement, individuals will not be likely to bring a lawsuit, let alone successfully. They will have difficulty obtaining an attorney because in most instances the damages are not sufficient to make a lawsuit worth it. Moreover, juries are far more likely to be sympathetic to police officers, especially when their actions succeeded in gaining evidence of illegal activities. Moreover, even if someone brings a lawsuit, the Court has made it almost impossible for anyone to sue cities for such violations, and it has made it difficult to sue police officers by providing them immunity to many suits for civil rights violations.

In a separate opinion, Justice Kennedy said that "the continued operation of the exclusionary rule . . . is not in doubt."[5] But *Hudson* made clear that in 2006 four justices—Scalia, Roberts, Thomas, and Alito—wanted to eliminate the exclusionary rule altogether in Fourth Amendment cases. Since then, in the decade and a half since *Hudson* was decided, the Court has only gotten significantly more conservative, and more opposed to the exclusionary rule.

· · · · · · · · ·

THREE YEARS AFTER *HUDSON*, in 2009 the Supreme Court significantly changed the law as to when courts must exclude evidence because of an unconstitutional police search, again in a 5–4 decision with the most conservative justices in the majority. The case, *Herring v. United States*,[6] is the most important change in the exclusionary rule since *Mapp v. Ohio* applied it to the states in 1961.[7]

In Coffee County, Florida, police learned that Bennie Dean Herring had driven to the sheriff's department to pick up an impounded truck. The officer, Mack Anderson, knew Herring from past encounters and checked to see if there were any outstanding warrants for him from other counties. Officer Anderson found an outstanding warrant from Dale County and arrested Herring based on it. Police searched Herring incident to his arrest and found methamphetamines in his pocket. It turned out, though, that five months earlier the other county had eliminated the warrant; the police computer system had not been updated. Thus the arrest and the resulting search had been illegal, though not because of any wrongdoing by the arresting officer. The issue was whether the exclusionary rule applies when police commit an illegal search based on good faith reliance on erroneous information from another jurisdiction.

Chief Justice Roberts, writing for the 5–4 majority, held that the exclusionary rule does not apply and that the evidence was properly admitted against Herring. The Court once more called the exclusionary rule the "last resort," to be used only where applying it would have significant additional deterrent effect on police violations of the Fourth Amendment.[8] The Court held that the exclusionary rule may be applied only if police intentionally or recklessly violate the Fourth Amendment or only if police department violations with regard to searches and seizures are systemic. For the first time in history, the Court concluded that the exclusionary rule does not apply if police violate the Fourth Amendment by good faith or even negligent actions.

The Court could have ruled in favor of the police in a far narrower holding. In a 1995 case, the Rehnquist Court had held that the exclusionary rule does not apply if police rely in good faith on erroneous information about a warrant from a court.[9] The Roberts Court could simply have ruled that the same exception applies when the police rely on erroneous information about a warrant from another jurisdiction. Instead, the Court's conservative majority that already wanted to limit the exclusionary rule issued a sweeping decision that evidence never has to be excluded if the police violate the Fourth Amendment in good faith or through negligence.

Exempting all negligent violations of the Fourth Amendment from the exclusionary rule is, in itself, a significant undermining of this protection. In reality, many police violations of the Fourth Amendment result not from systemic error or intentional disregard of constitutional rights but from carelessness and negligence. Also, the line between what is "negligent" as opposed to what is "reckless" is difficult to discern. Courts that do not want to exclude evidence—and they generally do not—can easily declare the police conduct to have been "negligent" and so admit as evidence the fruits of the illegal police search.

But Chief Justice Roberts went even further and said that the exclusionary rule applies only where the value of deterring police misconduct outweighs the costs of releasing a potentially guilty person: "To trigger the exclusionary rule, police conduct must be sufficiently deliberate that exclusion can meaningfully deter it, and sufficiently culpable that such deterrence is worth the price paid by the justice system."[10] This finding in itself created a major new exception to the exclusionary rule. Instead of being presumptively applicable for almost all Fourth Amendment violations, the exclusionary rule will now by law apply only if it would deter the specific police misconduct at issue and only if, on balance, the deterrence gained outweighs the cost of a possibly guilty person going free.

This erosion of the exclusionary rule has created significant problems. As Justice Ginsburg noted in her dissent, "[t]he exclusionary rule, it bears emphasis, is often the only remedy effective to redress a Fourth Amendment violation."[11] Rarely will a victim of a Fourth Amendment violation, such as the one in *Herring,* be able to successfully sue the officers for monetary damages. Without the exclusionary rule, nothing remains to deter police misconduct. In the context of *Herring,* without the exclusionary rule, Officer Anderson would have had no reason at all to check to make sure that the warrant for Herring was valid. Police are very savvy about this and quickly learn when they can violate the Fourth Amendment with impunity.

Moreover, Chief Justice Roberts's opinion errs in focusing on the exclusionary rule solely in terms of deterring police violations of the Fourth Amendment. The "rule also serves other important purposes," as Justice Ginsburg noted in her dissent: "It 'enabl[es] the judiciary to avoid the taint of partnership in official lawlessness,' and it 'assur[es] the people-all potential victims of unlawful government conduct-that the government would not profit from its lawless behavior, thus minimizing the risk of seriously undermining popular trust in government.' "[12]

To be sure, *Herring v. United States* did not eliminate the exclusionary rule. But it did significantly erode it and made clear that the majority on the Roberts Court wants to go very far in limiting it. Today, as the Court has become even more conservative, there may be five or six justices on the Court who will vote to abolish it. Opposition to the exclusionary rule is not new. Conservatives have vocally castigated it for decades, but now they finally may have a majority to substantially undermine it and perhaps to eliminate it. *Herring v. United States* was an unfortunate major step in that direction.

Why does it matter? The primary incentive for police to comply with the Fourth Amendment is their knowledge that violations will be counterproductive because illegally obtained evidence will be suppressed. The Fourth Amendment protects the privacy of all of us, not just those who have committed crimes. Without the Fourth Amendment, nothing keeps police from stopping and searching anyone at all, or searching anyone's home, anytime they want to. Surely it makes law enforcement more effective, but at a huge cost in terms of privacy. The Roberts Court's dramatic erosion of the exclusionary rule thus puts all our privacy and rights in jeopardy. And experience and studies tell us that it is people of color who will bear the brunt of this.

· · · · · · · · ·

THIS GUTTING of the exclusionary rule might be less troubling if citizens had other effective remedies for police misconduct. In calling for the elimination of the exclusionary rule, Justice Scalia argued that it was not needed because civil suits for monetary damages make it unnecessary.[13] Ironically, Justice Scalia and the other conservatives on the Court have made it extremely difficult to sue to recover money damages for police abuse.

Lawsuits to recover damages are essential, in the justice system and all other areas, to ensure accountability, to deter wrongdoing, and to compensate injured victims. The prospect of having to pay damages can be a crucial incentive for government to comply with the law. If cities were held liable for wrongs committed by police, they would have a greater incentive for care in hiring, training, supervising, and disciplining officers. When I examined the Los Angeles Police Department, I found that damage awards, and concern over them, motivated the municipal implementation of controls on police.[14] Also, if officers personally faced liability, they would be less likely to engage in wrongful behavior.

But the Rehnquist and Roberts Courts have made it much more difficult for people to sue both government entities and individual officers for monetary damages.

Over the last forty years, the Supreme Court has made it much harder for citizens to hold cities and counties liable when their police officers violate the Constitution. As explained earlier, the Burger Court, in *Monell v. Department of Social Services* in 1978, opened the door to such suits when it held that local governments can be sued. But the Court in *Monell* imposed a significant limit that over the years has become ever more daunting and difficult to overcome. A city or country cannot be held liable on the ground that its officers acted unconstitutionally; a municipality can be held liable only if it has a policy that violates the Constitution.[15] Although the George Floyd murder is a particularly heinous act, captured on video and ricocheted through social media across the world, the reality is that the City of Minneapolis could be held liable for damages only if it had a policy stating that officers could choke individuals under such circumstances. For obvious reasons, the city chose to settle with George Floyd's family rather than litigate, even though it might well have prevailed in court.

And in the last few decades, the Court has made it very difficult to prove the existence of such policies. No city ever will have an officially stated policy that its police officers should use excessive force, even if the culture in its police department condones it. Yet absent such an express policy, the Court has created an obstacle to proving municipal liability that is often insurmountable.

Consider, for example, the Court's decision in 1997 in *Bryan County, Oklahoma v. Brown*.[16] The Bryan County sheriff, B. J. Moore, hired his nephew's son, Stacy Burns, as a deputy even though Burns had a long criminal record that included guilty pleas for assault and battery, resisting arrest, and public drunkenness. Sheriff Moore obviously did not completely trust Burns; he authorized him to make arrests, but not to carry a weapon or operate a patrol car. Nonetheless Burns became involved in a high-speed car chase. Once the fleeing car finally stopped, Burns ordered the driver and passenger out of the car. When the passenger, Jill Brown, did not immediately comply, Burns pulled her from the car so violently that he caused permanent damage to both her knees. As the Supreme Court would note, Deputy Burns "used an 'arm bar' technique, grabbing [Brown's] arm at the wrist and elbow, pulling her from the vehicle, and spinning her to the ground. [Brown's] knees were severely injured, and she later underwent corrective surgery. Ultimately, she may need knee replacements."[17]

This should have been an easy case. Predictably, an officer who never should have been on the police force, given his prior history, inflicted great harm by using excessive force. In fact, the jury found that Sheriff Moore had been "deliberately indifferent" in his hiring and supervision of Burns.

But in a 5–4 decision, the Supreme Court ruled that there was not sufficient proof that the local government had caused Jill Brown's injuries. "[A] finding of culpability," Justice O'Connor wrote for the majority, "simply cannot depend on the mere probability that any officer inadequately screened will inflict any constitutional injury. Rather, it must depend on a finding that *this* officer was highly likely to inflict the *particular* injury suffered by the plaintiff."[18] In other words, Brown would have had to show that Burns was "highly likely" to inflict that "particular injury" on someone. In effect, she would have had to show that it was foreseeable that Deputy Burns would break someone's knees and not, say, dislocate a shoulder instead. This burden is, needless to say, often insurmountable.

The Court's decision is especially troubling because the jury in a lower court had found that the sheriff's deliberate indifference in hiring Burns had caused Brown's injuries. The Supreme Court had previously held that deliberate indifference by a local government was sufficient to show a municipal policy.[19] The record supported this decision: Sheriff Moore had deputized a close relative with a criminal record, fully aware that such a person, empowered to perform police duties, could cause great harm. It is unclear how much worse his criminal record would have had to have been for the Supreme Court to have allowed the verdict of liability to stand. That Burns would injure people as a deputy should have been obvious, but to require that it be foreseeable that he would cause a "particular injury" is an impossible obstacle to liability.

In the years that followed, the Court made it even harder to prove a municipal policy and hold local governments liable for their constitutional violations. *Connick v. Thompson* in 2011 was a case in which, like so many, race played a key role. John Thompson, an African American man, had been convicted of murdering a man and spent eighteen years in a Louisiana prison, fourteen of them on death row.[20] One month before he was to be executed, Thompson's defense lawyers found out that prosecutors had possessed, but never disclosed, blood evidence that exonerated Thompson for an armed robbery for which he had been convicted and that had greatly affected his murder trial.

Two days before Thompson's murder trial opened in New Orleans, the assistant district attorney had received the crime lab's report, which stated that the perpetrator had type B blood and that Thompson has type O blood. The defense was not told of this evidence at the trial. The assistant district attorney hid the report. Many years later, when he was dying of cancer, he told another assistant district attorney about it. That person, too, told no one, and in fact the Louisiana State Bar later disciplined him for not informing Thompson and his lawyers immediately.[21]

All the while, Thompson remained on death row with his execution date approaching. Only "through a serendipitous series of events" did his lawyer discover the blood evidence, a month before Thompson was to be executed.[22] New testing was done on blood that came from the perpetrator of the murders, and it didn't match Thompson's DNA or even his blood type. His conviction was overturned, and he was retried for the murder. This time he was acquitted of all charges.

The New Orleans district attorney's office conceded that by not turning over the blood evidence, it had violated its obligations under *Brady v. Maryland*[23]—a landmark 1963 case in which the Court ruled that withholding exculpatory evidence violates the due process clause of the Fourteenth Amendment. There was no way to argue otherwise. Thompson's lawyers, though, knew that they could not sue the district attorney or the lawyers who handled the case because the Supreme Court had ruled that prosecutors have absolute immunity to civil suits for monetary damages. So Thompson instead sued the local government that employed them. The New Orleans district attorney's office had a notorious history of not disclosing exculpatory information to defendants. The jury ruled in Thompson's favor and awarded him $14 million.

But the Supreme Court reversed, in a 5–4 decision, holding that the local government could not be held liable for the prosecutors' misconduct. John Thompson, who spent over eighteen years in prison because of prosecutorial misconduct for a murder that he did not commit, was left with no remedy at all.

Justice Thomas, writing for the Court, said that a single instance of prosecutorial misconduct was not enough to show deliberate indifference or establish liability of the city government. Thomas, as he almost always does, looked for and found a way to protect the government and its officers when they violate the Constitution, even tragically so.

But Justice Thomas was just wrong in characterizing this as a single instance of prosecutorial misconduct. As Justice Ginsburg observed in dissent, this "was no momentary oversight, no single incident of a lone officer's misconduct."[24] "Throughout the pretrial and trial proceedings against Thompson," she wrote, "the team of four engaged in prosecuting him for armed robbery and murder hid from the defense and the court exculpatory information Thompson requested and had a constitutional right to receive. The prosecutors did so despite multiple opportunities, spanning nearly two decades, to set the record straight."[25]

This was not even the only serious *Brady* violation prosecutors committed in the case. Police interviewed an eyewitness to the murder who described the assailant as having short hair. At that time, Thompson had a large Afro. That, too, was never disclosed to the defense. Thompson suffered one of the worst harms a government can inflict on a person, and the Court once more refused to allow any remedy.

The Supreme Court's decision in *Connick v. Thompson* has made it very difficult to hold local governments, or anyone at all, accountable for such prosecutorial misconduct. After the decision, I filed a petition for Supreme Court review, which was denied, on behalf of two men, Earl Truvia and Gregory Bright, who spent twenty-eight years in prison for a murder they did not commit.[26] They, like Thompson, were Black men. They were convicted in 1976. In 2002 the Orleans Parish Criminal District Court found that the Orleans Parish district attorney—the same office that had prosecuted John Thompson—had also suppressed crucial evidence in Truvia's and Bright's case. The criminal district court overturned their convictions, and the Louisiana Supreme Court subsequently denied review. In 2004, twenty-eight years after being wrongfully convicted, Truvia and Bright were released from prison.

After their convictions were vacated, Truvia and Bright filed a lawsuit against the local government, asserting claims for constitutional violations. They submitted substantial evidence to the federal district court that the Orleans Parish district attorney's office had a policy and custom of withholding exculpatory evidence, including that it failed to train its prosecutors of their obligations under the *Brady* decision. Truvia and Bright pointed to twelve other instances since 1990 of individuals whose convictions were overturned because of *Brady* violations committed by the Orleans Parish district attorney's office.[27] But the federal district court and the federal court of appeals ruled against them, saying that even this weight of evidence did not establish the existence of a municipal policy needed to hold the local government liable. The Supreme Court declined to review the case.

Municipal governments can be held liable for the conduct of their police officers only if it is shown that the city's own policy caused the unconstitutional conduct. Even a pattern of constitutional violations like that of the Orleans Parish district attorney's office is not enough to hold a local government liable. When it comes to constitutional violations by the police, including the use of excessive and even deadly force, it is extremely difficult and often impossible to successfully sue the local government.

· · · · · · · · ·

BECAUSE IT IS SO HARD for members of the public to sue cities, and it is usually impossible to sue the federal government or the states because of their sovereign immunity, the only possibility for litigation is often to sue individual police officers for monetary damages. But the Supreme Court has also made it increasingly difficult for citizens to sue to recover damages from government officials—federal, state, and local—when they violate the Constitution.

For the last forty years, the Supreme Court has increasingly closed the door to those who want to sue federal law enforcement officials for their unconstitutional actions, even when they cause great harm, including death. If a state or local official violates the Constitution or the laws of the United States, he or she can be sued pursuant to 42 U.S. Code Section 1983, which authorizes lawsuits against persons acting under state authority that violate the Constitution and laws of the United States. In 1971 the early Burger Court held that a federal officer who violates a constitutional right can be sued even though no statute expressly authorizes such litigation.[28] But since 1980, the Court has abandoned that decision. In every case since then, without exception, the Court has rejected people's ability to sue federal officers.

Most recently, in *Hernández v. Mesa* in 2020, the Roberts Court disallowed a civil suit against a border agent in El Paso, Texas.[29] In 2011 the agent had fired his gun across the U.S.-Mexico border and killed a fifteen-year-old boy on the Mexican side. The boy was one of a group of teenagers who, separated from the officer by a fence, were taunting him and maybe throwing rocks (though that was disputed). For the officer to fire his gun at the boys was inexcusable; he was in no danger, and even if rocks were being thrown, he could have just moved away from the fence and ignored the teenagers.

But Justice Alito, writing for the five conservative justices in a 5–4 decision, stressed the need to restrict suits against federal officials, here because it involved another country. Justice Thomas, joined by Justice Gorsuch, concurred and wrote separately to urge the complete overruling of *Bivens v. Six Unknown Federal Narcotics Agents*, the 1971 decision that had authorized such litigation.[30] Had the Court overruled *Bivens*, it would have left those injured by federal law enforcement—the FBI, ICE, the border patrol, the federal bureau of narcotics—with no ability to sue in federal court, no matter what constitutional violation the officers had committed and no matter how grave an injury the victim had suffered.

The Court, without expressly overruling *Bivens*, has nonetheless been effectively doing exactly that. As Justice Ginsburg pointed out, writing for the dissenters in *Hernández,* this case, like *Bivens,* involved a claim of excessive police force in violation of the Fourth Amendment. Even if the setting in *Hernández* could be characterized as "new," she wrote, "there is still no good reason why Hernández's parents should face a closed courtroom door."[31] Hernández's parents were left with no possible remedy; even though their son was killed by a federal law enforcement officer's unjustified use of deadly force, they could sue no one.

This is just one of many cases in which the Supreme Court has restricted suits against federal officers for their unconstitutional conduct. In *Hui v. Castenada* in 2010, the Court held that a prison inmate could not sue federal prison officials who refused to allow him to see a doctor for treatment for a lesion growing on his penis. By the time the prison guards allowed him to get medical treatment, he was suffering enormously, and it was too late; his penis had to be amputated and even that could not save him. A short time later he died from the cancer that had spread throughout his body.[32] Like Hernández's parents, the prisoner and ultimately his estate were left with no one they could sue.

But even in the rare instance in which a federal officer can be sued, and when state and local government officials are sued for monetary damages, they *always* can assert an "immunity defense," and this, too, will very often leave a person injured by police misconduct without any means of recovery. The Supreme Court has held that some government officials have *absolute immunity* and cannot be sued at all for monetary damages, no matter how egregious their constitutional violations. Absolute immunity exists for judges for their judicial acts, for prosecutors for their prosecutorial acts, for legislators for their legislative acts, for law enforcement personnel testifying as witnesses, and for the president for presidential acts. *All* other government officers are protected by qualified immunity and are liable only if they violate clearly established law that every reasonable officer should know and only if the right they violated is one that is established beyond dispute. In recent years, the Supreme Court has expanded the scope of both absolute immunity and qualified immunity, making it much harder—and often impossible—to sue government officials, including police officers, who violate the Constitution and inflict great harms.

These doctrines—the limitations on people's ability to sue federal officers and absolute and qualified immunity—are tremendous obstacles to enforcing the Constitution. Absolute immunity means just what it says: the person covered by it has no liability whatsoever, no matter how extreme their constitutional violation. In the area of criminal justice, prosecutors have absolute immunity to suits for damages for their prosecutorial misconduct. As discussed earlier, in *Imbler v. Pachtman* the Supreme Court accorded absolute immunity to a prosecutor who was sued for damages for knowingly using perjured testimony that resulted in an innocent person's conviction and incarceration for nine years.[33]

One consequence of absolute prosecutorial immunity is shown in the Roberts Court's decision in *Van de Kamp v. Goldstein*.[34] Thomas Lee Goldstein spent twenty-four years in prison for a murder that he did not commit. When Goldstein was tried, there were no eyewitnesses to the murder, and none testified against him. Additionally, no physical evidence, like DNA, linked him to the murder site. The primary evidence against him was the false testimony of a longtime jailhouse informant, Edward Floyd Fink. As the federal court of appeals explained: "Thomas Goldstein spent 24 years in prison after being convicted for murder based largely upon the perjured testimony of an unreliable jailhouse informant, the aptronymic Edward Fink."[35] Fink, a heroin addict with a long criminal record, testified that he had been in a cell with Goldstein in the Long Beach City Jail and that he had heard Goldstein admit to committing the murder.

At the time, in 1979, Goldstein was an engineering student and a Marine Corps veteran with no criminal history. Several eyewitnesses told the police that the shooter was a black or Hispanic man. Six eyewitnesses were shown a photo lineup, but none could identify the shooter. But after being shown the photo of Goldstein a second time, one witness—Loran Campbell—said it was possible Goldstein was the shooter. Based upon that equivocal positive identification, Long Beach police arrested Goldstein even though he was white.

While he was being detained in the Long Beach City jail, Goldstein had the misfortune of being placed in a cell with Edward Fink. Fink had a long history of getting deals from prosecutors, such as reduced sentences, in exchange for giving testimony against his fellow inmates. Fink testified at Goldstein's trial that Goldstein had admitted to the murders while they were together in the jail cell. On the basis of this testimony, Goldstein was convicted and ultimately spent twenty-four years in prison.

The Supreme Court held, and has often reaffirmed, that it violates due process of law for a prosecutor to fail to disclose to the defense evidence that could materially assist them at trial or at sentencing.[36] Police and prosecutors in their investigations often uncover information that is exculpatory, and they should not be able to hide this evidence. Additionally, in every state, the code of professional responsibility that regulates lawyer behavior requires that prosecutors turn over to the defense any potentially exculpatory information, including any that might help reduce the defendant's sentence.

The prosecutors in Goldstein's case indisputably had the constitutional duty to inform his defense counsel of Fink's long history of making deals in exchange for a reduction of charges and sentences. Had they done so, it would have provided a crucial basis for impeaching the key witness against Goldstein. Obviously, lawyers in the Los Angeles district attorney's office knew of these deals because they had negotiated them, and Goldstein's attorneys should have been informed about Fink. But no one ever disclosed the information to the defense.

After Goldstein spent over two decades in prison, a federal district court granted his habeas corpus petition. The court concluded that there was no reliable evidence linking Goldstein to the murders and that Fink's testimony was so lacking in credibility that it could not be the basis for a conviction. The federal court of appeals agreed, and finally Tommy Lee Goldstein was a free man.

Goldstein then sued the district attorney of Los Angeles County, John Van De Kamp, and other top officials, claiming that they had violated his constitutional rights "by purposefully or with deliberate indifference" failing to create a system that would ensure that key evidence would be turned over to defendants as required by the Constitution. Goldstein also argued that the district attorney had violated Goldstein's constitutional rights by failing to adequately train and supervise deputy district attorneys to ensure that they shared information regarding jailhouse informants with their colleagues.

The federal court of appeals ruled that Goldstein's suit could go forward against Van De Kamp and others in his office. The Supreme Court, though, unanimously reversed and ordered Goldstein's case dismissed. Justice Breyer, writing for the Court, said that prosecutors have absolute immunity to suits for monetary damages—they cannot be sued at all—and that this extends even to the administrative practices that Goldstein says led to his wrongful conviction. Although Goldstein spent twenty-four years in prison for murders he did not commit, the Court said the prosecutors were protected by absolute immunity. Such a clear case of injustice shows how absolute immunity keeps the federal courts from being able to enforce the Constitution. And of course, the case is not just about Tommy Lee Goldstein. All victims of such prosecutorial misconduct, no matter how long they are wrongly incarcerated, are kept from being able to sue.

Surprisingly, even the liberal justices on the Court accept absolute immunity, even though it usually leaves victims of prosecutorial misconduct with no recourse at all. I find it disturbing that not one justice was willing to say that Goldstein should have been able to sue to recover damages for this undeniable prosecutorial misconduct. Absolute immunity is unnecessary; something less than absolute immunity can achieve the goal of protecting prosecutorial discretion without completely undermining enforcement of the Constitution. Prosecutors should not have absolute immunity when they knowingly use

perjured testimony or intentionally hide evidence that they are constitutionally required to turn over to the defense.

Nor can police officers and other law enforcement personnel be
sued for monetary damages if they lie under oath and cause an innocent person to be convicted and imprisoned. Almost forty years ago,
soon after it granted prosecutors absolute immunity, the Court also
accorded police officers the same for testimony they give in court. In
general, police officers have only qualified, good faith immunity to
suits against them pursuant to Section 1983 or in a *Bivens* action.
However, in *Briscoe v. LaHue* in 1983, the Burger Court concluded
that police officers who commit perjury have absolute immunity in
suits against them for monetary damages.[37] In other words, a police
officer can intentionally lie under oath and cause an innocent person
to be convicted and imprisoned, yet he or she will be totally immune
to any civil liability for monetary damages. The officer might be subject to criminal prosecution or administrative discipline, but the victim of the police perjury who was wrongly convicted and imprisoned
will have no recourse at all. The Roberts Court has followed and
expanded this protection from any liability for law enforcement personnel who testify as witnesses.[38]

· · · · · · · · ·

AS ONE READS the absolute immunity cases, one senses that the
Court is worried that without such total protection, it would be too
easy to hold these government officials liable. The reality is just the
opposite. *All* government officials—local, state, and federal—who
are sued for monetary damages for constitutional violations are protected by qualified immunity if they do not have absolute immunity.
The Supreme Court has redefined qualified immunity and applied
it in such a way as to make it very difficult for plaintiffs to sue to
recover damages under this standard.

In the summer of 2020, after the death of George Floyd, the issue
of qualified immunity became part of the popular conversation over
policing, and bills were introduced into Congress to eliminate quali-

fied immunity. This is because at the end of the second decade of the twenty-first century, qualified immunity has made it ever more difficult to hold police officers liable for their wrongful actions.

Over the last forty years, the Court has continually expanded the scope of this doctrine to protect police officers and others who act unconstitutionally. In *Harlow v. Fitzgerald* in 1982, the Burger Court substantially reformulated the test for determining whether an officer acted in good faith.[39] An officer could be held liable, the Court said, and qualified immunity overcome, only if he or she violated clearly established law that a reasonable officer should know; the officer's intent, even malice, became irrelevant as a basis for liability for misconduct.

In the 2011 case *Ashcroft v. Al-Kidd,* the Roberts Court changed this legal test to make it even harder for citizens to hold government officials, including police officers, accountable.[40] In 2003 Abdullah al-Kidd, a U.S. citizen and a married man with two children, was arrested at a Dulles International Airport ticket counter. Over the next sixteen days, he was confined in high-security cells lit twenty-four hours a day in Virginia, Oklahoma, and then in Idaho, during which he was strip-searched on multiple occasions. Every time he was transferred to a different facility, he was handcuffed and shackled about his wrists, legs, and waist. He was released on "house arrest" and subjected to numerous restrictions on his freedom. By the time his confinement and supervision ended, fifteen months after his arrest, he had been fired from his job as an employee of a government contractor and had separated from his wife.

Al-Kidd had not been arrested and detained because he had committed a crime or even because there was probable cause that he had committed a crime. Rather, he was held under the federal material witness statute, which allows the government to hold a material witness who has essential testimony and otherwise is unlikely to be available to testify. But the government was not holding al-Kidd to secure his testimony, as that statute requires. His detention had absolutely nothing to do with obtaining testimony from him. Rather, he was detained because federal agents wanted to investigate him, and they used the material witness statute as a pretext because the government did not have enough evidence to arrest him on suspicion of any crime.

Al-Kidd was never charged with any crime, nor ever used as a material witness. After his release, he sued Attorney General John Ashcroft, who had authorized the detention. Ashcroft, who had been a senator from Missouri before becoming attorney general, had been aggressive after 9/11 in rounding up those of Middle Eastern descent, causing them to be subjected to brutal treatment.[41] Ashcroft claimed that he was protected by qualified immunity and moved to dismiss the lawsuit. The federal court of appeals rejected this claim, saying that any government official, and especially the U.S. attorney general, should know that it violates the Fourth Amendment to arrest and detain a person as a material witness if there is no desire to use the person as a witness and no probable cause that the person committed any crime.[42]

The Supreme Court, however, reversed and held that al-Kidd had no claim upon which he could sue to recover damages. Justice Scalia wrote for the Court that former attorney general Ashcroft was protected by qualified immunity because there was no clearly established law that his conduct was unconstitutional.

Surely, the attorney general knows that it is unconstitutional to detain a person as a material witness if there is no desire to use the person as a material witness. It is clearly established law that detaining a person without probable cause violates the Fourth Amendment, and that is exactly what was done to al-Kidd.

But the Court in *Ashcroft v. Al-Kidd* went even further and changed the law of qualified immunity. Justice Scalia, writing for the Court, declared that a government official can be held liable only if "*every 'reasonable official* would have understood that what he is doing violates that right.' "[43] The Court said that "existing precedent *must have placed the statutory or constitutional question beyond debate.*"[44] Never before had the Supreme Court said that the test was whether "every reasonable official" would have known that the conduct was impermissible. Never before had the Court said that a plaintiff could sue to recover damages for a constitutional violation only if existing law placed the question "beyond debate." Justice Scalia concluded his opinion by very broadly defining the protection of government officials from suit. Qualified immunity, he wrote, "protects all but the plainly incompetent or those who knowingly violate the law."[45]

As a result, it is now very difficult to successfully sue police officers even for egregious constitutional violations that cause great injury. In fact, in case after case, the Court has found qualified immunity based on the absence of a prior decision on point—that is, a decision involving the exact situation—even when the actions of the government officials are quite outrageous and unconstitutional in violating the Fourth Amendment.

In 2003 Savana Redding, a seventh-grade student at a public school in Arizona, was the victim of a deeply disturbing violation of her rights.[46] An assistant principal suspected her of giving prescription-strength ibuprofen to another student. The only difference between prescription-strength ibuprofen and regular-strength is the amount of the drug in the capsule; any of us can consume prescription-strength ibuprofen by taking a few regular-strength pills. Two female school officials took Redding into another room and subjected her to a strip search. They required her to remove all her outer clothes and to pull out her bra and underpants so that school officials could look in them for the drugs. They found nothing.

Redding and her parents sued the school officials who had subjected her to this degrading and humiliating search, contending that the search had violated the Fourth Amendment. The question wasn't close; of course subjecting a seventh-grade girl to a strip search to look for ibuprofen violates the Constitution. In an 8–1 decision, the Supreme Court said that the intrusiveness of the search violated the Fourth Amendment, especially given the relatively minor nature of the suspected offense and the lack of any reason to believe that the girl had hidden drugs in her underwear.

But the Court then proceeded to rule, 7–2, that the school officials could not be held liable because of qualified immunity. The
Court said that at the time of the search, the law concerning strip
searches was not clearly established, because the lower court cases
were conflicted on when strip searches in schools were permissible.
But wouldn't any reasonable teacher or school official have had "fair
notice" that it was wrong to strip search a seventh-grade girl and
look for ibuprofen in her underwear and at her breasts and genitals,
especially without any reason to believe she was hiding it there?

The Supreme Court has been especially aggressive about using qualified immunity to prevent police officers from being held liable when
they are sued for excessive force. There have been many instances in
the last decade and a half where the Supreme Court has reversed lower
courts and protected police officers from being held liable for misconduct that injured people. *Brosseau v. Haugen*, in 2004, involved Officer Rochelle Brosseau, a member of the Puyallup, Washington, Police
Department, shooting Kenneth Haugen in the back as he attempted
to flee from her in his vehicle.[47] Officer Brosseau was chasing Haugen,
who was wanted on a warrant, by foot. Haugen got into a car and
began backing it out of a driveway to get away from her. Brosseau
raised her gun and ordered him out of the car. When he refused and
continued to back out, she shot and seriously wounded him.

Haugen sued for the use of excessive force, and Brosseau raised
qualified immunity as a defense. The federal court of appeals said the
question of whether this should be deemed excessive force was to be
decided by a jury. The Supreme Court granted certiorari and decided
the case based entirely on the petition and opposition for certiorari;
the case was never briefed or argued. In an 8–1 decision, with only
Justice Stevens dissenting, the Court held that the officer was protected by qualified immunity. It stressed the lack of cases on point in
ordering the case dismissed based on qualified immunity. It concluded
by stating that the prior cases "by no means 'clearly establish' that
Brosseau's conduct violated the Fourth Amendment."[48] The Court
was saying that even though the police officer shot someone when

deadly force was unnecessary, she was immune from liability because there was no prior decision involving facts exactly like the ones in this situation. That approach, as later cases have made clear, makes it very difficult to ever hold police accountable for their wrongdoing.

The breadth of qualified immunity and the insurmountable obstacle that it presents to enforcing the Constitution is exemplified by two cases decided by the Supreme Court in 2014 that involved law enforcement officers who were sued for violating the Constitution.[49] In *Plumhoff v. Rickard,* the Court again found that police were protected by qualified immunity, even in a situation where their actions killed two people.[50] Police officers had pulled over a white Honda Accord because the car had only one operating headlight. Donald Rickard was the driver of the Accord, and Kelly Allen was in the passenger seat. The officer asked Rickard if he had been drinking, and Rickard responded that he had not. Because Rickard failed to produce his driver's license upon request and appeared nervous, the officer asked him to step out of the car. Rather than comply with the officer's request, he sped away.

A high-speed chase then occurred that lasted five minutes and reached speeds over one hundred miles per hour. At one point, the officers appeared to have Rickard's car pinned, but the car pulled away. The officers then fired three shots into the car. As the car attempted to speed away, they fired another twelve shots, killing both the driver and the passenger. The U.S. Court of Appeals for the Sixth Circuit concluded that the police had used excess force and violated the Fourth Amendment.

The Supreme Court unanimously reversed, ruling in favor of the police. Justice Alito, writing for the Court, held that there had been no violation of the Fourth Amendment. The driver's conduct had posed a "grave public safety risk" and the police were justified in shooting at the car to stop it: "It stands to reason that, if police officers are justified in firing at a suspect in order to end a severe threat to public safety, the officers need not stop shooting until the threat has ended."[51] Moreover, the Court said, even if there had been a

Fourth Amendment violation, the officers would have been protected by qualified immunity in that the law was not clearly established that the conduct violated the Fourth Amendment.

This holding is deeply troubling. The Supreme Court has now said that in any high-speed chase that officers perceive could injure others—and that would seem to be virtually all high-speed chases—the police can shoot at the vehicle and keep shooting until it stops. The officers had initially stopped Rickard's car for having only one working headlight. Rickard drove off, but why did the officers not just let the car go and track him down later? Why should death be his punishment for making the extremely poor choice to begin a high-speed chase? The Court has said that excessive force violates the Fourth Amendment. Shouldn't a jury at least have a chance to decide whether what was done constitutes excessive force?

So enveloping is the Roberts Court's desire to expand qualified immunity that in *Wood v. Moss*, another case from 2014, it found that Secret Service agents are protected by qualified immunity when they violate even the most basic rule of the First Amendment, that government officials cannot discriminate among speakers based on their viewpoint.[52] When President George W. Bush was in Oregon, Secret Service agents allowed his supporters to come closer and pushed his opponents farther away.

Nonetheless, the Court, in a unanimous decision with the majority opinion written by Justice Ginsburg, found that the agents were protected by qualified immunity because there were no cases on point concerning when Secret Service agents violate the First Amendment. But why are specific cases necessary when the law is clearly established that viewpoint discrimination violates the First Amendment?

Both of these cases were unanimous. Both found that qualified immunity applied because of the absence of cases on point. Together they show that the Court is very protective of government officials who are sued and makes it very difficult for victims of constitutional violations to bring lawsuits to recover damages. In all these cases, the Court did not allow the federal courts to enforce the Constitution.

It ruled that the government officials cannot be sued, and in all these instances it was highly unlikely that the government entity could be sued either. It is puzzling that even the most liberal justices, Ginsburg and Sotomayor, went along with this decision. Qualified immunity appears to be so deeply entrenched in the law that not a single justice dissented from barring victims of civil rights violations from having any recovery.

· · · · · · · · ·

IN MANY OTHER CASES since then, the Court has found that because of qualified immunity, police officers cannot be held liable for unnecessarily using deadly force, even though the law is clear that excessive police force violates the Fourth Amendment.[53] The Court has elevated qualified immunity to a bar never before seen, as in case after case it has reversed lower courts and held that the officers cannot be held liable because of this protection. By closing the courthouse doors to those whose rights have been violated, it has made qualified immunity, practically speaking, very much like absolute immunity.

City and County of San Francisco v. Sheehan, in 2015, is a particularly noteworthy case in this regard and has become a bellwether for subsequent decisions protecting police from liability.[54] It is also important in that it deals with how police officers should interact with mentally ill individuals.

Teresa Sheehan, who suffers from a schizoaffective disorder, lived in a group home for people dealing with mental illness. Although she shared common areas of the building with others, she had a private room. On August 7, Heath Hodge, a social worker who supervised the counseling staff in the building, attempted to visit Sheehan to conduct a welfare check. Hodge was concerned because Sheehan had stopped taking her medication, no longer spoke with her psychiatrist, and reportedly was no longer changing her clothes or eating. Hodge knocked on her door but received no answer. He then used a key to enter her room and found Sheehan on her bed. Initially, she would not respond to questions. But then she sprang up, reportedly yelling, "Get out of here! You don't have a warrant! I have a knife, and I'll kill you if I have to."

The police were called, and Sergeant Kimberly Reynolds and Officer Kathrine Holder responded. Accompanied by Hodge, the officers went to Sheehan's room, knocked on her door, announced who they were, and told Sheehan that "we want to help you." When Sheehan did not answer, the officers used Hodge's key to enter the room. Sheehan grabbed a kitchen knife with an approximately five-inch blade and began approaching the officers, yelling something along the lines of "I am going to kill you. I don't need help. Get out." The officers left the room and closed the door.

As explained by the Court, "Reynolds and Holder had to make a decision. They could wait for backup—indeed, they already heard sirens. Or they could quickly reenter the room and try to subdue Sheehan before more time elapsed." They decided to reenter. With pistols drawn, the officers moved in. When Sheehan, knife in hand, saw them, she again yelled for them to leave. Sheehan may have again threatened to kill them at that point but conceded that she had intended "to resist arrest and to use the knife." Reynolds pepper-sprayed Sheehan in the face, but Sheehan would not drop the knife. Holder shot her twice, but she did not collapse. Reynolds then fired multiple shots. After Sheehan finally fell, a third officer (who had just arrived) kicked the knife out of her hand.

Sheehan survived and sued, especially claiming that the police had failed to recognize her disability. The federal court of appeals said that it was for a jury to decide whether the police used excessive force and violated the Constitution. The Supreme Court, in an opinion written by Justice Alito, said that the officers were protected by qualified immunity because no prior case had held police officers liable under these specific circumstances.

The Court's insistence on a prior case as a prerequisite for holding the officers liable was misguided. Rarely will there be a case with a situation identical to the one under consideration, and insisting on one is just a way of protecting defendant officers from liability. Also, the ultimate question of qualified immunity is whether a police officer acted reasonably in using deadly force. That should be a question, as the court of appeals ruled, for a jury, not an issue of whether a prior case exists with similar facts on point.

The Court continually uses qualified immunity to protect the police and deny to those whose rights have been violated any ability to bring lawsuits to recover damages. In *Kisela v. Hughes* in 2018, the Court again found that officers who shot a mentally ill woman were protected by qualified immunity.[55]

In May 2010 police in Tucson, Arizona, got a 911 call that a woman was hacking at a tree with a kitchen knife. Officer Andrew Kisela and another officer went to the scene. The person who had called 911 flagged down the officers, described the woman with the knife, and told them she had been acting erratically. About the same time, another police officer, Lindsay Kunz, arrived on her bicycle.

The two officers then saw Amy Hughes emerge from the house carrying a large knife at her side, walk toward another woman, and stop "no more than six feet from her." A chain link fence stood between the officers and Hughes. Hughes matched the description of the woman who had been seen hacking a tree. The other woman was Sharon Chadwick, Hughes' roommate. All three officers drew their guns. At least twice they told Hughes to drop the knife. Hughes appeared calm but did not acknowledge the officers' presence or drop the knife. Her roommate, Chadwick, urged everyone to be calm. "Hughes stood stationary about six feet away from Chadwick, appeared 'composed and content,' and held a kitchen knife down at her side with the blade facing away from Chadwick. Hughes was nowhere near the officers, had committed no illegal act, was suspected of no crime, and did not raise the knife in the direction of Chadwick or anyone else."[56]

The top of the chain link fence blocked Kisela's line of fire, so he dropped to the ground and shot Hughes four times through the fence. Then the officers jumped over the fence, handcuffed Hughes, and called paramedics, who transported her to a hospital. There she was treated for non-life-threatening injuries. Less than a minute had transpired from the moment the officers saw Hughes to the moment Kisela fired shots.

Hughes sued Officer Kisela, and the federal court of appeals denied him qualified immunity. But the Supreme Court, in a 7–2 decision, ruled in favor of the officer, concluding that he was protected by qualified immunity. The Court stressed the absence of a case on point holding a police officer liable under such circumstances. Justice Sotomayor, joined by Justice Ginsburg, dissented, saying that a jury could find that it had been unreasonable for the officer to shoot Amy Hughes four times under these circumstances. Justice Sotomayor lamented the enormous expansion of qualified immunity and the way it leaves people like Amy Hughes, who are injured at the hands of police, without any form of remedy.

· · · · · · · · ·

ALL THESE DECISIONS about qualified immunity are part of a larger trend that began in the early 1980s when Ronald Reagan was president and the nation, or at least part of it, supported using force to combat crime. The war on drugs empowered the police and massively increased incarcerations, especially of people of color. Too often the ends of combating crime and stopping drugs led police to use means that were at odds with the Constitution and inflicted needless injuries.

It was in this context that the Supreme Court developed the rules for police officer liability. In the years since it first articulated the standard for qualified immunity in *Harlow v. Fitzgerald* in 1982, the Court has confronted the qualified immunity issue in more than thirty cases. Many of them involved claims of excessive police force. Only twice have the plaintiffs prevailed in the Court, and the last time was in 2004.[57] In nine of the cases, including *Brosseau v. Haugen* and *Kisela v. Hughes*, the Court reversed lower courts that had denied qualified immunity, without even briefing or oral argument.[58]

The Court's doctrine that police liability requires the existence of a prior case with virtually identical facts means that officers are protected by qualified immunity virtually always. Conservatives as well as liberals point to the unjustness of this outcome. U.S. Court of Appeals for the Fifth Circuit judge Don Willett, a Trump appointee, wrote of his "disquiet over the kudzu-like creep of the modern immunity regime. . . . Section 1983 meets Catch-22. Plaintiffs must produce precedent even as fewer courts are producing precedent. Important constitutional questions go unanswered precisely because those questions are yet unanswered. Courts then rely on that judicial silence to conclude there's no equivalent case on the books. No precedent = no clearly established law = no liability. An Escherian Stairwell. Heads defendants win, tails plaintiffs lose."[59]

This troubling trend was documented by a team of investigative reporters at Reuters who studied federal appeals court decisions involving suits against police officers where qualified immunity was raised as a defense. It found that "since 2005, the courts have shown an increasing tendency to grant immunity in excessive force cases. . . . The trend has accelerated in recent years." After analyzing the lower court decisions, the study concluded that the Supreme Court "has built qualified immunity into an often insurmountable police defense" and "has made it harder to hold police accountable when accused of using excessive force."[60]

Why has it done so? The Court's conservative majority—and it has had a conservative majority since 1969—identifies much more with police than with victims of excessive police force or police abuse. The resulting legal doctrines make it very difficult, often impossible, for people to bring lawsuits to recover damages from police who violate their constitutional rights.

Given the Court's increasingly conservative composition, it is unlikely in the coming years to ameliorate this trend; if anything, the immunity it gives to law enforcement is likely to increase. In the spring of 2020, ten petitions for Supreme Court review raised issues of qualified immunity, almost all in the context of excessive police force or police abuse. One was a petition I had filed on behalf of the parents of a young man whom they discovered unconscious in the cold; he died of hypothermia as police officers did nothing to try to resuscitate him. Both the police and the first responders ignored clear protocols for what to do in this situation.[61] From all we know about hypothermia, had the first responders followed proper procedures, they might have saved the boy's life. The federal court of appeals said the case had to be dismissed based on qualified immunity because there were no prior cases on point holding officers liable in these circumstances. Of course, the requirement for an almost identical case means that the most extreme misconduct gets excused because it has not happened before. The Supreme Court denied review in all ten qualified immunity cases, including this one.

. . . .

WHEN IT COMES TO POLICE, the story of the Rehnquist and Roberts Courts, from 1986 through the present and likely for years to come, can easily be summarized: the police almost always win. The Court has lessened the protections of the Fourth Amendment, making it possible for police to stop almost anyone at any time. It has undermined the Fifth Amendment privilege against self-incrimination by requiring that an individual expressly say that he or she wants to remain silent in order to have that protection. It has refused to acknowledge, let alone deal with, the problem of inaccurate eyewitness identifications. And even when there is a constitutional violation, the Court has gutted the remedies. It has dramatically lessened the application of the exclusionary rule, and it has made civil lawsuits to recover monetary damages against cities and individual officers very unlikely to succeed. Putting all this together, it is clear that the Supreme Court has contributed enormously to the problem of policing, and race-based policing, in the United States.

Nor is anything likely to change on the Supreme Court for the foreseeable future. With the appointment of three Trump justices, the Court has become even more conservative and therefore, given the pattern of the last half-century, more likely to side with police. But if the solution is not going to come from the Supreme Court, how can policing be significantly changed in the United States?

Part VI

IT CAN
BE DONE

Overcoming the Supreme
Court to Reform Policing

Demonstrators march down
Pennsylvania Avenue in
Washington during a protest
against police brutality and racism,
June 6, 2020. *(Photo by Drew Angerer/*
Getty Images)

19

The Path to Meaningful Police Reform

THE LATE SPRING AND SUMMER OF 2020 SAW UNPREC-
edented national and international protests against police
violence. Never before had Americans given such widespread and sustained attention to police violence and racism in policing. Never before had major league sports events been canceled as a
way of the players' expressing concern over the police. Never before
had so many Americans, of all races, taken to the streets to demand a
change in policing. "Black Lives Matter" was painted on streets, put
on lawn signs, written on the floor of professional basketball courts,
and worn by millions on T-shirts as a way of expressing the need to
change policing in the United States.

This new attention was triggered by a police killing in Minnesota
that quickly went viral over social media and galvanized the country
and the world. On May 25, 2020, Minneapolis police officer Derek
Chauvin pressed his knee onto George Floyd's neck for nine minutes
and twenty-nine seconds. Floyd, who was suspected of having passed
a counterfeit twenty-dollar bill, was killed by this choking. On the
evening of May 26 and into the morning of May 27, many Minneapolis residents protested; some graffitied police cars, while others went
to the precinct house where the four officers were assigned. Police
officers responded to the protests with tear gas and rubber bullets.

While most of the protesters were peaceful, some stripped local businesses of their stock and set stores ablaze.[1]

As the videos of Floyd being killed were played on television and social media, protests spread across the country, drawing demonstrators into the streets even as a pandemic was making such protests dangerous. On May 27 demonstrators in Memphis, Tennessee, protested the deaths of Floyd and of Breonna Taylor, who had died in March from a cross fire of police bullets in Louisville, Kentucky. Police had had a warrant to search Taylor's house because of allegations against an ex-boyfriend. When the police battered down the door and entered without knocking, her boyfriend, not knowing who was there, fired his gun. The police fired back, one of them shooting ten rounds blindly into the apartment. Six bullets struck and killed Taylor, a twenty-six-year-old emergency-room technician studying to become a nurse.

The demonstrators and their signs did not focus on the Supreme Court or even realize how much the Court was responsible for what they were protesting. The chokehold that killed George Floyd in Minneapolis continues to be used because, as discussed earlier, the Supreme Court refused to allow lawsuits to enjoin it in *City of Los Angeles v. Lyons* (discussed in Chapter 1).[2] The Louisville police were able to enter Taylor's home without knocking and announcing, leading to the gunshots that killed her, because the Supreme Court has explicitly allowed officers to obtain a warrant allowing them to enter without knocking and announcing.[3] Americans were taking to the streets to protest out of frustration and anger because constitutional limits have not been placed on police, and as a consequence racism manifests in policing every day.

The protests that spread across the country were on a scale that had not been seen since the April 1968 assassination of Martin Luther King, Jr. But where the 1968 protest mirrored the riots occurring in many U.S. cities in the 1960s, the 2020 protests were mostly peaceful and involved people of all races. Los Angeles saw a large protest—demonstrators even blocked a major freeway.[4] In St. Louis, protesters blocked a freeway; a man died after he was caught underneath and dragged by a FedEx truck.[5] In cities large and small, in every state, demonstrations called for a reform of policing, many demanding that police be "defunded," a word that suddenly took on currency in the whirlwind of protests that engulfed the nation in late May and early June.

Rather than express dismay over police violence or the deaths of innocent people at the hands of officers, President Trump inflamed the situation by issuing a tweet that referred to protesters as "thugs" and threatening that "when the looting starts, the shooting starts."[6] Many interpreted the tweet as a call to violence, but the president claimed ignorance of the phrase's racially charged language and history. The "looting, shooting" threat echoed words attributed to a white Miami police chief, Walter Headley, in 1967, who sought to thwart protesters by threating police shooting.[7] In response to President Trump's tweet, Twitter took the "unprecedented step" of hiding it due to its glorification of violence. Nearly fourteen hours later, the president backpedaled on this ultimatum, insisting his tweet had been "misinterpreted."[8]

If Twitter allowed President Trump to quickly reach a huge audience with his inflammatory words, social media also played the integral role of informing Americans about what was happening across the country and rallying citizens to take to the streets. Decades earlier Americans had learned about what was happening in cities only by watching the nightly news or reading the next day's newspaper. Social media and the internet allowed everyone to see it—and react to it—immediately, in real time.

Fueled by this access to information, protests against police violence continued throughout the country and abroad. In Atlanta, demonstrators protested near Centennial Olympic Park. Some climbed the CNN sign located in front of the network's headquarters and vandalized the exterior. Others climbed onto police cars, threw rocks at the Omni Hotel's glass doors, and broke windows of the College Football Hall of Fame and took items. That night Governor Brian Kemp called out the National Guard and declared a state of emergency in Fulton County.[9] In Brooklyn and lower Manhattan, thousands of protesters congregated at the Barclays Center.[10] In Oakland, protesters blocked a major freeway; ultimately police arrested twenty-two people there and detained sixty who were suspected of looting. Six Oakland police officers incurred injuries, seven members of outside organizations who responded were also injured, and a Federal Protective Services officer was fatally shot.[11] The challenge for mayors and police chiefs was to protect the peaceful protests, and stop any violence and looting, while avoiding a police overreaction. Excessive police force, exercised during protests against police violence, would only further inflame the situation, and social media would ensure it was seen immediately all over the world.

The next day, May 30, hundreds of thousands of Americans, perhaps millions, participated in demonstrations to protest the death of George Floyd and the crisis of police violence against Blacks. Overwhelmingly, the protests were peaceful, though occasionally there was looting.[12] On May 31, thousands of demonstrators gathered in front of the White House to peacefully protest, but at nightfall violence erupted as demonstrators clashed with riot police armed with plastic shields and "the two sides vied for control of Lafayette Square."[13] President Trump was moved into an underground bunker. The next day he threatened to deploy the military and referred to protesters as "terrorists."[14]

Seeking to demonstrate resolve, President Trump decided to visit nearby St. John's Episcopal Church. He called out military helicopters and troops, along with the National Guard, to clear out an entirely peaceful protest, something rarely seen in the United States. That done, he crossed the street to be photographed at the church displaying a Bible, awkwardly, in what critics called a "photo op."[15]

On June 2 The New York Times covered the eighth night of protesting by running photos taken across the country. Headlines read: "Police crackdown after curfew in the Bronx." "Police use tear gas to break up protest in Atlanta." "Protesters ride through Houston on horseback." "Police block protesters from entering Manhattan." "A show of force at the Lincoln Memorial." "Protesters gather in Hollywood and face off with the police."[16]

An estimated 15 million Americans participated in protests against police violence, even though much of the country was shut down because of the COVID-19 pandemic.[17] The issue of policing remained at the forefront of public attention throughout the summer of 2020. One study found that between May 24 and August 22, a total of more than 10,600 demonstrations occurred in all fifty states. Of them, 93 percent were peaceful.[18]

Meanwhile instances of police use of excessive force continued. On August 24 in Kenosha, Wisconsin, a white police officer shot Jacob Blake, a Black man, seven times in the back. Blake survived but was left paralyzed.[19] A video of the incident quickly circulated through social media. On August 26 the Milwaukee Bucks chose not to play in a scheduled National Basketball Association playoff game in protest of this shooting. The NBA then canceled all its games for a few days; there was talk of the playoffs being ended. Major league soccer also canceled all its games.[20] The Los Angeles Dodgers and San Francisco Giants postponed their game.[21] The U.S. Tennis Association and the Women's Tennis Association canceled all matches.

The Black Lives Matter movement, which gained national attention after the police killings of Michael Brown and Eric Garner in 2014, spread widely, and its name became a slogan to express the quest to reform police. Never before had the problems of racism in policing received such national attention. The media widely referred to it as a reckoning with the long history of anti-Blackness that dates back to 1619, when the first slaves were brought to the shores of North America.[22]

• • • • • • • • • •

WE MUST HOPE that all this attention will pressure all branches of government at every level to take action to change policing in the United States. But the Supreme Court has become ever more conservative over the last half-century, especially in the last few years, and the protests are unlikely to resonate with these justices. The

six conservative justices—Roberts, Thomas, Alito, Gorsuch, Kavanaugh, and Barrett—do not openly acknowledge the Court's role,
let alone its complicity, in worsening the problems of policing in the
United States. None of these justices has even once expressed concern
in a judicial opinion about the racism that infects policing. Nor does
anything they have ever said or done, on or off the bench, indicate
that they will reconsider the legal rules described in this book that
empower the police. The most recent Supreme Court decision about
policing, *Kansas v. Glover* in 2020, was an 8–1 decision that allowed
police officers to stop a car if they learn that it was registered to someone without a valid driver's license.[23] The majority opinion made no
mention of the fact that Glover was Black, and only Justice Sotomayor
dissented, lamenting a further increase in the ability of police to easily
stop individuals. Sotomayor, alone among the justices, has been willing to speak of the problem of racism in policing; not even the liberal
Ruth Bader Ginsburg joined her eloquent opinions.[24]

The composition of the current Court is a product of the historical accidents as to when vacancies have occurred as well as a deliberate manipulation of the confirmation process by Senate Republicans.
Between 1960 and 2020, there were twenty-eight years with a Democratic
president and thirty-two years with a Republican president. During this
time, Democratic presidents have appointed eight justices to the Court
and Republican presidents have appointed fifteen. Since 1988—and I
choose that year because no current justice was appointed earlier than the
George H. W. Bush presidency—there have been sixteen years of Democratic presidents (Clinton and Obama) and sixteen years of Republican
presidents (Bush, Bush, and Trump.) But the Republican presidents have
nominated seven justices, while the Democratic presidents have selected
only four. On a Court that is so often divided 5–4, including on issues
concerning race and the police, that makes all the difference.

In part, the current disparity is due to Senate Republicans block-
ing the nomination of Chief Judge Merrick Garland to the Supreme
Court in 2016. That February Justice Scalia died, and President
Obama quickly nominated Judge Garland to replace him. Garland,

by all accounts, is a moderate and is superbly qualified by any measure to be a justice. No one, not even Senate Majority Leader Mitch McConnell, raised the slightest question about Garland's suitability for the position. But McConnell refused to hold hearings on Garland's nomination or allow a vote, saying it would be inappropriate in the last year of a presidential term. He thereby held the seat open for the next president and hoped for a Republican victory that November. Prior to 2016, a vacancy had opened in the last year of a president's term twenty-four times in American history. In twenty-one instances the Senate had confirmed the nominee, and in three instances it had not. But never before had the Senate disallowed hearings and a vote.

McConnell's strategy worked. After President Trump took office, he nominated conservative federal appeals court judge Neil Gorsuch to replace Justice Scalia. The difference between Garland and Gorsuch in that seat made all the difference in many 5–4 cases, including those involving police. A year later, in 2018, President Trump got to replace Justice Kennedy with Judge Brett Kavanaugh. That did not change the overall ideological balance, though Kavanaugh is likely more conservative than Kennedy on many issues. But it does likely ensure that this seat will be occupied by a conservative justice appointed by a Republican president for decades to come.

The ideological composition of the Court changed dramatically after Justice Ruth Bader Ginsburg died on September 18, 2020. In stunning hypocrisy, the Republicans, who had blocked Merrick Garland's confirmation by claiming that a Supreme Court vacancy should not be filled in an election year, rushed through the confirmation of the very conservative judge Amy Coney Barrett. Barrett, who had been a Notre Dame law professor before President Trump nominated her for the federal court of appeals, is as conservative as any federal judge in the United States and is as different ideologically from Ginsburg as two jurists could be. Decisions that formerly had a 5–4 conservative majority now will probably be 6–3. And the chances that conservatives will join the liberal justices for the occasional 5–4 liberal victory have become much more remote. Throughout American history, and especially since the advent of the Burger Court in 1969, conservatives have consistently favored the powers of law enforcement over the rights of individuals. This view is now even more entrenched on the Supreme Court.

The current Court is the crowning achievement of a conservative political movement that began with Richard Nixon's campaign against the Warren Court in 1969. In the early 1980s, during the Reagan presidency, conservatives openly articulated the goal of gaining control of the Supreme Court and the federal judiciary. Republican presidents became ever more careful to nominate justices who have proven conservative ideologies and are young enough to be on the Court for decades.

Thus no change in the Court's ideological balance is likely to occur in the foreseeable future. At this writing, in 2020, Chief Justice Roberts is sixty-five years old, and Justice Thomas is seventy-two, Justice Alito is seventy, Justice Gorsuch is fifty-three, Justice Kavanaugh is fifty-five, and Justice Barrett is forty-eight. It is easy to imagine that these justices will continue on the bench for another decade or more. And even the Democratic appointees do not necessarily vote to limit the police power: Justice Breyer, for one, has often been a key vote in favor of police in Fourth Amendment cases.[25]

Unexpected vacancies obviously may occur, but otherwise, with these justices, it is hard to imagine the Supreme Court changing course with regard to policing. Someday, with different justices, the Court may confront the consequences of its rulings and dramatically change the course of American law, deciding to protect the constitutional rights that limit the police and create meaningful remedies for police misconduct. But given its current composition, the Court is unlikely to change for many years.

· · · · · · · · ·

AMID ALL THIS highly justifiable gloom, I contend that Americans should not perceive themselves as helpless victims of a Supreme Court that throughout history has failed to control the police. Those who advocate changing police can find other ways to confront the problems, ways that circumvent the Supreme Court. Given the demographic shifts that are sweeping the country, I believe that police reform could realistically succeed at the state and local level in ways that most people today cannot imagine. I think it is possible, and even likely, that policing will be changed by means other than the justices and the federal judiciary.

One possibility would be for state and local governments to follow the call that was increasingly heard in the summer of 2020 and abolish the police. If that option is neither possible nor desirable, as I believe, then other institutions must act. State supreme courts could alter state constitutions to protect people in their encounters with the police. Congress, state legislatures, and local governments could take legislative action. And finally, the U.S. Department of Justice can enforce existing laws much more aggressively.

All these possibilities could make a real difference in how policing is done, though admittedly all have limitations as well. Using these institutional avenues, there are many ways to change policing in this country,[26] to reform police departments and to provide remedies for police misconduct. Some of them include:

- ✦ eliminate stops and frisks based on reasonable suspicion, requiring that all seizures, arrests, and searches be based on probable cause;
- ✦ require written consent for police searches;
- ✦ restore citizens' ability to raise Fourth Amendment claims on habeas corpus;
- ✦ eliminate pretextual police stops and exclude evidence gained as a result of illegal stops;
- ✦ provide counsel for everyone being interrogated by police;
- ✦ eliminate the requirement that a suspect must expressly invoke the right to remain silent or the right to counsel;
- ✦ allow counsel at all identification procedures;
- ✦ eliminate the most suggestive forms of police identification;

- ✦ exclude suggestive eyewitness identifications from being heard by juries;
- ✦ strengthen the exclusionary rule when police violate the Constitution so that any evidence gained as a result of unconstitutional police behavior cannot be used at trial;
- ✦ expand the civil liability of police officers who violate the Constitution and that of the cities that employ them; and
- ✦ eliminate dangerous police practices, such as by barring the use of the chokehold by the police and end "no knock" warrants.

How can these and other essential changes be accomplished?

Abolish the Police?

In the summer of 2020, Americans heard loud calls to "abolish the police" or to "defund the police." Those calls can mean many things.[27] Defunding could mean decreasing police budgets and shifting some tasks and money to social service agencies, including mental health agencies, so that they, rather than police, might provide those services.[28] This change seems highly desirable, and many cities are pursuing it. Some, though, treat the slogan "defund the police" as if it meant the same thing as "abolish the police": making police obsolete. Those who advocate abolishing police believe it is the only solution because meaningful reform of police departments is impossible.[29] These voices are sufficiently loud and prominent that they cannot be ignored.[30]

The "abolish the police" movement originated not in movements of our own time but in W.E.B. Du Bois's 1935 book *Black Reconstruction in America*. Du Bois coined the term *abolition-democracy* to refer to the fight for "freedom, intelligence, and power for all men," a fight that began with the abolition of slavery but that Reconstruction did not win.[31] Abolition-democracy aimed to eliminate the institutions that had arisen to keep black people poor and powerless and that tried to push them back toward slavery. Du Bois, in critiquing many aspects of the criminal justice system, characterized white police as being instruments of "domination." The 1980s and '90s saw the emergence of the prison abolition movement, and two prominent leaders, Angela Davis and Ruth Wilson Gilmore, expanded their critiques to target policing.[32] In 2014 and 2015 activists began using "abolish the police" as a rallying cry, and it received national and local attention in the summer of 2020.

Activists who call for abolishing the police begin by pointing to the fact that police have brutalized Black Americans and other people of color throughout American history.[33] From the slave patrols in the 1700s and 1800s to the first municipal police departments in the mid-1800s, policing has facilitated the suppression of marginalized groups and worked to preserve the status quo. Police have suppressed worker activism, often using violence to do so, as in the bloody repression of the 1877 railroad strike, the brutality directed at pacifists, socialists, and labor activists in the 1910s, and the violent opposition of efforts to prevent unionization of industry, mining, and agriculture in the first third of the twentieth century.

Those who urge abolition argue that liberal policing reforms have failed and that reform efforts are futile.[34] They point to the fact that Black Americans are three times as likely to be killed by police as their white counterparts.[35] They also point to the ineffectiveness of police in solving and preventing crimes.[36] In 2018 FBI data revealed that the national clearance rate—the percentage of reported crimes that resulted in arrests by police—for murder was 62.3 percent.[37] Aggravated assault and rape had clearance rates of 52.5 percent and 33.4 percent, respectively. For property crimes, the clearance rate was below 20 percent.

In 2018 *The Washington Post* analyzed murders in fifty-two of the largest U.S. cities over the previous decade and found that Blacks accounted for the majority of homicide victims, but they were the least likely racial group to have their murders result in the arrest of a perpetrator.[38] Meanwhile another study reported that for every one thousand sexual assaults, only 230 are reported to the police, and of those, less than five result in incarceration.[39] This means that 75 percent of sexual assaults go unreported and 99 percent go unpunished. A 2020 *New York Times* analysis found that less than 4 percent of police time is dedicated to handling violent crime.[40] Activists are convinced that every year police surveil, arrest, and imprison millions of people whose "crime" is being poor, homeless, or disabled.[41]

Advocates of abolishing the police say that communities of color would be better off with no police at all. This position is becoming mainstream on many college campuses. At UC Berkeley in the spring of 2020, hundreds of students and faculty signed a petition calling for the elimination of the campus police.

Although I am sympathetic to the history and urgency behind that demand, my own view is that the idea of abolishing police is utopian and is neither possible nor desirable. Contrary to the views of those who call for it, meaningful reform of policing is the only possible path. One reason is obvious: every society needs a criminal justice system to punish the dangerous. I strongly agree that the United States incarcerates far too many people, especially people of color. As I mentioned earlier, the United States has only 5 percent of the world's population but 25 percent of the world's prisoners. Our country punishes too many things that should be dealt with not by criminal sanctions but in other ways; drugs, for example, should be thought of as a public health issue and not handled through incarceration. As California's former governor Jerry Brown was fond of saying, "Not every problem deserves a law."[42] Criminal sentences are often far too long. The first case that I argued before the Supreme Court was in 2002, on behalf of a man who had stolen $153 worth of videotapes; under California's "three strikes" law, he had been sentenced to fifty years to life in prison.[43] The Court ruled against my client and rejected the argument that such a sentence was cruel and unusual punishment.

I agree with those who argue that many functions now being performed by police might well be transferred to social service agencies.
Mental health professionals can deal with mentally ill individuals
better than armed police officers can. Even routine traffic enforcement might be done by people dedicated to that task rather than by
armed police.[44]

But every society has violent crimes, and they must be investigated
and their perpetrators prosecuted and punished. In a society without
any police or any form of punishment, individuals would have little
deterrent against committing crimes. Substantial literature in criminology, economics, and sociology demonstrates that larger police
forces lead to less violent crime via deterrence,[45] and that police produce deterrence by reducing criminal opportunities.[46] When the University of Pennsylvania's campus police increased patrols within its
defined zone in West Philadelphia, crime fell about 60 percent in the
targeted areas, particularly violent crime.[47] I certainly am not arguing
for expanding police forces, and I support the idea of shifting some
tasks currently done by police to social service agencies. My point is
that police do play a role in deterring and solving violent crimes.

Nor will abolishing the police end policing; it will merely result
in the establishment of private police. Those who want protection
and can afford it will pay for it, thereby creating a private structure
that will likely be even more regressive. Private police forces have
the potential to "become a sort of elite praetorian guard to protect
the rich and well-connected," as one critic has pointed out.[48] Private police do not have to comply with the Constitution because the
Constitution applies only to the government and government actors.
Private police would be subject to state tort law, but they would not
have to comply with the Fourth, Fifth, and Sixth Amendments. In
early America, policing was done that way, and it worked poorly. Private police forces employed by residents, without training or supervision by city departments, are not a recipe for improving policing and
dealing with the racial injustices of the current system.

Abolishing police would thus create a new type of inequity:

wealthier communities would have a form of policing and poor communities would not. Perhaps intuiting that inequity, most Americans, including people of color, are not in favor of abolishing the police. Only 15 percent of Americans overall said in a Gallup poll that they support it, and 22 percent of Black and 20 percent of Hispanic Americans expressed support.[49] Meanwhile 38 percent of Black Americans support an increased police presence, even though a majority of Blacks think police treat them unfairly.[50] The concern, which I share, is that predominantly minority communities suffer not only from overpolicing and excessive police violence but also from underpolicing and insufficient attention to violent crimes.[51]

Abolishing a city's police department would merely shift policing to other levels of local government. The county or state police would step in instead. Students and faculty at UC Berkeley urged the chancellor to eliminate the campus police, as I mentioned, but doing so would mean that the Berkeley city police and the Alameda County sheriff would do more policing on campus; they now generally defer to campus police except in the most serious matters. My experience, having been a professor on many campuses, is that campus police are generally more understanding of students and more compassionate in their policing than city or county police forces would be. Eliminating campus police would not end policing on campus and would actually be worse for students.

I worry that the focus on abolishing police will only increase frustration and tension among those activists who call for it. Since police are not going to be abolished, they are sure to be disappointed. In the United States, then, we have no choice but to focus on reforming police. But how do we finally achieve meaningful reforms?

State Constitutions

In 1977 Justice William Brennan wrote a famous article, published in the *Harvard Law Review,* that encouraged the use of state constitutions to protect constitutional rights.[52] State constitutions, he argued, "are a font of individual liberties."[53] A former justice of the New Jersey Supreme Court was extolling the virtues of state courts and state constitutions, but it was more than that. By 1977, Brennan had seen the Burger Court's retrenchment on constitutional rights, especially in the area of criminal procedure. As the Court narrowed and sometimes overruled the Warren Court precedents that he had supported, his frustration was palpable. In light of the Court's failure to protect federal constitutional rights, Brennan urged the use of state constitutions as an alternative.

In his article, Justice Brennan pointed to examples where state courts had interpreted state constitutions and reached conclusions that were opposite to those taken by the Supreme Court and instead followed the approaches of his own dissents. In *Schneckloth v. Bustamonte* in 1973, the Court had held that when police want to search someone, they need not inform that individual that he or she has the right to decline the request; he or she is considered to have consented regardless.[54] But Brennan pointed out that in 1975, the New Jersey Supreme Court, in *State v. Johnson,* came to the opposite conclusion: it held that an "essential element" of a valid consent "is knowledge of the right to refuse consent."[55] Similarly, in 1974 the Michigan Supreme Court required counsel to be present at photo identification procedures, rejecting the Supreme Court's holding that counsel was not needed.[56]

Brennan's advocacy of the development of state constitutional law is even more important today, as the Supreme Court has become increasingly conservative, especially as to criminal procedure. State constitutions thus provide a way for our society to limit police conduct in instances where the Supreme Court has failed to do so through the Constitution.

States can provide more protection of rights under their constitutions than exists under the U.S. Constitution. To take a simple example, the Supreme Court has held that citizens have no First Amendment right to use privately owned shopping centers for speech purposes.[57] But the California Supreme Court interpreted the state constitution to create a right in the state to use shopping centers for expression. The Supreme Court upheld this interpretation as permissible.[58] Similarly, several state supreme courts found that state laws prohibiting same-sex marriage violated *state* constitutions, before the Supreme Court came to the same conclusion under the U.S. Constitution in 2015.[59]

In fact, if a state supreme court explicitly says that it is relying on state constitutional law for its decision, and there is no federal issue, the Supreme Court cannot review the state court's ruling at all.[60] This opens a way for state supreme courts to expand the protection of individual rights, including for criminal defendants, without any chance that the Supreme Court will reverse it. Every state has its own constitution, and state courts can interpret them to impose limits on police behavior even when the Supreme Court has refused to do so.

One example is in the area of searches and seizures. The Court has held that police do not need a warrant to search a person's garbage because, it concluded, a person has no reasonable expectation of privacy with regard to discarded trash.[61] But many state courts have come to the opposite conclusion in interpreting their state constitutions and require a warrant for police searches of trash.[62]

In *California v. Hodari D.* in 1991, the Court held that a person who is being chased by the police is not considered to be seized until he or she is actually tackled by the officer; chasing the individual does not constitute a seizure within the meaning of the Fourth Amendment.[63] But fifteen states have rejected this idea and said that under their state constitutions, chasing a suspect is sufficient to constitute a seizure and thus requires at least reasonable suspicion.[64]

As explained earlier, the Court decision in *Whren v. United States* expanded the power of the police to stop almost anyone at any time.[65] The Court held that in evaluating the legality of a stop or a frisk or a search, the officer's motivations are irrelevant. An officer who wants to search the driver of a car can easily use a minor traffic violation—driving through a yellow light, changing lanes without a signal, stopping not quite long enough at a stop sign—as a pretext to engage in racial profiling. But several state supreme courts have rejected *Whren* and held that pretextual stops violate their state constitutions.[66]

The Supreme Court has held that physical evidence is admissible at trial even when it is gained as a result of interrogation done in violation of *Miranda*.[67] But several state supreme courts—such as in Ohio, Wisconsin, and Massachusetts—have interpreted their state constitutions to bar the admissibility of the physical fruits of police questioning that was done without the proper administration of *Miranda* warnings.[68] This takes away one police incentive for disregarding the *Miranda* decision.

The development of state constitutional law is particularly essential in controlling police procedures in eyewitness identifications. As discussed earlier, inaccurate eyewitness identifications often lead to the conviction of innocent people. But the Supreme Court has almost entirely ignored this serious failure of the criminal justice system. Prior to 1967, not one Court decision imposed any limit on the way police conduct identifications. During the entire Rehnquist and Roberts era— from 1986 through today—the Court decided only one case that dealt with the issue, and it ruled in favor of the police. A huge body of social psychology research has documented the problems with eyewitness identification, but the Supreme Court has almost entirely ignored it.

This is another place where state courts can step in, and some have already created the limits that the Supreme Court refuses to impose on police. For example as described earlier, the Supreme Court held in *Kirby v. Illinois,* that a suspect has no right to have an attorney present at an eyewitness identification procedure—a lineup or a showup—conducted before an indictment.[69] Counsel is required for such identifications after an indictment, but as a result of *Kirby,* police can easily circumvent that requirement simply by conducting the identification before it occurs. But a number of states have interpreted their constitutions to hold that suspects have a right to an attorney at a preindictment identification procedure.[70]

The Supreme Court has held that eyewitness identifications, no matter how suggestive the police behavior, are admissible as long as a court deems them "reliable."[71] But some state courts have explicitly rejected this approach. Massachusetts and New York require unnecessarily suggestive identifications to be excluded from trial, even if they would be reliable and admissible under the Supreme Court's approach.[72] Wisconsin has found that showup procedures—where the witness sees just the suspect—are inherently suggestive and has barred them from being used as evidence unless they are shown to be necessary.[73] Other states, too, have created limits on identification procedures that are much more protective of the rights of criminal suspects than the Supreme Court's hands-off approach.[74]

· · · · · · · · ·

SIMPLY PUT, in light of the Supreme Court's failure to impose limits on police, state courts can and should invoke state constitutions in order to do so. I do recognize limitations of this approach: obviously, state law can regulate only state and local police officers; federal law enforcement officials do not have to comply with state law. For over two hundred years the Supreme Court has held that states cannot regulate the federal government or its officers. The importance of this limit on state authority is not hypothetical: in 2020 when President Trump was dissatisfied with local law enforcement in Portland and Chicago, he sent in federal law enforcement officers, apparently border control agents. Officers without identification reportedly apprehended peaceful protesters and put them in unmarked cars.[75] But no matter whether and how these federal officers violated the Constitution, they could not be prosecuted or sued under state law. Still, the vast majority of criminal cases are tried in state courts, giving state courts a potentially significant role in changing policing in the United States.

Another limitation to relying on state constitutions is that they will never provide more than partial success in advancing liberties and curtailing police misconduct, because on any given issue, the chance of success in all or even most states is small. Consider the right to marriage equality for gay and lesbian couples: at most, how many state supreme courts would have been likely to recognize it as a right under their state constitutions? Even in the absence of state constitutional amendments precluding it, it is difficult to imagine that more than half the states would recognize the right and likely significantly less. Given that even the New York Court of Appeals refused to recognize it,[76] it would not be realistic to imagine the South Carolina or Mississippi or Oklahoma Supreme Court doing so. Where state courts have developed state constitutional rights to overcome Supreme Court decisions, it is usually only a handful of states that have done so.

It is disquieting, to say the least, to think of a person in one state going to jail for a coerced confession, knowing that that person under the same circumstances in California would have gone free. The disparity is bad enough when the issue is whether people can exercise their fundamental right to marry, but for someone to be locked up or even executed in one state, when their case would have been dismissed in another, is revolting. Using state constitutions to control the police and protect liberties is important, but we must acknowledge the limitations as well.

For structural reasons, significant advances in individual liberties are unlikely to occur in most states. In thirty-nine states, state court judges face some form of electoral accountability.[77] In some of these states, state supreme court justices run in partisan elections. In others, justices face retention elections. In the last few decades, a number of state supreme court justices—such as Rose Bird, Joseph Grodin, and Cruz Reynoso in California, Penny White in Tennessee, and David Lanphier in Nebraska—have lost their seats because of rulings they made in favor of criminal defendants.[78]

It is revealing that among the seven state supreme courts that initially recognized some form of marriage equality, none make use of contested judicial elections.[79] This suggests that states with such systems are unlikely to recognize controversial new rights.

To be sure, many issues of state constitutional law, even those advancing rights, are unlikely to make much difference in elections. And some justices on state supreme courts will be courageous and pay no attention to their coming electoral review. But the next time such justices are being considered at the polls, their controversial rulings, including those overturning convictions in criminal cases, will make them a target for attack. The late California Supreme Court justice Otto Kaus said that for a judge who must face voters, electoral review is like having a crocodile in one's bathtub; it is impossible to forget that it is there.[80] Elected judges and those facing retention elections thus are far less likely than are federal judges with life tenure to take controversial steps to protect the rights of criminal suspects and defendants and to control the police.

We must also recognize that many states have no tradition of using their constitutions to provide rights greater than that in the U.S. Constitution. Many states have "what can only be characterized as a general unwillingness among state supreme courts to engage in any kind of analysis of the state constitution at all."[81] This unwillingness might change in the future, but such states' long history of lacking separate protection for rights under state constitutional law would have to be overcome.

Turning to state constitutions to protect rights means accepting inherently limited success across the country. State-level successes in the face of failures in the Supreme Court are surely better than nothing, but it would be a mistake to pretend that they are more than a distant second best.

Litigating under state constitutions requires each state to undertake a separate effort. There will be some wins and many losses. It is not the same as the Supreme Court creating a uniform rule across the country to protect individual rights and limit police abuses.

And even successes that are achieved via state constitutional law often can be undone through the initiative process. In most states, it is easier to amend the state constitution than the U.S. Constitution; many states allow their state constitutions to be amended through ballot initiatives. Thus, state court decisions that interpret the state constitution to control police may be undone by voters. In some states, including Florida, voters have amended their state constitution to say that its particular provisions must be construed in conformity with the U.S. Constitution and to bar any greater protection of rights than exist under it.[82]

By raising these difficulties, I am not arguing against using state constitutions to curtail police misconduct. On the contrary, I strongly support use of state constitutions to develop rights that limit police abuses. But the limitations of this avenue for change must also be recognized.

Legislative Reforms

Congress, state legislatures, and local governments can adopt laws to regulate policing, and they legislate remedies for victims of police misconduct. My fervent hope is that the current unprecedented national attention to policing will cause laws to be adopted.

After the killing of George Floyd, two comprehensive bills addressing police reform were introduced in Congress, one in the House and one in the Senate. The George Floyd Justice in Policing Act was introduced on June 8, 2020, by Representative Karen Bass (D-CA) and as amended passed the House on June 25.[83] The Just and Unifying Solutions to Invigorate Communities Everywhere (JUSTICE) Act of 2020 was introduced by Senator Tim Scott (R-SC) on June 17.[84]

Although neither bill became law in 2020, they both show that many reforms can be enacted through legislation. These bills can and should be the basis for legislation that a future Congress can enact and for reforms at all levels of government. Also, state legislatures can adopt laws controlling police in their borders, as city councils and county boards of supervisors can regulate their officers. For example, in 2020, state legislatures in California, Delaware, Iowa, New York, Oregon, and Utah adopted laws banning police from using a chokehold on suspects.[85]

What legislative reforms of policing are crucial? Five are especially important: (1) expand the liability standards for police officers and the departments that employ them; (2) outlaw particularly dangerous police practices; (3) authorize suits against federal law enforcement officials who violate the Constitution; (4) mandate data collection about policing; and (5) increase transparency as to policing. Congress could legislate such reforms for the entire country, using its authority under section five of the Fourteenth Amendment to enact laws that enforce due process and equal protection of the law. Congress could also make compliance with these standards a condition for state and local governments to receive federal law enforcement funds. But even if Congress does not act, any state government could take these steps, as can cities and counties for their police departments.

Consider each of these five reforms.

Expand the liability standards for police officers and the departments that employ them

The Supreme Court, in its interpretation of 42 U.S. Code Section 1983, has made it far too difficult for people whose rights have been violated to sue either police officers or the local governments that employ them. Because the Court's decisions in this area are based on a statute and not on the Constitution, Congress can revise the statute to expand liability of officers and local governments.

One important way to expand liability for police officers who violate the Constitution would be to legislatively revise the standard for qualified immunity. As discussed earlier, the Supreme Court has construed Section 1983 to allow officers to avoid liability based on the defense of qualified immunity. The Court has broadly interpreted qualified immunity to preclude victims of police misconduct from bringing suits and recovering damages. In case after case involving claims of excessive police force, the Court has said that the officers cannot be held liable because of qualified immunity. Lower courts have followed this lead, creating a serious obstacle to holding police officers accountable. Because qualified immunity is based on the Supreme Court's interpretation of a federal statute, Congress can change that law. Some urge the complete elimination of qualified immunity, at least with regard to police, which would make officers liable any time they violate a person's constitutional rights.

The House bill, the George Floyd Justice in Policing Act, would not abolish qualified immunity, but it would allow police officers only two defenses to liability: that the officer was "acting in good faith" on a belief that the conduct was lawful or that the rights that the officer infringed were not "clearly established." But this provision does not go far enough in reforming qualified immunity to keep it from being used to shield officers from responsibility for their constitutional violations and to ensure that those police harm receive compensation. Under current qualified immunity law, a major obstacle to citizens' suing officers for their impermissible conduct and recovering damages is the Supreme Court's protection of police by pointing to the absence of cases of similar conduct in almost identical situations. The language in the House bill does not clearly reject or preclude that approach.

Instead, I would urge Congress to completely eliminate qualified immunity for intentional police violations of the Constitution, especially where police conduct causes serious injury or death. At the very least, no defense of qualified immunity should be available to an officer who is shown to have acted with malice in violating a person's rights. The statute also should make clear that an officer is liable, and qualified immunity is to be denied, if the officer had "fair notice" that the conduct was illegal; there need not be a case on point to deny qualified immunity. Additionally, Congress should make clear that in every case where qualified immunity is asserted, the Court must decide whether there is a constitutional violation before considering whether there is clearly established law that the reasonable officer should know. This would return the law to what it was before 2009 and ensure the development of rights for the future.

I suggest that Congress make several more additions to the existing bills, to cover what is missing there now. For one, Congress should eliminate absolute immunity for prosecutorial misconduct and for police officers who commit perjury. Those who engage in wrongful conduct, particularly when it leads to the conviction of innocent people, should not be shielded from civil liability.

Congress also should change the federal civil rights statute, 42 U.S. Code Section 1983, to hold cities liable for the misconduct of their police officers. This change must be part of any effort to reform policing in the United States. As shown earlier, the Supreme Court has interpreted Section 1983 to allow local governments to be held liable only if their own policies or customs violate the Constitution.[86] If I could make one change in existing law, it would be to allow the public to hold cities liable when their police officers violate the Constitution. It would create an incentive for cities to improve their hiring, training, supervising, and disciplining of police officers. If cities were vicariously liable for the damages that officers inflict, they would have a much stronger financial incentive to prevent and punish police excessive force.

The role of police unions in blocking effective discipline of officers and meaningful reform has recently come under discussion. Liability rules for cities play a crucial role in bargaining with unions. Imagine that a police department is negotiating with a police union about discipline.[87] Because the city rarely pays damages to victims of police violence, it makes financial sense for the city to trade smaller salary increases for greater protections against discipline. The city saves money on salary and gives up nothing economically significant by agreeing for protections for officers. But if the city faced the prospect of a multimillion-dollar judgment in every case in which an officer kills, maims, or wounds a member of the public, its cost of tolerating violence goes up enormously. The city would have a much stronger financial incentive to ensure that it doesn't hire bad cops and to fire those accused of misconduct.

Revising the laws concerning municipal and officer liability also would change the incentives of unions negotiating over discipline. If union negotiators know that the money the city spends on paying damages for officers' civil rights violations is money that is not available to pay salaries, they would think hard before negotiating disciplinary rules that make it difficult to fire officers responsible for excessive force. If the majority of the rank and file realize that they didn't get a pay raise because the city spent its police budget paying for harms caused by officers who use excessive force, the union leadership would respond or be voted out.

As I said earlier in this chapter, the legal doctrines protecting local governments and police officers from liability are based on the Supreme Court's interpretation of federal civil rights statutes, not the U.S. Constitution. Congress can and should change these laws to ensure much greater police accountability nationwide. But if Congress does not do so, state governments can accomplish the same reforms piecemeal, as a matter of state law. Obviously, state governments cannot change the content of federal law, but a state can create its own civil rights law and determine when officers and police departments within that state are liable.

Outlaw particularly dangerous police practices

The 2020 House bill included several essential reforms to protect people against racist policing. It would outlaw police use of the chokehold, defined as the "application of any pressure to the throat or windpipe, the use of maneuvers that restrict blood or oxygen flow to the brain, or carotid artery restraints that prevent or hinder breathing or reduce intake of air of an individual." It would condition federal funding for law enforcement on the police department prohibiting law enforcement officers' use of chokeholds or carotid holds. It would make the use of chokeholds or carotid holds a criminal civil rights violation. In other words, the U.S. Department of Justice could criminally prosecute a police officer using the chokehold. The chokehold is what killed George Floyd, Eric Garner, and many others, and it was the basis for the lawsuit in *City of Los Angeles v. Lyons*.[88] Study after study has shown that the chokehold is not needed to protect officers' safety yet inherently risks seriously injuring or killing those being choked. It is long overdue to prohibit its use. And as mentioned above, several states in 2020 prohibited police use of the chokehold. Others should do the same, especially if Congress does not do so.

The congressional legislation must also impose greater limits on law enforcement officers' use of lethal force. The House bill would prohibit the use of deadly force unless it is necessary and proportional in order to carry out the arrest of a person who the officer has probable cause to believe has committed a criminal offense, and reasonable alternatives to the use of less lethal force have been exhausted. The bill also prohibits federal law enforcement officers from using deadly force unless (1) it is necessary as a last resort to prevent imminent and serious bodily injury or death to the officer or another person; (2) it creates no substantial risk of injury to a third person; and (3) reasonable alternatives have been exhausted. This is a great improvement over current law, which allows deadly force to be used as long as it is reasonable. Here, too, if Congress does not enact this provision as a national standard, state and local governments should adopt it for their own officers.

Another crucial reform is to explicitly prohibit racial profiling. No current federal law does this, and no Supreme Court precedent ever has disapproved the practice. The House bill would do so and would forbid "relying, to any degree, on actual or perceived race, ethnicity, national origin, religion, gender, gender identity, or sexual orientation in selecting which individual to subject to routine or spontaneous investigatory activities." The bill would allow members of the public to enforce this prohibition in civil actions for declaratory or injunctive relief. A national law outlawing racial profiling would be a huge step toward acknowledging and attempting to deal with racism in policing.

Congress must also enact legislation to ban the issuing of no-knock warrants in drug cases. It should amend the Controlled Substances Act and condition federal funding on a state or local government's implementation of a law prohibiting no-knock warrants in such cases. When police enter a residence without knocking, those inside do not know who is intruding, and violence often ensues. This is what led to the death of Breonna Taylor in the spring of 2020.

Authorize suits against federal law enforcement officials who violate the Constitution

Although Section 1983 authorizes suits against state and local officials who violate the Constitution, no such statute exists allowing people to sue federal officers who violate the Constitution. Although in 1971 the Court said such suits could be brought directly under the Constitution, in the last forty years the Supreme Court has made it very difficult for citizens to bring such suits, stressing the absence of statutory authority for them. In *Hernández v. Mesa* in 2020, the Court held, 5–4, that a border agent who fired his gun across the border and killed a teenage boy on the other side could not be sued. By any reasonable standard, this use of force was unjustified and outrageous. But the boy's family could sue no one.

The Court, in an opinion by Justice Alito, stressed that no federal statute expressly authorized suits against federal officers who violate the Constitution. So Congress must create one. The statute easily could parallel Section 1983 and permit federal officers to be sued when they violate the Constitution.

Mandate data collection about policing

Data collection can not only provide the information necessary to assess how policing is done; by itself it can change policing as well.

Experience has shown that requiring police to record the race of individuals stopped has a significant effect in lessening the disproportionate stops of people of color. Federal law should require law enforcement agencies at every level to report data on traffic stops, frisks and body searches, and officers' use of deadly force. Additionally, federal law should require that all police departments record and report all uses of force. A single form can be distributed to all police departments in the country so the information would be uniform.

Increase transparency as to policing

In my study of the Los Angeles Police Department, I was surprised to learn that it had no system for tracking the disciplinary record of a specific officer. The consent decree to reform the LAPD mandated the creation of such a system, but many cities still do not have one. A provision of the 2020 House bill concerning data collection would require the attorney general to establish a National Police Misconduct Registry, to be maintained by the DOJ. The registry would contain data on federal and local law enforcement officers, including (1) complaints that were found to be credible or that resulted in disciplinary action, complaints pending review, and complaints that were determined to be unfounded or not sustained; (2) discipline records; (3) termination records; (4) records of certification; (5) records of lawsuits against officers and settlements; and (6) records of officers who resign or retire while under active investigation related to use of force. The registry would be made available to the public online, and it would be searchable for an individual officer's records of misconduct involving use of force or racial profiling. Again, collecting information by itself can change policing, and such a registry would make it possible for members of the public to identify patterns of constitutional violations and abusive policing. That information could then be a catalyst for reform.

The provisions of the House and Senate bills introduced in 2020 show how much could be done by legislation. Congress, state legislatures, and city councils could and should all enact these reforms for their officers. The only question is whether they will have the political will to do so.

Enforce existing laws

Changing the law through state constitutions and through legislation is desirable and indeed essential. But we could also make progress by better enforcing existing laws. For example, 42 U.S. Code Section 14141 allows the U.S. Department of Justice to sue local and state governments if it finds a pattern of constitutional violations there. Adopted in 1994, this federal law prohibits "a pattern or practice of conduct by law enforcement officers . . . that deprives persons of rights, privileges, or immunities secured or protected by the Constitution or laws of the United States." It says that whenever the attorney general has "reasonable cause to believe" that a violation has occurred, the Justice Department may sue for "appropriate equitable and declaratory relief to eliminate the pattern or practice."

This provision is potentially enormously powerful: it allows the U.S. government to investigate state and local police departments and to bring lawsuits to reform them. During the Obama administration, almost three-quarters of the Justice Department's investigations found a pattern or practice of violating civil rights, or a reform agreement, or both.[89] When the Justice Department has sued law enforcement agencies, it has only lost once,[90] and even in that instance the police department ultimately entered a settlement agreement to implement significant reforms.[91] Although under this law the Justice Department can sue a city, in most instances cities settle rather than litigate and enter a consent decree.

A consent decree is a "court-ordered and court-enforceable settlement, overseen by a federal judge." In a consent decree, the Justice Department and a city or state enter into an agreement requiring that specific reforms be instituted. Usually a monitor is appointed to oversee the process. The federal court retains the case and can impose sanctions on the government if it does not meet the terms of the agreement. Consent decrees therefore "give federal courts substantial leverage over law enforcement agencies to facilitate real change."[92]

The Justice Department has used this authority to reform police departments in Baltimore, Cincinnati, Los Angeles, New Orleans, and Pittsburgh. In each instance, major changes in policing resulted. I am most familiar with the case of Los Angeles, having done a report on the LAPD in the wake of the 2000 Rampart scandal.[93]

In the Rampart scandal, police officers were found to have planted evidence on innocent people and lied in court to gain convictions, which focused national attention on the LAPD. The Justice Department investigated and found a pattern and practice of civil rights violations by the LAPD. Justice informed the city that it would sue unless a settlement was reached. In June 2001 the city agreed to settle, and a consent decree of over one hundred pages long was entered.

The consent decree affected almost every aspect of policing in Los Angeles and included a large number of overdue reforms. It created a database to track police use of force and police discipline. It required police to record information about every stop they made. It changed how police use of force was to be investigated. It altered control of the antigang units, as it was an antigang unit in the Rampart Division that led to the scandal. It required regular audits of many aspects of policing. A monitor was appointed, and for twelve years, until 2013, a federal judge oversaw its implementation.

The Harvard Kennedy School did a detailed study—*Policing Los Angeles Under a Consent Decree: The Dynamics of Change at the LAPD*—and found that the consent decree significantly changed policing in Los Angeles.[94] Serious use-of-force incidents, for example, decreased by 15 percent.[95] Chief Bill Bratton committed to enforcing the consent decree and took the bold step of appointing reformer Gerald Chaleff and prominent civil rights lawyer Connie Rice to be the department's constitutional policing advisers. Many people, including police officers, told me that all this significantly changed the culture of the LAPD.

Did the consent decree solve all the problems in the LAPD? Of course not. But by any measure its reforms improved policing in a city that had a long pattern of police misconduct. And for those who worry that enforcing a higher standard of police behavior might hinder crime fighting, it is worth noting that crime declined precipitously in Los Angeles during the years that the consent decree was in effect.

The federal government's aggressive use of Section 14141 authority made a major difference elsewhere as well. A 2017 study of twenty-three police departments that had been subject to consent decrees found that "civil rights suits against these departments dropped anywhere from 23 percent to 36 percent after a federal intervention." Consent decrees overseen by a monitor have led to a 29 percent decrease in civilian fatalities at police hands.[96]

Unfortunately, the Trump administration refused to use this statutory power; it did not enforce existing consent decrees or seek new ones. At Jeff Sessions's confirmation hearings for attorney general, the Alabama senator expressed an unwillingness to use Section 14141, saying it was too intrusive of local governments. On April 5, 2017, Attorney General Sessions issued a memo saying that the department was reviewing existing agreements. In November 2018, the day before he left office, he again made clear that he regarded Section 14141 as an intrusion on local police departments and announced a new policy greatly limiting the ability of the Justice Department to use this statutory authority.[97] Attorney General William Barr continued that approach. Hence a crucial tool for police reform went unused during the Trump years. We will never know whether a Justice Department that had been willing to use this law might have mandated reforms in Minneapolis that could have prevented the George Floyd tragedy and others across the country.

But Section 14141 remains a federal law, and the Biden administration can and should use it as a powerful tool for reforming police departments. In April 2021, Attorney General Merrick Garland repealed the Trump-era policy and announced that the Department of Justice again would use its authority under Section 14141. Cities often have great difficulty reforming their own police departments. Police unions frequently exercise significant political influence that obstructs major changes. High-profile instances of police abuse can trigger efforts at reform, but as public attention wanes, reform efforts fade as well. This certainly had been the experience in Los Angeles over several decades. Federal intervention using Section 14141 mandated needed changes and provided the mechanisms, through a monitor and court enforcement, to ensure that reforms were implemented.

· · · · · · · · · ·

POLICE ARE A singular component of society because they have the ability to take away people's liberty by arresting them and even to deprive them of life by using deadly force. Experience shows that police exercise of power needs to be checked. Black Lives Matter implores us to remember George Floyd and Breonna Taylor and Michael Brown and Eric Garner and Laquan McDonald and Walter Scott and so many others over the course of American history who died unnecessarily at the hands of the police. Today videos and social media inform us quickly about every one of these instances, but long before we had those tools, police used violence against Blacks, behind closed doors, in a long and despicable history.

Even the best-intentioned police officers can be overly zealous in their goal to fight crime and protect society from dangerous individuals. Too easily they can come to see the end of catching criminals as justifying means that compromise basic rights. That is why constraints on police searches, arrests, interrogations, and eyewitness identifications are essential. That was why the Framers of the Constitution, recognizing the need to control police, put limits on policing in the Bill of Rights.

Our country has been infected by racism since its inception, and inevitably police, like all of us, have implicit biases. But their biases affect who they stop and how they act, too often with deadly consequences. Study after study has documented significant and unconscionable racial disparities in who police stop and what happens when they do. Any police department will have some who should not be police officers and whose impulses are to abuse the authority they are given. Throughout American history, some officers have been overtly racist in their policing, and recent studies show that some today have ties to white supremacist groups.[98] None of us should forget the story of Robert Hall, a Black man in Baker County, Georgia. In 1943 Sheriff M. Claude Screws arrested Hall on suspicion of stealing a tire and beat him to death with a baton for thirty minutes. Nor should any of us forget the 1991 image of Rodney King, a Black man, being savagely beaten by four police officers who later joked about what they had done. None of us should forget Walter Scott, an unarmed Black man in North Charleston, South Carolina, who in 2016 was shot in the back by a white police officer, Michael Slager, who had stopped him for a nonfunctioning brake light.

The crucial questions are, how do we control police behavior in order to protect people's liberty and lives? How do we eliminate the racism that too often has affected law enforcement? The U.S. Constitution provides crucial checks on police behavior: it limits searches and arrests, it protects the privilege against self-incrimination, it ensures the right to counsel, and it guarantees due process of law. Ideally, over time, the Supreme Court would have created rules limiting officers' conduct in routine police actions like searching, arresting, interrogating, and conducting identifications. And ideally, the Court would have developed effective remedies to redress violations in order to ensure implementation of those limits. That certainly was possible. All the Court's decisions empowering police could have come out differently; many powerful dissents could have instead been majority decisions that imposed greater limits on policing.

Presumed Guilty is the story of how, tragically, that didn't happen. The Court, to a large extent, has failed to develop rules to constrain the police, and too often it has developed rules that do just the opposite. The majestic promise of the Constitution to check and limit government power, when it comes to policing, has gone largely unrealized, especially for communities of color. At the same time, the Court has largely failed to develop remedies for violations in order to enforce the rules that do exist. All these failures empower, rather than check, police. They mean that far too often officers can act with impunity, knowing that their actions will bring few if any adverse consequences. Cultures even develop within police departments that actually encourage disregard of rights and racist policing.

I wrote this book to show that the Supreme Court deserves a significant share of blame for the problems of policing in the United States. Of course, it is not too late for the Court to change course and develop a jurisprudence to hold police accountable. Perhaps its own history could still inspire the justices to confront the need to enforce constitutional limits on policing.

But alas, we have no indication that this is likely to occur in the foreseeable future, certainly not with the Court as currently constituted. Perhaps someday another Warren Court will emerge that sees the need to protect people's rights and control police. Perhaps the breezes of justice will surprise us and shift in an unexpected direction. Until then, the crucial question is whether other institutions in society will act to control the police.

The intense attention to policing in the summer of 2020 offers hope that this is possible. Will other institutions of government make a sustained effort to hold police accountable? Or will they too fail to bring about meaningful change? And if reform doesn't happen, popular anger at society's failure—and the Supreme Court's failure—to control the police is sure to grow.

ACKNOWLEDGMENTS

ANYONE WHO HAS WRITTEN A BOOK KNOWS THAT IT reflects the support of a team of people. I am so grateful to the many individuals who helped make this book possible.

This book would not exist without Bob Weil, my editor at Norton, and his enthusiasm for the project. As an author, I simply cannot imagine a better editor. The approach of the book and its structure are very much based on his suggestions. His brilliant editing immeasurably improved the book. He has truly been a pleasure to work with at every step along the way.

My wonderful literary agent, Bonnie Nadell, helped me develop the idea for this book and prepare the proposal. As always, she pushed me to sharpen my focus and to think through the book's thesis. It is hard to believe that this is my sixth book with Bonnie, and I look forward to many more.

Writing a book while being dean of a law school, let alone in the midst of a pandemic, is a daunting task. Like all that I accomplish, it would not have been possible without the assistance of my outstanding assistant, Whitney Mello.

I have tremendously benefited from the assistance of great research assistants. I am very grateful to Téa Bartlett, Chelsea Bray, Julia Bront, Daria Butler, Eli Freedman, and Rachel Thompson for all their hard work. My son, Alex Chemerinsky, provided assistance in finding the photographs and talking through many of the book's ideas.

Many friends took time out from their own work to read a draft of the manuscript and to give me invaluable suggestions that made this book much better. I am so grateful to Joan Biskupic, Barry Friedman, Laurie Levenson, Jim Newton, and Marcy Strauss. All gave me detailed, terrific suggestions, and their ideas, and often their words, appear on pages throughout the book. I tried to address all their comments, but the book would undoubtedly be better if I followed even more of their advice.

I am grateful to Haley Bracken and Gabriel Kachuck, at Norton, for help in so many ways in preparing the manuscript for publication. Janet Biehl did a superb job of copyediting. And I also want to thank Rebecca Karamehmedovic for securing the approvals for the use of the photographs.

I was supported, as always, by my wonderful family. They are the best part of my very blessed life: Jeff, Kim, Adam, Katherine, Alex, and Mara, and my grandchildren, Andrew and Sarah.

This book is dedicated to my wife, Catherine Fisk. Her ideas are reflected in every part of it, though I know there are places where we disagree. She patiently allowed me to hijack our nightly walks to talk through parts of the book. She believed I could get it done when I had doubts. She read a draft and gave me superb suggestions on every chapter. And this does not begin to thank her for the far more important things, as she fills my life with joy and love every day.

NOTES

Chapter 1: "I CAN'T BREATHE"

1. *See* Paul Butler, Chokehold: Policing Black Men (2017).
2. Graham v. Conner, 490 U.S. 386 (1989) (excessive police force violates the Fourth Amendment).
3. 461 U.S. 95 (1983).
4. Petition for a Writ of Certiorari by the City of Los Angeles, City of Los Angeles v. Lyons, 461 U.S. 95 (1983); 1981 U.S. S.Ct. Briefs LEXIS 1411 at 41. *See also* 461 U.S. at 114-115 (Marshall, J., dissenting).
5. *See* Jerome H. Skolnick and James J. Fyfe, *Perspective on Law Enforcement; Chokehold Defenders Crying Wolf*, Los Angeles Times, May 6, 1993 (Lyons "mouthed off in protest of a traffic ticket" to the officers).
6. Petition for a Writ of Certiorari by the City of Los Angeles, City of Los Angeles v. Lyons, 1981 U.S. Briefs 1064; 1981 U.S. S.Ct. Briefs LEXIS 1411, at 11 n.7.
7. *Id*. Brief for Petitioner, at 9-10.
8. *Id*. at 11.
9. *Id*. at 16.
10. This description is from the petition for certiorari by the City of Los Angeles, *id*. at 11.
11. 461 U.S. at 98 n.1.
12. 461 U.S. at 117 (Marshall, J., dissenting).
13. Declaration of Alex Griswold, M.D., A.365, 367, quoted in Brief for Respondent, City of Los Angeles v. Lyons, at 22.
14. *Id*. at 23.
15. Brief for Petitioner at 11.
16. Brief for Respondent at 30.
17. 461 U.S. at 116 n.3.
18. Quoted in Gregory Howard Williams, *Controlling the Use of Non-Deadly*

Force: Policy and Practice, 10 Harvard BlackLetter Law Journal 79 n.34 (1993).

19. Lyons v. City of Los Angeles, 615 F.2d 1243, 1246 (9th Cir. 1980).

20. *Id.* at 1250.

21. 410 U.S. 113 (1973) (White, J., dissenting).

22. 384 U.S. 436 (1966) (White, J., dissenting).

23. 461 U.S. at 105.

24. *Id.*

25. *Id.* at 109.

26. *Id.* at 113 (Marshall, J., dissenting).

27. *Id.* at 137.

28. *See, e.g.,* Jones v. Bowman, 664 F. Supp. 433 (N.D. Ind. 1987) (no standing to challenge strip searches of women performed by county jail); John Does 1-100 v. Boyd, 613 F. Supp. 1514 (D. Minn. 1985) (no standing to challenge strip searches of people brought to the city jail for minor offenses).

29. Curtis v. City of New Haven, 726 F.2d 65 (2d Cir. 1984) (no standing to challenge police use of mace); Brown v. Edwards, 721 F.2d 1442 (5th Cir. 1984) (no standing to challenge state policy awarding money to constables for each arrest they made that led to a conviction); 664 F. Supp. at 433; 613 F. Supp. at 1514.

30. Corbett v. Transportation Security Administration, 930 F.3d 1225 (11th Cir. 2019) (holding no standing for traveler to challenge TSA screening protocol); J W and through Tammy Williams v. Birmingham Board of Education, 904 F.3d 1248 (11th Cir. 2018) (holding no standings against police use of chemical incapacitation spray); American Civil Liberties Union v. National Sec. Agency, 493 F.3d 644 (6th Cir. 2007) (holding no standing for challenging NSA warrantless wiretaps); Shain v. Ellison, 356 F.3d 211 (2d Cir. 2004) (ruling no standing for challenge blanket policy of strip/cavity searching); Hodgers-Durgin v. de la Vina, 199 F.3d 1037 (9th Cir. 1999) (holding no standing to challenge unreasonable searches for those stopped near the Mexican border).

31. Monell v. Department of Social Services, 436 U.S. 658 (1978) (cities are liable only for their own policies and customs and not on a respondeat superior basis).

32. All government officers have either absolute immunity or qualified immunity from suits for monetary damages. Absolute immunity is accorded to judges performing in a judicial capacity, legislators in a legislative capacity, prosecutors in a prosecutorial capacity, police officers testifying as witnesses, and the U.S. president for acts done in office. All other government officers can be sued only if qualified immunity is overcome; that is, an officer is liable only if it is shown that he or she violated clearly established law that a reasonable officer should know. For a description of these immunities, *see* Erwin Chemerinsky, Federal Jurisdiction, ch. 8 (8th ed. 2020).

33. *See* Memphis Community School Dist. v. Stachura, 477 U.S. 299 (1986)

(damages cannot be based on the abstract value or the importance of constitutional rights).

34. Petition for a Writ of Certiorari by the City of Los Angeles, City of Los
Angeles v. Lyons, 1981 U.S. Briefs 1064; 1981 U.S. S.Ct. Briefs LEXIS
1411, at 11 n.7.

35. *See, e.g.*, David A. Harris, Profiles in Injustice: Why Racial Profiling Cannot Work (2002) (describing racial profiling by U.S. police departments).

36. Connie Rice, Power Concedes Nothing (2012); Lou Cannon, Official Negligence: How Rodney King and the Riots Changed Los Angeles and the
LAPD (1997).

37. Indep. Comm'n on the L.A. Police Dep't, Report of the Independent Commission on the Los Angeles Police Department xiv, 1 (1991).

38. David D. Dotson, *A Culture of War,* Los Angeles Times, February 27,
2000.

39. David Shaw, *Chief Parker Molded LAPD Image—Then Came the '60s,*
Los Angeles Times, May 25, 1992.

40. *Id.*

41. My report is published as Erwin Chemerinsky, *An Independent Analysis
of the Los Angeles Police Department's Board of Inquiry Report on the
Rampart Scandal,* 34 Loy. L.A. L. Rev. 545, 568 (2001).

42. Darlene Ricker, *Does Society Condone Police Brutality in Exchange for
Getting Criminals off the Streets?,* ABA Journal, 77 A.B.A.J. 45 (July 1991).

43. *Id.*

44. *Id.* at 46.

45. Jerome H. Skolnick and James J. Fyfe, *Perspective on Law Enforcement;
Chokehold Defenders Crying Wolf,* Los Angeles Times, May 6, 1993.

Chapter 2: CONFRONTING THE REALITIES OF RACE AND POLICING

1. *See* Michelle Alexander, The New Jim Crow (2010) (describing the racism
of the criminal justice system).

2. *See* Paul Butler, Chokehold (2017); For an excellent discussion of police
behavior in the United States, *see* Barry Friedman, Unwarranted: Policing
without Permission (2017).

3. Barack Obama, *The President's Role in Criminal Justice Reform,* 130
Harv. L. Rev. 811, 820 (2017).

4. Elizabeth Hinton et al., *An Unjust Burden: The Disparate Treatment of
Black Americans in the Criminal Justice System* 2 (2018), https://www
.vera.org/downloads/publications/for-the-record-unjust-burden-racial
-disparities.pdf.

5. Andrew Lehren, *The Disproportionate Risks of Driving While Black,*
New York Times, October 24, 2015.

6.   Adam Cohen, Supreme Inequality: The Court's Fifty-Year Battle for a More Unjust America 295 (2020).
7.   Jon Swaine and Ciara McCarthy, *Young Black Men Again Faced Highest Race of US Police Killings in 2016,* Guardian, January 6, 2017. For an excellent discussion of police shootings, *see* Franklin Zimring, When Police Kill (2017).
8.   *Id.*
9.   Sirry Alang et al., *Police Brutality and Black Health*, Am. J. Public Health (May 2017), http://ajph.aphapublications.org/doi/abs/10.2105/AJPH.2017.303691.
10. U.S. Commission on Civil Rights, Police Use of Force: An Examination of Modern Policing Practices 23-24 (November 2018).
11. *See* Franklin Zimring, When Police Kill (2017).
12. Center for Policing Equity, Data Science for Justice, https://policingequity.org.
13. Timothy Williams, *Study Supports Suspicion that Police Are More Likely to Use Force on Blacks*, New York Times, July 7, 2016.
14. Alexei Jones, *Police Stops Are Still Marred by Racial Discrimination, Data Shows*, Prison Policy Initiative (October 12, 2018), https://www.prisonpolicy.org/blog/2018/10/12/policing.
15. Report of the National Advisory Committee on Civil Disorders 3 (1968).
16. *Id.* at 1, 8.
17. The examples and powerful stories are countless. A particularly moving one can be found in Gilbert King, Devil in the Grove: Thurgood Marshall, the Groveland Boys, and the Dawn of a New America (2013).
18. Connie Hassett-Walker, *The Racist Roots of American Policing: From Slave Patrols to Traffic Stops*, Chicago Reporter, June 7, 2019.
19. Michael German, Hidden in Plain Sight: Racism, White Supremacy, and Far-Right Militancy in Law Enforcement, Brennan Center for Justice, August 27, 2020.
20. Erwin Chemerinsky, An Independent Analysis of the Los Angeles Police Department's Board of Inquiry Report on the Rampart Scandal, 34 Loy. L.A. L. Rev. 545, 564 (2001).
21. Bryan Stevenson, *A Presumption of Guilt: The Legacy of America's History of Racial Injustice,* Policing the Black Man 4-5 (Angela Davis ed. 2017).

Chapter 3: THE SUPREME COURT'S ESSENTIAL ROLE IN ENFORCING THE CONSTITUTION AND CONTROLLING POLICE

1.   Graham v. Conner, 490 U.S. 386 (1989).
2.   384 U.S. 436 (1966).
3.   5 U.S. (1 Cranch) 137 (1803).

4. Barry Friedman, Unwarranted: Policing Without Permission 61 (2017).
5. *Id.*
6. United States v. Carolene Prod. Co., 304 U.S. 144 fn. 4 (1938).
7. I actually fear I overstate here. The changes instituted as a result of the Christopher Commission, such as limiting the term of the police chief and strengthening the role of the police commission, also helped change the LAPD.
8. Christopher Stone, Todd Foglesong, and Christine M. Cole, Policing Los Angeles Under a Consent Decree: The Dynamics of Change at the LAPD 2 (2009), http://assets.lapdonline.org/assets/pdf/Harvard-LAPD%20Study .pdf (presenting evidence that the consent decree successfully reformed the LAPD).
9. Utah v. Strieff, 136 S.Ct. 2056 (2016). This case is discussed in detail in Chapter 15.
10. Terry v. Ohio, 392 U.S. 1 (1968).
11. Floyd v. City of New York, 959 F. Supp. 2d 540 (S.D.N.Y. 2013).
12. Ben Poston and Cindy Chang, *LAPD Searches Blacks and Latinos More. But They're Less Likely to Have Contraband than Whites,* Los Angeles Times, October 8, 2019.
13. *Id.*
14. Devon W. Carbado, *From Stop and Frisk to Shoot and Kill:* Terry v. Ohio's *Pathway to Police Violence,* 64 UCLA L. Rev. 1508, 1537 (2017).
15. McCulloch v. Maryland, 17 U.S. (4 Wheat.) 415 (1819). I developed the criticism of originalism in Erwin Chemerinsky, We the People: A Progressive Reading of the Constitution for the Twenty-First Century 27-50 (2018).
16. Pew Research Institute, cited in Charles M. Blow, *In the Wake of Protests,* New York Times, August 10, 2020.

Chapter 4: WHY THE SUPREME COURT IGNORED POLICING FOR MUCH OF AMERICAN HISTORY

1. Eric H. Monkkonen, *History of Urban Police,* 15 Crime & Just. 547, 549 (1992).
2. Roger Lane, *Urban Police and Crime in Nineteenth-Century America,* 15 Crime & Just. 1, 5 (1992) (saying that they were supposed to do this "in theory," suggesting that they rarely actually broke up fights).
3. United States v. Wade, 388 U.S. 218, 225 (1967).
4. Monkkonen, *supra* note 1, at 549; Craig D. Uchida, *The Development of the American Police,* in Critical Issues in Policing, 14 (7th ed. 2015).
5. Monkkonen, *supra* note 1, at 549.
6. Lane, *supra* note 2, at 5.
7. *Id.; see* Nicholas Parrillo, *The De-Privatization of American Warfare:*

How the U.S. Government Used, Regulated, and Ultimately Abandoned Privateering in the Nineteenth Century, 19 Yale J.L. & Human. 1, 3 (2007).

8. Roger Roots, *Are Cops Constitutional?,* 11 Seton Hall Const. L. J. 685, 692 (2001).

9. *Id.*

10. Lane, *supra* note 2, at 6.

11. Wesley N. Oliver, The Prohibition Era and Policing: A Legacy of Misregulation 16 (2018).

12. *Id. at* 17-18.

13. *Id.* at 20.

14. *Id.*

15. Eleanor Lumsdon, *How Much Is Police Brutality Costing America,* 40 Hawai'i L. Rev. 141, 145 (2017); Brandon Hasbrouck, *Abolishing Racist Policing,* 68 UCLA L. Rev. Discourse 200, 206 (2020).

16. Jeffrey R. Hummel, review of Slave Patrols: Law and Violence in Virginia and the Carolinas, http://eh.net/book_reviews/slave-patrols-law-and -violence-in-virginia-and-the-carolinas.

17. Philip L. Reichel, *Southern Slave Patrols as a Transitional Police Type,* 7 Am. J. Police 51, 66-67 (1998).

18. *Id.* at 67.

19. Eric H. Monkkonen, *From Cop History to Social History: The Significance of Police in American History,* 15 J. Soc. His. 575, 578 (1982).

20. Lumsdon, *supra* note 17, at 145.

21. Hasbrouck, *supra* note 17, at 206; Larry H. Spruill, *Slave Patrols, "Packs of Negro Dogs," and Policing Black Communities,* 53 Phylon 42, 44 (1960).

22. Reichel, *supra* note 19, at 63.

23. 41 U.S. (16 Pet.) 539 (1842).

24. *Id.* at 611.

25. *Id.*

26. *Id.* at 613.

27. Moore v. Illinois, 55 U.S. (14 How.) 13, 18 (1852).

28. In *The Antelope,* 23 U.S. (10 Wheat.) 66 (1825), the Court suggested that slavery was inconsistent with national law and therefore had to be authorized by statute.

29. 60 U.S. 393 (1857).

30. *Id.* at 52-53.

31. Oliver, *supra* note 11, at 21.

32. Monkkonen, *supra* note 1, at 550.

33. *Id.* at 551. Monkkonen's theory is that uniforming the police was the key moment when they became modern forces. However, other scholars evaluate modern police force by a certain set of criteria.

34. *Id.*

35. *Id.*

36. *Id.* at 553; Reichel, *supra* note 19, at 9.

37. Uchida, *supra* note 4, at 18.

38. Oliver, *supra* note 11, at 24.

39. *Id.*; Wesley MacNeil Oliver, *The Neglected History of Criminal Procedure, 1850-1940,* 62 Rutgers L. Rev. 447, 471 (2010).

40. Oliver, *supra* note 41, at 469.

41. *Id.* at 477.

42. Reichel, *supra* note 19, at 9.

43. Monkkonen, supra note 1, at 556.

44. *See* Rich Rosell, *New York City Police Commissioner Teddy Roosevelt America's First Progressive Police Leader,* Blue Magazine, May 18, 2020.

45. 41 U.S. 65, 70 (1842)

46. 55 U.S. 584 (1852)

47. 32 U.S. (7 Pet.) 243 (1833).

48. *Id.* at 247.

49. *Id.* at 250.

50. *See* Marbury v. Madison, 5 U.S. (1 Cranch) 137 (1803); McCulloch v. Maryland, 17 U.S. (4 Wheat.) 136 (1819) (upholding the constitutionality of the Bank of the United States).

51. *Barron,* 32 U.S. at 250-251.

52. John Ely, Democracy and Distrust 196 n.58 (1980) ("In terms of the original understanding, *Barron* was almost certainly decided correctly").

53. 166 U.S. 226 (1897).

54. 211 U.S. 78 (1908).

55. *Id.* at 99.

56. 268 U.S. 652 (1925).

57. *Id.* at 666.

58. 274 U.S. 380 (1927).

59. 287 U.S. 45 (1932).

60. *Id.* at 68.

61. 316 U.S. 455 (1942).

62. *Id.* at 473.

63. 372 U.S. 335 (1963).

64. In *Palko v. Connecticut,* 302 U.S. 19 (1937), the Court said that the Fifth Amendment's protection against double jeopardy did not apply in state courts.

65. Adamson v. California, 332 U.S. 46, 54 (1947).

66. *Id.* at 54.

67. 332 U.S. 46, 71-72 (1947) (Black, J., dissenting) ("My study of the historical events that culminated in the Fourteenth Amendment . . . persuades me that one of the chief objects . . . [of] the first section . . . was to make the Bill of Rights applicable to the states.")

68. Charles Fairman, *Does the Fourteenth Amendment Incorporate the Bill of Rights? The Original Understanding,* 2 Stan. L. Rev. 5, 132 (1949).

69. Adamson v. California, 332 U.S. at 68 (Frankfurter, J., concurring).
70. Oliver, *supra* note 41, at 501.
71. *Id*. at 495.
72. *Id*. 471.
73. *Id*. at 496.
74. Oliver, supra note 11, at 39.
75. Oliver, *supra* note 11, at 498.
76. Oliver, *supra* note 41, at 1140 (emphasis added).
77. *Id*.
78. *Id*. at 1141.
79. *Id*.; Wan v. United States, 266 U.S. 1 (1924).
80. Oliver, supra note 41, at 1143.
81. *Id*.
82. Bivens v. Six Unknown Federal Narcotics Agents, 403 U.S. 388 (1971), discussed in Chapter 14.
83. Monroe v. Pape, 365 U.S. 167 (1961), discussed in Chapter 10.
84. 59 U.S. 396 (1855).
85. *Id*. at 401.
86. *Id*. at 402-403.
87. *Id*. at 403.
88. Charles H. Whitebread and Christopher Slobogin, Criminal Procedure 831 (3d ed. 1993).
89. Brown v. Allen, 344 U.S. 443 (1953).

Chapter 5: JUDICIAL SILENCE ON CONSTITUTIONAL PROTECTIONS AND REMEDIES BEFORE 1953

1. Edwin M. Borchard, Convicting the Innocent 3-5 (1932).
2. Katz v. United States, 389 U.S. 347 (1967), discussed in Chapter 7.
3. 116 U.S. 616 (1886).
4. Justice Scalia, in his decision in United States v. Jones, 565 U.S. 400 (2012), cited Entick v. Carrington, 95 Eng. Rep. 807 (C.P. 1765), as a basis for explaining why the police putting a GPS device on a car without a warrant constituted a search.
5. 116 U.S. at 626.
6. *Id*. at 626-627.
7. Olmstead v. United States, 277 U.S. 438, 464 (1928).
8. *See, e.g.,* Board of Education v. Earls, 536 U.S. 822 (2002) (upholding random drug testing for students participating in extracurricular activities); National Treasury Employees Union v. Von Raab, 489 U.S. 656 (1989) (upholding random drug testing for customs workers).
9. *See, e.g.,* Michigan Department of State Police v. Sitz, 496 U.S. 444 (1990) (upholding sobriety checkpoints).

10. 277 U.S. 438 (1928).

11. *Id.* at 456.

12. *Id.* at 456-57.

13. *Id.* at 457.

14. *See* Lochner v. New York, 198 U.S. 45 (1905) (invalidating a law limiting bakers to working no more than sixty hours a week).

15. Adkins v. Children's Hospital, 261 U.S. 525 (1923).

16. Hammer v. Dagenhart, 247 U.S. 251 (1918).

17. Champion v. Ames, 188 U.S. 321 (1903) (upholding federal lottery act); Caminetti v. United States, 242 U.S. 470 (1917) (upholding the Mann Act, which prohibits taking a woman across state lines, as applied to extramarital sexual relations without monetary compensation).

18. Buck v. Bell, 247 U.S. 200 (1927).

19. 277 U.S. at 464.

20. *Id.* at 465.

21. *Id.* at 478.

22. *Id.*

23. Katz v. United States, 389 U.S. 347 (1967).

24. 316 U.S. 129 (1942).

25. *Id.* at 131.

26. 343 U.S. 747 (1952).

27. *Id.* at 751.

28. *Id.* at 754.

29. 365 U.S. 505, 512 (1961).

30. 265 U.S. 57 (1924).

31. *Id.* at 58.

32. 110 U.S. 574 (1884).

33. *Id.* at 584.

34. *Id.* at 585.

35. 168 U.S. 532, 537 (1897).

36. *Id.* at 561-562.

37. *Id.* at 562.

38. 266 U.S. 1 (1924).

39. *Id.* at 12.

40. *Id.* at 14-15.

41. *Id.* at 17.

42. 297 U.S. 278 (1936).

43. *Id.* at 281-282.

44. *Id.*

45. *Id.* at 282.

46. 297 U.S. at 279 ("Aside from the confessions, there was no evidence sufficient to warrant the submission of the case to the jury.")

47. *Id.* at 287.

48. For a compelling example of the failure of state courts, *see* Gilbert King,

Devil in the Grove: Thurgood Marshall, the Groveland Boys, and the Dawn of a New America (2013).

49. 309 U.S. 227 (1940).
50. *Id.* at 241.
51. 316 U.S. 547 (1942).
52. *Id.* at 549.
53. *Id.*
54. 142 U.S. 547 (1892).
55. *Id.* at 555.
56. Yale Kamisar, *A Look Back on a Half-Century of Teaching, Writing, and Speaking About Criminal Law and Criminal Procedure*, 2 Ohio St. J. Crim. L. 69, 83 (2004).
57. 232 U.S. 383 (1914).
58. *Id.* at 394.
59. Wolf v. Colorado, 338 U.S. 25, 29 (1949)
60. *Id.*
61. *Id.* at 34.
62. 325 U.S. 91 (1945).
63. *Id.* at 92.
64. *Id.* at 139.
65. Korematsu v. United States, 323 U.S. 214 (1944).

Chapter 6: "EACH ERA FINDS AN IMPROVEMENT IN LAW FOR THE BENEFIT OF MANKIND"

1. These are the facts of Mapp v. Ohio, 367 U.S. 643 (1961).
2. *Id.* at 644.
3. *Id.* at 645.
4. 338 U.S. 25 (1949).
5. 232 U.S. 383 (1914).
6. 367 U.S. at 655.
7. *Id.* at 657.
8. *Id.* at 659.
9. Olmstead v. United States, 277 U.S. 438, 485 (1928) (Brandeis, J., dissenting).
10. *See, e.g.,* Draper v. United States, 358 U.S. 307 (1959) (rejecting defendant's Fourth Amendment claim).
11. For an excellent biography of Warren, *see* Jim Newton, Justice for All: Earl Warren and the Nation He Made (2007).
12. *See* William Manchester, The Glory and the Dream: A Narrative History of America 297 (1973).
13. *Id.* at 300.
14. *Id.* at 297.

15. Jim Newton, Eisenhower: The White House Years 113 (2011).
16. *Id*. at 114.
17. 347 U.S. 483 (1954).
18. Baker v. Carr, 369 U.S. 186, 266 (1962) (Frankfurter, J., dissenting).
19. H. N. Hirsch, The Enigma of Felix Frankfurter (1981)
20. For an unflattering portrayal of Douglas, *see* Bruce Murphy, Wild Bill: The Legend and Life of William Douglas (2003).
21. In Terry v. Ohio, 392 U.S. 1 (1968), only Justice Douglas dissented.
22. Korematsu v. United States, 323 U.S. 214 (1944).
23. Noah Feldman provides a vivid portrayal of these justices and their interpersonal dynamics in his excellent book Scorpions: The Battles and Triumphs of FDR's Great Supreme Court Justices (2010).
24. *See* Richard Kluger, Simple Justice (1975).
25. For a detailed account of the appointment of Brennan, *see* Seth Stern and Stephen Wermiel, Justice Brennan: Liberal Champion 71-95 (2010).
26. For example, in Justice Brennan's last opinion for the Court, Metro Broadcasting v. FCC, 497 U.S. 547 (1990), the Court upheld an affirmative action program and gave the federal government more latitude to enforce affirmative action. This decision was overruled five years later, after Justice Marshall was replaced by Justice Thomas. Adarand Constructors v. Pena, 515 U.S. 200 (1995).
27. 348 U.S. 436 (1966).
28. 378 U.S. 478 (1964), discussed below.
29. 372 U.S. 335 (1963), discussed below.
30. 366 U.S. 717 (1961).
31. *Id.*
32. *Id*. at 727.
33. 370 U.S. 660 (1962).
34. *Id*. at 667-668.
35. 372 U.S. 335 (1963).
36. 287 U.S. 45 (1932).
37. 316 U.S. 455 (1942).
38. *Id*. at 796.
39. American Bar Association Standing Committee on Legal Aid and Indigent Defenders, Gideon's Broken Promise: America's Quest for Equal Justice 38 (2004).
40. Haskell v. Berghuis, 2013 WL 163965 (6th Cir. 2013) (rejecting claim of ineffective assistance of counsel).
41. Wilkinson v. Polk, 227 Fed.Appx. 210 (4th Cir. 2007) (rejecting claim of ineffective assistance of counsel).
42. 150 Cong. Rec. S11612-13 (2004) (statement of Senator Patrick Leahy).
43. American Bar Association Standing Committee on Legal Aid and Indigent Defenders, *supra* note 46, at 9.
44. Report of the National Right to Counsel Committee, Justice Denied:

America's Continuing Neglect of Our Constitutional Right to Counsel 6-7 (2009).

45. *Id*. at 7.

46. James Anderson and Paul Heaton, *How Much Difference Does the Lawyer Make?: A Comparison of Retained and Appointed Counsel in Cases of Capital Murder,* 122 Yale L. J. 154, 188-197 (2012).

47. For example, in 2006, Judith Kaye, chief judge of the New York Court of Appeals, said, "New York's current fragmented system of county-operated and largely county-funded indigent defense services fails to satisfy the State's constitutional and statutory obligations to protect the rights of indigent accused." Comm'n on the Future of Indigent Defense Services, Final Report to the Chief Judge of the State of New York (2006). *See also* National Legal Aid and Defender Association, An Assessment of Trial-Level Indigent Defense Services in Louisiana 40 Years After Gideon (2004) (describing the method of funding lawyers for indigents in Louisiana).

48. Dorothy E. Roberts, *The Social and Moral Cost of Mass Incarceration in African American Communities,* 56 Stan. L. Rev. 1271, 1272 (2004).

49. *See* Michelle Alexander, The New Jim Crow (2012) (describing incarceration rates especially among African Americans).

50. Douglas W. Vick, *Poorhouse Justice: Underfunded Indigent Defense Services and Arbitrary Death Sentences,* 43 Buff. L. Rev. 329, 459 (1995).

51. 378 U.S. 1 (1964).

52. Twining v. New Jersey, 211 U.S. 78 (1908); Adamson v. California, 332 U.S. 46 (1947).

53. Pointer v. Texas, 380 U.S. 400 (1965).

54. 386 U.S. 213 (1967).

55. 391 U.S. 45 (1968).

56. *Id*. at 155, 157-158.

57. 130 S.Ct. 3020 (2010).

58. Timbs v. Indiana, 139 S.Ct. 682 (2019).

59. A notable exception is Justice Thomas's repeated statement that he does not believe that the establishment clause of the First Amendment—the provision forbidding laws respecting the establishment of religion—should apply to state and local governments. *See, e.g.,* Town of Greece v. Galloway, 134 S.Ct. 1811, 1835-37 (2014) (Thomas, J., concurring in part and concurring in the judgment); Elk Grove Unified School Dist. v. Newdow, 542 U.S. 1, 46 (2004) (Thomas, J., concurring in the judgment); Zelman v. Simmons-Harris, 536 U.S. 639, 679 (2002) (Thomas, J., concurring). Justice Gorsuch recently joined an opinion by Justice Thomas arguing this. Espinoza v. Montana Department of Revenue, 140 S.Ct. 2246 (2020).

60. In fact, in its most recent decision about incorporation, in 2020, the Court overruled earlier decisions and held that the Sixth Amendment required that jury verdicts in criminal cases be unanimous in state courts. Ramos v. Louisiana, 140 S.Ct. 1390 (2020).

Chapter 7: BOTH LIMITING AND EMPOWERING POLICE

1. 389 U.S. 347 (1967).
2. 392 U.S. 1 (1968).
3. The Court's statement of the facts in *Katz* is quite brief. These facts are drawn from Harvey A. Schneider, Katz v. United States: *The Untold Story*, 40 McGeorge L. Rev. 13 (2009). Schneider argued the case for Katz in the Supreme Court.
4. 277 U.S. 438 (1928).
5. *Id.* at 15.
6. 389 U.S. at 353.
7. Jacobellis v. Ohio, 378 U.S. 184 (1964) (Stewart, J., dissenting).
8. *See* Laurence Tribe, The Constitution in Cyberspace (1991); *see also* https://news.harvard.edu/gazette/story/2020/06/laurence-tribe-speaks-on -his-career-in-constitutional-law/.
9. 389 U.S. at 353.
10. *Id.* at 359.
11. *Id.* at 369 (Harlan, J., concurring).
12. 138 S.Ct. 2206 (2018).
13. The officers had obtained a court order pursuant to the federal Stored Communications Act. The key difference is that probable cause is required for a warrant but is not needed under the Stored Communications Act.
14. Riley v. California, 573 U.S. 373 (2014).
15. *Id.* at 2217.
16. Orin Kerr, *Katz Has Only One Step: The Irrelevance of Subjective Expectations,* 82 U. Chi. L. Rev. 113 (2015) (arguing that there really is only one prong, an objective one, to the *Katz* analysis).
17. 488 U.S. 445 (1989).
18. *Id.* at 450-451.
19. California v. Greenwood, 486 U.S. 35 (1988).
20. *Id.* at 4041.
21. *Katz v. United States,* 389 U.S. 351 (1967).
22. *Smith v. Maryland,* 442 U.S. 735 (1979).
23. *Id.* at 743-744.
24. Carpenter v. United States, 138 S.Ct. 2206 (2018).
25. 392 U.S. 1 (1968).
26. *Id.* at 16.
27. *Id.* at 16-17.
28. *Id.* at 27.
29. *Id.* at 31.
30. *Id.* at 37 (Douglas, J., dissenting).
31. "Although a mere 'hunch' does not create reasonable suspicion, the level of suspicion the standard requires is considerably less than proof of wrong-

doing by a preponderance of the evidence, and obviously less than is necessary for probable cause." Prado Navarette v. California, 572 U.S. 393,
397 (2014).

32. Kansas v. Glover, 140 S.Ct. 1183, 1190 (2020).

33. 392 U.S. 14-15 (1968).

34. Brief for the N.A.A.C.P. Legal Defense and Educational Fund, Inc., as
    Amicus Curiae at 3, Terry v. Ohio, 392 U.S. 1 (1967) WL 113672, at *3.

35. Floyd v. City of New York, 959 F. Supp. 2d 540 (S.D.N.Y. 2013).

36. Emma Pierson et al., *A Large Scale Analysis of Racial Disparity in Police
    Stops Across the United States*, 4 Nat. Hum. Behav. 736 (2020).

37. Devon W. Carbado, *From Stop and Frisk to Shoot to Kill: Terry v. Ohio's
    Pathway to Police Violence*, 64 UCLA L. Rev. 1508, 1511 (2017).

38. John Q. Barrett, *Deciding the Stop and Frisk Cases: A Look Inside the
    Supreme Court's Conference*, 72 St. John's L. Rev. 749 (1998).

39. *Id*. at 797.

40. *Id*. at 838.

41. Carbado describes this as well as a cause for the Court's decision in *Terry*.
    Carbado, *supra* note 37, at 1528.

Chapter 8: *MIRANDA*

1. 384 U.S. 436 (1966).

2. Spano v. New York, 360 U.S. 315 (1959) (psychological pressure made the
   confession involuntary).

3. *See* Payne v. Arkansas, 356 U.S. 560 (1958) (the fact that the suspect was
   given no food for twenty-four hours was important to the Court's conclusion that the confession was involuntary).

4. Colorado v. Connelly, 479 U.S. 157 (1986) (confession is admissible if voluntary even if the product of mental illness).

5. Joseph D. Grano, *Voluntariness, Free Will, and the Law of Confessions*,
   65 Va. L. Rev. 859, 863 (1979).

6. 377 U.S. 201 (1964).

7. 378 U.S. 478 (1964).

8. *Id*. at 482.

9. *Id*. at 481.

10. *Id*. at 490.

11. *Id*. at 491-492.

12. *Id*. at 461.

13. *Id*. at 457.

14. *Id*. at 468-469.

15. The Court said: "Once warnings have been given, the subsequent proce-
    dure is clear. If the individual indicates in any manner, at any time prior

to or during questioning, that he wishes to remain silent, the interrogation must cease. At this point he has shown that he intends to exercise his Fifth Amendment privilege; any statement taken after the person invokes his privilege cannot be other than the product of compulsion, subtle or otherwise. Without the right to cut off questioning, the setting of in-custody interrogation operates on the individual to overcome free choice in producing a statement after the privilege has been once invoked. If the individual states that he wants an attorney, the interrogation must cease until an attorney is present. At that time, the individual must have an opportunity to confer with the attorney and to have him present during any subsequent questioning. If the individual cannot obtain an attorney and he indicates that he wants one before speaking to police, they must respect his decision to remain silent." *Id.* at 474-475.

16. *Id.* at 475.
17. *Id.* at 483-484.
18. *Id.* at 480.
19. Charles Weisselberg, *Saving Miranda*, 84 Cornell L. Rev. 109, 121 (1998).
20. 18 U.S.C. §3501.
21. United States v. Dickerson, 530 U.S. 428 (2000).
22. Stephen J. Schulhofer, Miranda's *Practical Effect: Substantial Benefits and Vanishingly Small Social Costs*, 90 Nw. U. L. Rev. 500 (1996) (reviewing these studies).
23. *See, e.g.*, Michael Wald et al., *Interrogations in New Haven: The Impact of* Miranda, 76 Yale L. J. 1519 (1967); Richard J. Medalie, *Custodial Police Interrogation in Our Nation's Capital: The Attempt to Implement* Miranda, 66 Mich. L. Rev. 1347 (1969).
24. Medalie, *supra* note 23, at 1347.
25. Schulhofer, *supra* note 22, at 506.
26. Richard Leo, Police Interrogation and American Justice (2009). This sentiment is not unanimous among scholars. Paul Cassell argues that *Miranda* has decreased the confessions obtained by police. *See* Paul G. Cassell, Miranda's *Social Costs: An Empirical Reassessment*, 90 Nw. U. L. Rev. 387 (1996). The methodology of Cassell's study is disputed. *See* Schulhofer, *supra* note 22, at 500.
27. Gerald M. Caplan, *Questioning* Miranda, 38 Vand. L. Rev. 1417, 1466 (1986).
28. Paul G. Cassell and Bret S. Hayman, *Police Interrogation in the 1990s: An Empirical Study of the Effects of Miranda*, 43 UCLA L. Rev. 839, 860 (1996).
29. Saul M. Kassin et al., *Police Interviewing and Interrogation: A Self-Report Survey of Police Practices and Beliefs*, 31 Law & Hum. Behav. 381, 394 (2007).
30. *See, e.g.,* Oregon v. Mathiason, 429 U.S. 492 (1977).

31. Irene Merker Rosenberg and Yale L. Rosenberg, *A Modest Proposal for the Abolition of Custodial Confessions*, 68 N.C. L. Rev. 69, 112 (1990) (suggesting that police circumvent *Miranda* by conducting coercive non-custodial interviews in suspects' homes).

32. Charles Weisselberg, *Mourning* Miranda, 96 Calif. L. Rev. 1519, 1267 (2008).

33. Richard A. Leo and Welsh S. White, *Adapting to* Miranda: *Modern Inter-rogators' Strategies for Dealing with the Obstacles Posed by* Miranda, 84 Minn. L. Rev. 397, 432 (1999).

34. Harris v. New York, 401 U.S. 222 (1971).

35. United States v. Pattane, 542 U.S. 630 (2004).

36. Weisselberg, *supra* note 19, at 109, 132.

37. Weisselberg, *supra* note 32, at 1547.

Chapter 9: **PROTECTING THE INNOCENT FROM WRONGFUL CONVICTIONS**

1. Edwin M. Borchard, Convicting the Innocent 3-5 (1932).

2. Brandon L. Garrett, *Judging Innocence*, 108 Colum. L. Rev. 55, 60 (2008).

3. United States v. Wade, 388 U.S. 228 (1967).

4. *See* Elizabeth F. Loftus, Eyewitness Testimony (1979).

5. For an excellent summary of the factors that lead to inaccurate identifi-cation, *see* National Research Council, Identifying the Culprit: Assessing Eyewitness Identification 45-70 (2014).

6. *See* Christian A. Meissner and John C. Brigham, *Thirty Years of Investi-gating the Own-Race Bias in Memory for Faces,* 7 Psychol., Pub. Pol'y & L. 3, 15, 21 (2001).

7. Gary L. Wells, *What Price Justice? Exploring the Relationship of Lineup Fairness to Identification Accuracy,* 4 Law & Hum. Behav. 275, 278 (1980).

8. Brian L. Cutler, and Steven D. Penrod, Mistaken Identification: The Eye-witness, Psychology and the Law 819-822 (1995).

9. *See* Nancy Steblay et al., *Eyewitness Accuracy Rates in Police Showup and Lineup Presentations: A Meta-Analytic Comparison,* 27 Law & Hum. Behav. 523, 532 (2003).

10. 388 U.S. 218 (1967).

11. *Id.* at 228.

12. *Id.* at 228–229.

13. *Id.* at 229.

14. *Id.* at 236–237 (citations omitted).

15. *Id.* at 240.

16. *Id.* at 242.

Chapter 10: **RIGHTS NEED REMEDIES**

1. S. Rep. No. 1, 42d Cong., 1st Sess. (1871).
2. Wilson v. Garcia, 471 U.S. 261, 276 (1985).
3. Monell v. Department of Social Services, 436 U.S. 658, 685 (1978). For other Supreme Court discussions of the historical background of Section 1983, *see* Patsy v. Board of Regents of Fla., 457 U.S. 496 (1982); Allen v. McCurry, 449 U.S. 90 (1980); Mitchum v. Foster, 407 U.S. 225 (1972); Monroe v. Pape, 365 U.S. 167 (1961). For a discussion of the history of Section 1983 and the Court's inconsistent uses of it, *see* Gene R. Nichol, *Federalism, State Courts, and Section 1983,* 73 Va. L. Rev. 959 (1987).
4. 365 U.S. at 180.
5. Patsy v. Board of Regents of Fla., 457 U.S. 502-503 (1982) (Section 1983 as a "basic alteration" of our federal system).
6. 407 U.S. at 242 (citations omitted).
7. *Comment, The Civil Rights Act: Emergence of an Adequate Federal Civil Remedy?,* 26 Ind. L. J. 361, 363 (1951).
8. *See* Eugene Gressman, *The Unhappy History of Civil Rights Legislation,* 50 Mich. L. Rev. 1323 (1952); Robert J. Harris, The Quest for Equality 56, 82-89 (1960).
9. *See, e.g.,* Plessy v. Ferguson, 163 U.S. 537 (1896) (upholding state laws mandating separate accommodations for whites and blacks); The Civil Rights Cases, 109 U.S. 3 (1883) (holding unconstitutional the Civil Rights Act of 1875 as exceeding Congress's authority on account of its regulation of private conduct); The Slaughterhouse Cases, 83 U.S. (16 Wall.) 36 (1873) (narrowly construing the provisions of the Fourteenth Amendment).
10. Giles v. Harris, 189 U.S. 475, 485 (1903). At the time Holmes made this statement, the civil provision of the Civil Rights Act of 1871 was numbered 1979. In the codification of the U.S. Code, it became 42 U.S.C. §1983.
11. Peter W. Low and John C. Jeffries, Federal Courts and the Law of Federal-State Relations 917 (4th ed. 1998). *See, e.g.,* Smith v. Allwright, 321 U.S. 649 (1944); Lane v. Wilson, 307 U.S. 268 (1939); Rice v. Elmore, 165 F.2d 387 (4th Cir. 1947); Chapman v. King, 154 F.2d 460 (5th Cir. 1946).
12. Theodore Eisenberg, Civil Rights Legislation: Cases and Materials 86 (2d ed. 1987), citing statistics from the Administrative Office of the U.S. Courts, Annual Report of the Director 232 (1960).
13. "U.S. District Clourts—Civil Cases Filed . . . ," table 4.4 in Administrative Office of the U.S. Courts, Annual Report of the Director: Judicial Business of the United States (2019), https://www.uscourts.gov/sites/default/files/data_tables/jff_4.4_0930.2019.pdf.
14. *Id.*
15. 365 U.S. 167 (1961).

16. State governments cannot be sued under Section 1983. Will v. Michigan Department of State Police, 491 U.S. 58 (1989). This, in large part, is because states have sovereign immunity protected under the Eleventh Amendment.
17. Low and Jeffries, *supra* note 11, at 917.
18. 365 U.S. at 169
19. *Id*. at 184.
20. *Id*. at 183 (emphasis added).
21. *Id*. at 173-174.
22. *Id*. at 236 (Frankfurter, J., dissenting).
23. *Id*. at 191.
24. Monell v. Department of Social Services, 436 U.S. 658 (1978).

Chapter 11: "ONLY THE GUILTY HAVE SOMETHING TO HIDE"

1. These are the facts of Schneckloth v. Bustamonte, 412 U.S. 218 (1973).
2. Subsequently, in Stone v. Powell, 428 U.S. 465 (1976), the Supreme Court held that a federal court cannot hear Fourth Amendment claims on habeas corpus.
3. Bustamonte v. Schneckloth, 488 F.2d 699 (9th Cir. 1971).
4. 412 U.S. at 223.
5. *Id*. at 227.
6. *Id*. at 232-233.
7. *Id*. at 242: "The protections of the Fourth Amendment are of a wholly different order, and have nothing whatever to do with promoting the fair ascertainment of truth at a criminal trial."
8. *Id*. at 246.
9. Alafair S. Burke, *Consent Searches and Fourth Amendment Reasonableness*, 67 Fl. L. Rev. 509, 511 (2016) ("multiple scholars have estimated that consent searches comprise more than 90% of all warrantless searches by police").
10. Marcy Strauss, *Reconstructing Consent*, 92 J. Crim. L. & Criminology 211, 213 (2001).
11. Frank R. Baumgartner, Derek A. Epp, and Kelsey Shoub, Suspect Citizens: What 20 Million Traffic Stops Tell Us About Policing and Race (2018).
12. Neil Gross, *Still Guilty of Driving While Black*, New York Times, September 10, 2020.
13. Comm'n to Investigate Allegations of Police Corruption and the Anti-Corruption Procedures of the Police Dep't, City of New York, Commission Report 36 (1994); *see also* Joe Sexton, *New York Police Often Lie Under Oath, Report Says,* New York Times, April 22, 1994.
14. Stuart Taylor, Jr., *For the Record*, Am. Law. 72 (1995).
15. Christopher Slobogin, *Testilying: Police Perjury and What to Do About It,* 67 Colo. L. Rev. 1037, 1041 (1996).

16. Joseph D. McNamara, *Law Enforcement: Has the Drug War Created an Officer Liars' Club?*, Los Angeles Times, February 11, 1996.

17. Susan Bandes, *Police Accountability and the Problem of Regulating Consent Searches*, 2018 U. Ill. L. Rev. 1759 (2018).

18. John Massaro, *LBJ and the Fortas Nomination for Chief Justice*, 97 Poli. Sci. Q. 603 n.2 (1983).

19. Quoted in Brian R. Gallini, Schneckloth v. Bustamonte: *History's Unspoken Fourth Amendment Anomaly*, 79 Tenn. L. Rev. 233, 253 (2012).

20. Bryon J. Moraski and Charles R. Shipan, *The Politics of Supreme Court Nominations: A Theory of Institutional Constraints and Choices*, 43 Am. J. Pol. Sci. 1069, 1093 (1999).

21. Frederick Wilmot-Smith, Equal Justice: Fair Legal Systems in an Unfair World 160 (2019).

22. Laura Kalman, The Long Reach of the Sixties: LBJ, Nixon, and the Making of the Contemporary Supreme Court 237 (2017); Bruce H. Kalk, *The Carswell Affair: The Politics of a Supreme Court Nomination in the Nixon Administration*, 42 Am. J. Legal Hist. 261, 284 (1998).

23. 403 U.S. 713 (1971).

24. For an excellent description of this evolution, *see* Linda Greenhouse, Becoming Justice Blackmun: Harry Blackmun's Supreme Court Journey (2006).

25. Asad Rahim, *Diversity to Deradicalize* 17, 37, 39, https://ssrn.com/abstract=3469365.

26. Lewis F. Powell, Jr., Confidential Memorandum to Eugene B. Sydnor: Attack on American Free Enterprise System 1 (August 23, 1971), https://scholarlycommons.law.wlu.edu/powellmemo/1.

27. *Id.* at 6.

28. Richard Kluger, Simple Justice 606 (1975).

29. San Antonio Board of Education v. Rodriguez, 411 U.S. 1 (1973).

30. Milliken v. Bradley, 418 U.S. 717 (1974).

31. 410 U.S. 113 (1973).

32. 426 U.S. 229 (1976).

33. *See* Joan Biskupic, Sandra Day O'Connor: How the First Woman on the Supreme Court Became Its Most Influential Justice (2005).

34. For example, Justice Stevens initially voted with the conservatives to limit affirmative action; *see* City of Richmond v. J. A. Croson Co., 488 U.S. 469 (1989). But he subsequently shifted and voted with the more liberal justices to uphold affirmative action. *See, e.g.,* Grutter v. Bollinger, 539 U.S. 306 (2003); Adarand Constructors v. Pena, 515 U.S. 200 (1995).

35. 428 U.S. 465 (1976).

36. 344 U.S. 443 (1953). For an excellent discussion of *Brown,* see Eric M. Freedman, *Milestones in Habeas Corpus III: Brown v. Allen,* 51 Ala. L. Rev. 1541 (2000).

37. 344 U.S. at 511.

38. Kaufman v. United States, 394 U.S. 217, 226 (1969).

39. *See, e.g.,* Stephen Bright and Patrick Keenan, *Judges and the Politics of Death: Deciding Between the Bill of Rights and the Next Election in Capital Cases,* 75 B.U.L. Rev. 759 (1995).

40. 412 U.S. at 250 (Powell, J., concurring).

41. *Id.* at 274-275.

42. 428 U.S. 465 (1976).

43. *Id.* at 494.

44. *Id.* at 495.

45. *Id.* at 490-491.

46. *Id.* at 493-494 n.35.

47. For an excellent article criticizing *Stone v. Powell* and arguing in favor of allowing relitigation of issues on habeas corpus, *see* Gary Peller, *In Defense of Federal Habeas Corpus Relitigation,* 16 Harv. C.R.-C.L. L. Rev. 579 (1982).

48. *See* 28 U.S.C. §§2241, 2254.

49. *See* The Antiterrorism and Effective Death Penalty Act of 1996 (restricting the availability of habeas corpus).

50. *See, e.g.,* Burt Neuborne, *The Myth of Parity,* 90 Harv. L. Rev. 1105 (1977); Peller, *supra* note 47, at 665-666.

51. 412 U.S. 218, 257-58 (1973). *See generally* Henry Friendly, *Is Innocence Irrelevant? Collateral Attack on Criminal Judgments,* 38 U. Chi. L. Rev. 142 (1970) (arguing for a limit of habeas corpus to cases where there is a colorable showing of innocence).

52. Stone v. Powell, 428 U.S. at 524 (Brennan, J., dissenting); *see also* Ira P. Robbins and James E. Sanders, *Judicial Integrity, the Appearance of Justice, and the Great Writ of Habeas Corpus: How to Kill Two Thirds (or More) with One Stone,* 15 Am. Crim. L. Rev. 63 (1977).

53. 425 U.S. 435 (1976).

54. *Id.* at 442.

55. *Id.* at 443.

56. *Id.* at 451 (Brennan, J., dissenting).

57. 442 U.S. 735 (1979).

58. *Id.* at 742.

59. *Id.* at 743.

60. United States v. Forrester, 512 F.3d 500 (9th Cir. 2008).

61. 138 S.Ct. 2206 (2018).

62. Wayne LaFave, Search and Seizure: A Treatise on the Fourth Amendment 747 (4th ed. 2004).

63. United States v. Jones, 565 U.S. 400, 413 (2012). For a defense of the third-party doctrine, *see* Orin Kerr, *The Case for the Third Party Doctrine,* 107 Mich. L. Rev. 561 (2007).

64. Joshua Dressler, Alan C. Michaels, and Ric Simmons, Understanding Criminal Procedure, vol. 1, Investigations 209 (7th ed., 2017).

65. 267 U.S. 132 (1925).
66. *Id.* at 153.
67. 399 U.S. 402 (1970).
68. *Id.* at 48.
69. 413 U.S. 433 (1973).
70. *Id.* at 441.
71. *Id.* at 442.
72. *Id.* at 441.
73. 417 U.S. 583 (1974).
74. 471 U.S. 386 (1985).
75. *Id.* at 393.
76. California v. Acevedo, 500 U.S. 565 (1991).
77. Wyoming v. Houghton, 526 U.S. 295 (1999).
78. Sarah A. Seo, Policing the Open Road: How Cars Transformed American Freedom 253 (2019) ("the police would need a warrant to search a briefcase if the owner was carrying it—and then would be free to search it without a warrant once the owner placed the briefcase in a car").
79. In its most recent decision, the Court recognized the need for a limit on car searches: it did not allow the automobile exception to be applied to a motorcycle parked in front of a house. Collins v. Virginia, 138 S.Ct. 1663 (2018).

Chapter 12: HOLLOWING OUT *MIRANDA*

1. *See, e.g.,* Rhode Island v. Innis, 446 U.S. 291 (1980).
2. 453 U.S. 355 (1981).
3. *Id.* at 359.
4. 492 U.S. 195 (1989).
5. *Id.* at 202.
6. *See, e.g.,* New York v. Quarles, 467 U.S. 649 (1984) (creating a public safety exception to the requirement for *Miranda* warnings).
7. 401 U.S. 222 (1971).
8. *Id.* at 232 (Brennan, J., dissenting).
9. Charles Weisselberg, *Saving* Miranda, 84 Cornell L. Rev. 109, 132–138 (1999).
10. *Id.* at 136.
11. *Id.* at 139.

Chapter 13: REFUSING TO CHECK POLICE EYEWITNESS IDENTIFICATION PROCEDURES

1. Daniel Epps, *The Consequences of Error in Criminal Justice*, 128 Harv. L. Rev. 1067, 1067-68 (2015).
2. 388 U.S. 218 (1967).

3.   406 U.S. 682 (1972).

4.   Joshua Dressler, Alan C. Michaels, and Ric Simmons, Understanding Criminal Procedure, vol. 1, Investigations 512 (7th ed., 2017).

5.   413 U.S. 300 (1973).

6.   *Id*. at 312.

7.   *Id*. at 326-327 (Brennan, J., dissenting).

8.   *Id*. at 317.

9.   *Id*. at 321.

10. *Id*. at 326 (Brennan, J., dissenting).

11. Stovall v. Dennis, 388 U.S. 293 (1967).

12. Foster v. California, 394 U.S. 440 (1969). The police structured a lineup of three men. The suspect was over six feet tall; the other two men in the lineup were at least six inches shorter. The witness could not make an identification. Over a week later, the police did a second lineup. Only the suspect was in both, and this time the witness made an identification.

13. 388 U.S. at 302.

14. *Id*.

15. 409 U.S. 188 (1972).

16. *Id*. at 201.

17. Gary S. Wells and Deah Quinlivan, *Suggestive Eyewitness Identification and the Supreme Court's Reliability Test in Light of Eyewitness Science: 30 Years Later*, 33 L. & Hum. Behav. 1, 11 (2009).

18. 432 U.S. 98 (1977).

19. *Id*. at 107.

20. *Id*. at 109.

21. *Id*. at 114.

22. Sherri Lynn Johnson, *Cross-Racial Identification Errors in Criminal Cases*, 69 Cornell L. Rev. 934, 938 (1984).

23. David Bazelon, *Eyewitness News,* Psychology Today 105 (March 1980).

Chapter 14: **ERODING REMEDIES FOR POLICE MISCONDUCT**

1.   468 U.S. 796 (1984).

2.   *Id*. at 805.

3.   487 U.S. 533 (1988).

4.   *Id*. at 541.

5.   *Id*. at 544.

6.   468 U.S. 897 (1984).

7.   *Id*. at 907.

8.   *Id*.

9.   *Id*. at 922.

10. *Id*. at 928-929 (Brennan, J., dissenting).

11. 423 U.S. 362 (1976).
12. Id at 367.
13. *Id*. at 372, quoting O'Shea v. Littleton, 414 U.S. 488, 495 (1974).
14. Younger v. Harris, 401 U.S. 37 (1971).
15. *Id*. at 38.
16. 403 U.S. 388 (1971).
17. 409 F.2d 718, 719 (2d Cir. 1969), *rev'd*, 403 U.S. 388 (1971).
18. 403 U.S. at 394-395.
19. *Id*.
20. *Id*. at 402-403 (Harlan, J., concurring).
21. *Id*. at 409-410.
22. *Id*. at 410-411.
23. *Id*. at 412 (Burger, C.J., dissenting).
24. *Id*. at 420 (Burger, C.J., dissenting).
25. *See* Carlson v. Green, 446 U.S. 14 (1980); Davis v. Passman, 442 U.S. 228 (1979).
26. *See, e.g.,* Hernandez v. Mesa, 130 S.Ct. 735 (2020); Ziglar v. Abassi, 137 S.Ct. 1843 (2020); Hui v. Castaneda, 130 S.Ct. 1845 (2010); Wilkie v. Robbins, 551 U.S. 537 (2007); Correctional Services Corp. v. Malesko, 534 U.S. 61 (2001).
27. Ziglar v. Abassi, 137 S.Ct. 1843, 1857 (2017) ("a *Bivens* remedy will not be available if there are 'special factors counselling hesitation in the absence of affirmative action by Congress'") (internal citations omitted); *id*. at 1859 ("The proper test for determining whether a case presents a new *Bivens* context is . . . If the case is different in a meaningful way from previous *Bivens* cases decided by this Court, then the context is new").
28. 140 S.Ct. 735, 750 (2020) (Thomas, J., concurring).
29. *See, e.g.,* Stump v. Sparkman, 435 U.S. 349 (1978); Pierson v. Ray, 386 U.S. 547 (1967); Bradley v. Fisher, 80 U.S. 335 (1871).
30. Bradley v. Fisher, 80 U.S. at 347; Pierson v. Ray, 386 U.S. at 554 (a judge should not have to "fear that unsatisfied litigants may hound him with litigation charging malice or corruption"); *see also* Mireles v. Waco, 502 U.S. 9 (1991) (upholding absolute immunity for a judge that allegedly ordered excessive force be used in arresting a suspect).
31. 435 U.S. 349 (1978).
32. Rebecca Cepko, *Involuntary Sterilizations of Mentally Disabled Women,* 8 Berkeley Women's Law Journal 122, 123 (1993).
33. Skinner v. Oklahoma, 316 U.S. 535 (1942).
34. 424 U.S. 409 (1976).
35. *Id*. at 423.
36. Van de Kamp v. Goldstein, 555 U.S. 335 (2009).
37. *See, e.g.,* Pierson v. Ray, 386 U.S. 547 (1967) (police officers have qualified immunity in suits for damages).

38. 460 U.S. 325 (1983).

39. *Id*. at 343.

40. *See, e.g.,* The City of New York Commission to Investigate Allegations of Police Corruption and the Anti-Corruption Procedures of the Police Department, Commission Report 38 (1994) (Hon. Milton Mollen, Chair).

41. 416 U.S. 232 (1974).

42. *Id*. at 247-248.

43. *See, e.g.,* Wood v. Strickland, 420 U.S. 308 (1975).

44. 457 U.S. 800 (1982).

45. Nixon v. Fitzgerald, 457 U.S. 731 (1982).

46. 457 U.S. at 818.

47. The Burger Court, and especially the Rehnquist Court, greatly expanded the sovereign immunity of state governments, including for conduct by state police forces. *See* Erwin Chemerinsky, Federal Jurisdiction ch. 7 (8th ed. 2020).

48. Lincoln Cnty v. Luning, 133 U.S. 529 (1890); Mt. Healthy City Sch. Dist. Bd. of Educ. v. Doyle, 429 U.S. 274 (1977).

49. 365 U.S. 167 (1961).

50. *Id*. at 188.

51. 436 U.S 658 (1978).

52. *Id*. at 683.

53. *Id*. at 690 (emphasis included).

54. *Id*. at 694.

55. *See, e.g.,* David Jacks Achtenberg, *Taking History Seriously: Municipal Liability Under 42 U.S.C. §1983 and the Debate over Respondeat Superior,* 73 Fordham L. Rev. 2183 (2005); Karen M. Blum, *From* Monroe *to* Monell: *Defining the Scope of Municipal Liability in Federal Courts,* 51 Temp. L. Q. 409 (1978); Christina B. Whitman, *Government Responsibility for Constitutional Torts,* 85 Mich. L. Rev. 225, 236 n.43 (1986).

56. Bd. of the Cnty. Comm'rs v. Brown, 520 U.S. 397, 437 (1997) (Breyer, J., dissenting).

57. *Id*. at 431-433.

Chapter 15: THE POLICE CAN STOP ANYONE, AT ANY TIME, AND SEARCH THEM

1. 136 S.Ct. 2056 (2016).

2. The phrase "fruit of the poisonous tree" was used by the Court in Nardone v. United States, 308 U.S. 338 (1939).

3. *Id*. at 2068 (Sotomayor, J., dissenting).

4. *Id*. at 2064.

5. *Id*. at 2070.

6. Richard Kluger, Simple Justice 606 (1975).

7. Plessy v. Ferguson, 163 U.S. 537 (1896) (concluding that "separate, but equal" does not violate equal protection).

8. *See, e.g.,* Obergefell v. Hodges, 576 U.S. 644 (2015) (state laws prohibiting same-sex marriage violate equal protection and due process); Whole Women's Health v. Hellerstedt, 136 S.Ct. 2292 (2016) (striking down state law imposing restrictions on abortions).

9. 384 U.S. 436 (1966) (White, J., dissenting).

10. Similarly, in Navarette v. California, 572 U.S. 393 (2014), Justice Breyer was the fifth vote in ruling that police could stop a car based on an anonymous tip that the car was driving erratically. And in Maryland v. King, 539 U.S. 435 (2013), Justice Breyer was also the fifth vote in ruling that police could take DNA from a person arrested for a serious crime to see if it matched an unsolved crime in the police database. Interestingly, Justice Scalia dissented in both of these cases.

11. *See, e.g.,* June Medical Services v. Russo, 140 S.Ct. 2103 (2020) (Louisiana's Unsafe Abortion Protection Act, which required doctors who perform abortions to have admitting privileges at a nearby hospital, is unconstitutional); Bostock v. Clayton County, Georgia, 140 S.Ct. 1731 (2020). The prohibition in Title VII of the Civil Rights Act of 1964, 42 U.S.C. §2000e-2(a)(1), against employment discrimination "because of . . . sex" encompasses discrimination based on an individual's sexual orientation or gender identity; Department of Homeland Security v. Regents of the University of California, 140 S.Ct. 1891 (2020) (the Department of Homeland Security's decision to wind down the Deferred Action for Childhood Arrivals program is judicially reviewable; and DHS's decision to rescind DACA was arbitrary and capricious under the Administrative Procedure Act.).

12. One exception would be United States v. Carpenter, 138 S.Ct. 2206 (2018), where Chief Justice Roberts wrote for the majority in a 5–4 decision holding that the police must obtain a warrant or have an emergency in order to obtain stored cellular location information. *Carpenter* is discussed in Chapter 7. For an excellent biography of Roberts, *see* Joan Biskupic, The Chief: The Life and Turbulent Times of Chief Justice John Roberts (2019).

13. *See* Schuette v. Coalition to Defend Affirmative Action, 572 U.S. 291 (2014) (Sotomayor, J., dissenting). *See also* Joan Biskupic, Breaking In: The Rise of Sonia Sotomayor and the Politics of Justice (2014).

14. For an excellent description of the fight over Kavanaugh's nomination, *see* Ruth Marcus, Supreme Ambition: Brett Kavanaugh and the Conservative Takeover (2020).

15. 517 U.S. 806 (1996).

16. *Id*. at 809.

17. *Id*. at 810.

18. *Id*. at 813.

19. Pennsylvania v. Mimms, 434 U.S. 106 (1977) (police can order a driver out of a car when there has been a traffic stop); Maryland v. Wilson, 519 U.S. 408 (1997) (police can order passengers out of a car).

20. New York v. Belton, 453 U.S. 454 (1981). Subsequently, the Court said that this ability to search the car does not apply to situations where the car was already pulled over before the officer approached it and where the driver and passenger were not near the vehicle. Arizona v. Gant, 556 U.S. 332 (2009).

21. 532 U.S. 318 (2001).

22. Virginia v. Moore, 553 U.S. 164 (2008).

23. South Dakota v. Opperman, 428 U.S. 364 (1976).

24. The Court said there might be a claim for denial of equal protection, but establishing an equal protection violation is enormously difficult, and even if it is established, it is not a basis for excluding the evidence gained as a result of the stop.

25. 543 U.S. 146 (2004).

26. District of Columbia v. Wesby, 138 S.Ct. 577, 594 (2018).

27. 572 U.S. 293 (2014).

28. See, e.g., Florida v. J.L., 529 U.S. 266 (2000).

29. 572 U.S. at 404.

30. *Id*. at 405 (Scalia, J., dissenting).

31. United States v. Arvizu, 534 U.S. 266 (2002).

32. *Id*. at 270.

33. *Id*. at 270.

34. *Id*. at 277.

35. For an excellent discussion of the history of police and cars, *see* Sarah Seo, Policing the Open Road: How Cars Transformed American Freedom (2019).

36. Illinois v. Wardlow, 528 U.S. 119 (2000).

37. *Id*. at 122.

38. *Id*. at 121.

39. *Id*. at 124.

40. *Id*.

41. The City of New York Commission to Investigate Allegations of Police Corruption and the Anti-Corruption Procedures of the Police Department, Commission Report 38 (1994) (Hon. Milton Mollen, Chair).

42. *Id*.

43. *See* Graham v. Connor, 490 U.S. 386 (1989); Tennessee v. Garner, 471 U.S. 1 (1985).

44. Graham v. Connor, 490 U.S. at 388.

45. Osagie Obasogie and Zachary Newman, *The Futile Fourth Amendment: Understanding Police Excessive Force Doctrine Through an Empirical Assessment of* Graham v. Connor, 112 Nw. U. L. Rev. 1465 (2018).

Chapter 16: YOU DON'T REALLY HAVE THE RIGHT TO REMAIN SILENT

1. 530 U.S. 428, 443 (2000).
2. Omnibus Crime Control and Safe Streets Act of 1968, Pub. L. No. 90-351, §701(a), 82 Stat. 197.
3. Justice Scalia observed: "In fact, with limited exceptions the provision has been studiously avoided by every Administration, not only in this Court, but in the lower courts, since its enactment more than 25 years ago." Davis v. United States, 512 U.S. 452, 463-464 (1994) (Scalia, J., concurring).
4. United States v. Dickerson, 166 F.3d 667, 673-677 (4th Cir. 1999) (Michael J., dissenting) (quoting appellant's opening brief at 34).
5. 530 U.S. at 437.
6. *Id.* at 465 (Scalia, J., dissenting).
7. Stephen J. Schulhofer, *Reconsidering* Miranda, 54 U. Chi. L. Rev. 435 (1987) (arguing that *Miranda* rules pose no serious problems that would make law enforcement more difficult).
8. Missouri v. Seibert, 542 U.S. 600, 608-609 (2004).
9. Berkemer v. McCarty, 468 U.S. 420, 433 n.20 (1984) ("cases in which a defendant can make a colorable argument that a self-incriminating statement was 'compelled' despite the fact that law enforcement authorities adhered to the dictates of *Miranda* are rare").
10. 560 U.S. 370 (2010).
11. Davis v. United States, 512 U.S. 452 (1994)
12. 560 U.S. at 384.
13. 384 U.S. at 475.
14. *Id.* at 476.
15. Withrow v. Williams, 507 U.S. 680, 692 (1993).
16. 542 U.S. 630 (2004)

Chapter 17: IGNORING THE PROBLEM OF FALSE EYEWITNESS IDENTIFICATIONS

1. Perry v. New Hampshire, 565 U.S. 228, 257 (2012) (Sotomayor, J., dissenting).
2. *Id.* at 263-264.
3. 565 U.S. 228 (2012).
4. *Id.* at 245.
5. *See., e.g.,* Neil v. Biggers, 409 U.S. 188 (1972).
6. 565 U.S. at 257 (Sotomayor, J., dissenting) (citations omitted).

Chapter 18: THE VANISHING REMEDIES FOR POLICE
MISCONDUCT

1. 547 U.S. 586 (2006).
2. Wilson v. Arkansas, 514 U.S. 927 (1995).
3. 547 U.S. at 591.
4. Bivens v. Six Unknown Federal Narcotics Agents, 403 U.S. 388, 411 (1971)
    (Burger, C.J., dissenting).
5. 547 U.S. at 603 (Kennedy, J., concurring).
6. 555 U.S. 135 (2009).
7. 367 U.S. 643 (1961). *Mapp* is discussed in detail in Chapter 6.
8. 555 U.S. at 140.
9. Arizona v. Evans, 514 U.S. 1 (1995).
10. 555 U.S. at 144.
11. *Id*. at 153 (Ginsburg, J., dissenting).
12. *Id*. at 152.
13. Hudson v. Michigan, 547 U.S. at 598.
14. For an excellent description of the reform of the LAPD, *see* Connie Rice,
    Power Concedes Nothing (2012).
15. Monell v. Department of Social Services, 436 U.S. 658 (1978).
16. Bd. of the Cnty. Comm'rs v. Brown, 520 U.S. 397 (1997)
17. *Id*. at 400–401
18. *Id*. at 412 (emphasis in original).
19. City of Canton v. Harris, 489 U.S. 378 (1989).
20. Connick v. Thompson, 563 U.S. 51 (2011).
21. *Id*. at 56 n.1.
22. Earl Truvia, Greg Bright, Dan Bright, State v. Bright, 875 So.2d 37 (La.
    2004); Shareef Cousin, State v. Cousin, 710 So.2d 1065 (La. 1998); Roland
    Gibson, Gibson v. State, Case No. 203-904, Orleans Parish Crim. Dist.
    Ct.; Isaac Knapper, State v. Knapper, 579 So.2d 956 (La. 1991), Curtis Lee
    Kyles, Kyles v. Whitley, 514 U.S. 419, 441 (1995); Dwight Labran, Labran
    v. State, Case No. 388-287, Orleans Parish Crim. Dist. Ct.; John Thomp-
    son, State v. Thompson, 825 So.2d 552 (La. App. 4 Cir. 2002); Hayes Wil-
    liams, Williams v. State, Case No. 199-523, Orleans Parish Crim. Dist.
    Ct.; Calvin Williams, In re Calvin Williams, 984 So.2d 789 (La. App. 1
    Cir. 2008); and Juan Smith, Smith v. Cain, 565 U.S. 73 (2012).
23. 373 U.S. 83 (1963).
24. 563 U.S. at 80 (Ginsburg J. dissenting).
25. *Id*. at 79.
26. Truvia v. Connick, 577 F. App'x 317 (5th Cir. 2014)
27. See cases *supra* note 22.
28. Bivens v. Six Unknown Federal Narcotics Agents, 403 U.S. 388 (1971).
29. 140 S.Ct. 735 (2020).

30. *Id*. at 750 (Thomas, J., concurring).
31. *Id*. at 757 (Ginsburg, J., dissenting).
32. Hui v. Castenada, 559 U.S. 799 (2010).
33. 424 U.S. 409 (1976).
34. 555 U.S. 335 (2009).
35. Goldstein v. City of Long Beach, 715 F.3d 750, 751 (9th Cir. 2013).
36. 373 U.S. 83 (1963). *See also* Giglio v. United States, 405 U.S. 150 (1972) (impeachment evidence must be disclosed by prosecutors to defendants).
37. 460 U.S. 325 (1983).
38. *Rehberg v. Paulk*, 566 U.S. 356 (2012).
39. 457 U.S. 800 (1982).
40. 563 U.S. 731 (2011).
41. *See* Ziglar v. Abassi, 137 S.Ct. 1843 (2017) (suit against Ashcroft for abusive treatment of those of Middle Eastern descent).
42. Al-Kidd v. Ashcroft, 580 F.3d 949, 973 (9th Cir. 2009).
43. 563 U.S. at 741.
44. *Id*. (emphasis added).
45. *Id*. at 743.
46. Safford Unified School Dist. No. 1 v. Redding, 557 U.S. 364 (2009).
47. 543 U.S. 194 (2004).
48. *Id*. at 201.
49. Lane v. Franks, 573 U.S. 228, 242-243 (2014).
50. 572 U.S. 744 (2014).
51. *Id*. at 777.
52. 572 U.S. 744 (2014).
53. Graham v. Connor, 490 U.S. 386 (1989); Tennessee v. Garner, 471 U.S. 1 (1985).
54. 575 U.S. 600 (2015).
55. 138 S.Ct. 1148 (2018).
56. *Id*. at 1155 (Sotomayor, J., dissenting).
57. Hope v. Pelzer, 536 U.S. 730 (2002) and Groh v. Ramirez, 540 U.S. 551 (2004).
58. William Baude, *Is Qualified Immunity Unlawful?* 106 Cal. L. Rev. 45, 82 (2018).
59. Zadeh v. Robinson, 902 F.3d 483 (5th Cir. 2018) (Willett, J., concurring).
60. Andrew Chung et al., *For Cops Who Kill, Special Supreme Court Protection*, Reuters, May 8, 2020.
61. Anderson v. City of Minneapolis, 934 F.3d 836 (8th Cir. 2018).

Chapter 19: THE PATH TO MEANINGFUL POLICE REFORM

1. Derrick Bryson Taylor, *George Floyd Protests: A Timeline*, New York Times, July 10, 2020.
2. 461 U.S. 95 (1983).

3. Arkansas v. Wilson, 514 U.S. 927 (1995) (allowing police to enter without knocking and announcing with a warrant to do so).

4. Matthew Ormseth, Richard Winton, and Jessica Perez, *Protesters, Law Enforcement Clash in Downtown L.A. During Protest over George Floyd's Death*, Los Angeles Times, May 27, 2020.

5. Dori Olmos, *St. Louis Protesters Shut Down Interstate Demanding Justice in George Floyd's Death*, KSDK, May 30, 2020, https://www.ksdk.com/article/news/local/st-louis-protests-interstate-closed-george-floyd/63-c58336a6-f87d-4cde-8909-a3fb959d2dfd.

6. Maggie Haberman and Alexander Burns, *Trump's Looting and "Shooting" Remarks Escalate Crisis in Minneapolis,* New York Times, May 29, 2020.

7. Barbara Sprunt, *The History Behind "When the Looting Starts, The Shooting Starts,"* NPR, May 29, 2020, https://www.npr.org/2020/05/29/864818368/the-history-behind-when-the-looting-starts-the-shooting-starts.

8. Haberman and Burns, *supra* note 6.

9. Richard Fausset and Michael Levenson, *Atlanta Protesters Clash with Police as Mayor Warns "You Are Disgracing Our City,"* New York Times, May 29, 2020.

10. Edgar Sandoval, *Protests Flare in Brooklyn Over Floyd Death as De Blasio Appeals for Calm,* New York Times, May 30, 2020.

11. Alex Wigglesworth, *Federal Officer Killed by Gunfire Outside U.S. Courthouse in Oakland,* Los Angeles Times, May 30, 2020.

12. Harmeet Kaur, *About 93% of Racial Justice Protests in the US Have Been Peaceful, a New Report Says,* CNN, September 4, 2020, https://www.cnn.com/2020/09/04/us/blm-protests-peaceful-report-trnd/index.html.

13. Peter Baker and Maggie Haberman, *As Protests and Violence Spill Over, Trump Shrinks Back*, New York Times, May 31, 2020.

14. Katie Rogers, Jonathan Martin, and Maggie Haberman, *As Trump Calls Protesters "Terrorists," Tear Gas Clears a Path for His Walk to a Church*, New York Times, June 1, 2020.

15. Zach Montague, *Holding It Aloft, He Incited a Backlash. What Does the Bible Mean to Trump*, New York Times, June 2, 2020.

16. *Here's What Happened on the 8th Night of George Floyd Protests*, New York Times, July 10, 2020.

17. Charles M. Blow, *In the Wake of Protests,* New York Times, August 10, 2020.

18. The study was conducted by the U.S. Crisis Project, a joint effort of the Armed Conflict Location and Event Data Project (ACLED) and the Bridging Divides Initiative (BDI) at Princeton University. *See* Kaur, *supra* note 11.

19. Christina Morales, *What We Know About the Shooting of Jacob Blake*, New York Times, November 7, 2020.

20. Kurt Streeter, *With Walkouts, a New High Bar for Protests in Sports Is Set*, New York Times, August 27, 2020.

21. Jorge Castillo, *Dodgers, Giants Decide Not to Play to Protest the Shooting of Jacob Blake*, Los Angeles Times, August 26, 2020.

22. *The New York Times* published its 1619 Project, which seeks to recast American history from this date when the first slaves arrived.

23. 140 S.Ct. 1183 (2020).

24. In Utah v. Strieff, 136 S.Ct. 2056 (2016) (discussed in Chapter 15), Justice Sotomayor wrote an eloquent dissent focusing on the problems of racism in policing. Although Justices Ginsburg and Kagan also dissented, they joined the rest of Justice Sotomayor's opinion, but not the section lamenting the role of race in policing in the United States.

25. *See, e.g.,* Utah v. Strieff, 136 S.Ct. 2056 (2016), and Navarette v. California, 573 U.S. 293 (2014), both discussed in Chapter 15. *See also* Maryland v. King, 565 U.S. 439 (2013).

26. For example, Barry Friedman has powerfully defended a shift to what he calls "democratic policing." *See* Barry Friedman, Unwarranted: Policing Without Permission (2017).

27. Ruairi Arrieta-Kenna, *The Deep Roots—and New Offshoots—of "Abolish the Police,"* Politico, June 12, 2020.

28. Dionne Searcey and John Eligon, *Minneapolis Will Dismantle Its Police Force, Council Members Pledge*, New York Times, Jun. 7, 2020.

29. *See* Amna Akbar, *An Abolitionist Horizon for (Police) Reform,* 108 Calif. L. Rev. (2020).

30. *See, e.g.,* Paul Butler, Chokehold: Policing Black Men (2017); Akbar, *supra* note 31.

31. W.E.B. Du Bois, Black Reconstruction in America: An Essay Toward a History of the Part Which Black Folk Played in the Attempt to Reconstruct Democracy in America, 1860–1880 (1935).

32. Angela Y. Davis, Are Prisons Obsolete? (2003); and Rachel Kushner, *Is Prison Necessary? Ruth Wilson Gilmore Might Change Your Mind*, New York Times, April 17, 2019.

33. Derecka Purnell, *How I Became a Police Abolitionist*, Atlantic, July 6, 2020.

34. Dionne Searcey, *What Would Efforts to Defund or Disband Police Departments Really Mean?*, New York Times, June 8, 2020.

35. Police Violence Map, Mapping Police Violence, https://mappingpolice violence.org.

36. John Gramlich, *Most Violent and Property Crimes in the U.S. Go Unsolved,* Pew Research Center, March 1, 2017.

37. FBI, 2018 Crime in the United States, https://ucr.fbi.gov/crime-in-the-u.s /2018/crime-in-the-u.s.-2018/topic-pages/clearances.

38. Wesley Lowery, Kimbriell Kelly, and Steven Rich, *An Unequal Justice*, Washington Post, July 25, 2018.

39. RAINN, The Criminal Justice System: Statistics, https://www.rainn.org/statistics/criminal-justice-system.

40. Jeff Asher and Ben Horwitz, *How Do the Police Actually Spend Their Time?*, New York Times, June 19, 2020.

41. *See* Michelle Alexander, The New Jim Crow (2010).

42. Jerry Brown and Jim Newton, Man of Tomorrow 353 (2020).

43. Lockyer v. Andrade, 538 U.S. 63 (2003). In 2012 California voters amended the "three strikes" law to require that the third strike be a serious or violent felony. This amendment was made retroactive to those already convicted. Andrade was released pursuant to this change in the law.

44. *See* Sarah Seo, Policing the Open Road: How Cars Transformed American Freedom (2019).

45. Steven D. Levitt, *Understanding Why Crime Fell in the 1990s: Four Factors that Explain the Decline and Six that Do Not,* 18 J. Econ. Perspect. 163 (2004).

46. Daniel S. Nagin, Robert M. Solow, and Cynthia Lum, *Deterrence, Criminal Opportunities, and Police,* 53 Criminology 74 (2015); Daniel S. Nagin, *Deterrence in the Twenty-First Century,* 42 Crime Justice 199 (2013).

47. Jonathan Klick, John MacDonald, and Ben Grunwald, *The Effect of Private Police on Crime: Evidence from a Geographic Regression Discontinuity Design,* 179 J. Royal Stat. Soc. A 831 (2015).

48. Jack Lessenberry, *Privatizing the Police Would Be a Dangerous Policy*, Michigan Radio, October 5, 2017.

49. Dionne Searcey, *What Would Efforts to Defund or Disband Police Departments Really Mean?*, New York Times, June 8, 2020.

50. *Id.*

51. *See* Jill Leovy, Ghettoside: A True Story of Murder in American (2015).

52. William J. Brennan, Jr., *State Constitutions and the Protection of Individual Rights*, 90 Harv. L. Rev. 489 (1977). For an excellent recent advocacy of the development of state constitutional law, *see* Jeffrey Sutton, 51 Imperfect Solutions: States and the Making of American Constitutional Law 82 (2018).

53. *Id.* at 491.

54. 412 U.S. 218 (1973).

55. 68 N.J. 349, 353-354 346 A.2d 66, 68 (1975).

56. *Compare* People v. Jackson, 391 Mich. 323, 217 N.W.2d 22 (1974), *with* United States v. Ash, 413 U.S. 300 (1973).

57. Hudgens v. NLRB, 424 U.S. 507 (1976).

58. Pruneyard Shopping Center v. Robins, 447 U.S. 74 (1980).

59. Massachusetts was the first state to do this in Goodridge v. Dept. of Public Health, 798 N.E.2d 941 (Mass. 2003). The Supreme Court did so in Obergefell v. Hodges, 576 U.S. 644 (2015).

60. Michigan v. Long, 463 U.S. 1032 (1983).

61. California v. Greenwood, 486 U.S. 35 (1988).

62. *See, e.g.,* State v. Tanaka, 701 P.2d 1274 (Haw. 1985); State v. Goss, 834 A.2d 316 (N.H. 2003); State v. Boland, 800 P.2d 1112 (Wa. 1990).

63. 499 U.S. 621 (1991).

64. Sutton, *supra* note 51, at 82.

65. 517 U.S. 806 (1996).

66. *See, e.g.,* State v. Sullivan, 74 S.W.3d 315 (Ark. 2002); State v. Ladson, 979 P.2d 833 (Wash. 1999).

67. United States v. Patane, 542 U.S. 630 (2004).

68. *See, e.g.,* State v. Farris, 849 N.E.2d 985 (Ohio 2006); State v. Knapp, 700 N.W.2d 899 (Wis. 2005); Commonwealth v. Martin, 827 N.E.2d 198 (Mass. 2005).

69. 406 U.S. 682 (1972).

70. See, e.g., State v. Boyd, 294 A.2d 459 (Me. 1972); People v. Hawkins, 55 N.Y.2d 474, 450 N.Y.S.2d 159, 435 N.E.2d 376 (1982); People v. Delahunt, 121 R.I. 565, 401 A.2d 1261 (1979); State v. Taylor, 60 Wis.2d 506, 210 N.W.2d 873 (1973).

71. *See, e.g.,* Manson v. Brathwaite, 432 U.S. 98 (1977); Neil v. Biggers, 409 U.S. 188 (1972).

72. *See* Commonwealth v. Johnson, 650 N.E.2d 1257 (Mass. 1995); People v. Adams, 423 N.E.2d 379 (N.Y. 1981).

73. State v. Dubose, 2005 WI 126, ¶ 2, 285 Wis. 2d 143, 699 N.W.2d 582.

74. State v. Henderson, 27 A.3d 872, 885-912 (N.J. 2011); State v. Lawson, 291 P.3d 673, 690 (Or. 2012)

75. Mark Hosenball, *U.S. Homeland Security Confirms Three Units Sent Paramilitary Officers to Portland*, Reuters, July 21, 2020.

76. Hernandez v. Robles, 855 N.E.2d 1, 5 (N.Y. 2006).

77. Williams-Yulee v. Florida Bar, 575 U.S. 433, 437 (2015).

78. Rachel Paine Caufield, *Reconciling the Judicial Ideal and the Democratic Impulse in Judicial Retention Elections*, 74 Mo. L. Rev. 573, 587 (2009) (describing defeat of incumbent justices).

79. Neal Devins, *How State Supreme Courts Take Consequences Into Account: Towards a State-Centered Understanding of State Constitutionalism*, 62 Stan. L. Rev. 1629, 1675-1679 (2010).

80. Dan Morain, *Kaus to Retire from State Supreme Court: Deplores Strident Attacks on Justices in Anti-Bird Effort,* Los Angeles Times, July 2, 1985.

81. James A. Gardner, *The Failed Discourse of State Constitutionalism,* 90 Mich. L. Rev. 761, 781 (1992).

82. Article I, Section 17 of the Florida Constitution.

83. George Floyd Justice in Policing Act of 2020, H.R. 7120, 116th Cong. (2020).

84. Just and Unifying Solutions to Invigorate Communities Everywhere (JUSTICE) Act of 2020, S. 3985, 116th Cong. (2020). The JUSTICE Act was introduced by Senator Tim Scott (R-SC) on June 17, 2020.

85. *New Laws Address Virus, Police Reform*, Los Angeles Times, January 3, 2021.

86. Monell v. Department of Social Services, 436 U.S. 658 (1978).
87. Erwin Chemerinsky and Catherine Fisk, *Cities Must Be Legally Account-able for Police Reform,* San Francisco Chronicle, June 16, 2020.
88. 461 U.S. 95 (1983).
89. U.S. Dep't of Justice, Civil Rights Div., The Civil Rights Division's Pattern and Practice Police Reform Work: 1994–Present (2017), https://www.justice.gov/crt/file/922421/download.
90. Joanna Schwartz, *Who Can Police the Police?,* 11 U. Chi. Legal F. 437, 447 (2016).
91. Brianna Hathway, *A Necessary Expansion of State Power: A "Pattern or Practice" of Failed Accountability,* 41 NYU Review of Law & Social Change 61, 78 (2019).
92. *Id.*
93. Erwin Chemerinsky, *An Independent Analysis of the Los Angeles Police Department's Board of Inquiry Report on the Rampart Scandal,* 34 Loy. L.A. L. Rev. 545, 568 (2001).
94. Christopher Stone, Todd Foglesong, and Christine M. Cole, Policing Los Angeles Under a Consent Decree: The Dynamics of Change at the LAPD 2 (2009), http://assets.lapdonline.org/assets/pdf/Harvard-LAPD%20 Study.pdf.
95. *Id.* at 1.
96. Ian Milheiser, *Trump's Justice Department Has a Powerful Tool to Fight Police Abuse. It Refuses To Use It,* Vox, June 30, 2020.
97. *Id.*
98. *Hidden in Plain Sight: Racism, White Supremacy, and Far-Right Militancy in Law Enforcement,* Brennan Center for Justice, August 27, 2020, https://www.brennancenter.org/our-work/research-reports/hidden-plain -sight-racism-white-supremacy-and-far-right-militancy-law.

INDEX

ABOUT THE AUTHOR

ERWIN CHEMERINSKY IS DEAN AND THE JESSE H. CHOPER Distinguished Professor of Law at the University of California, Berkeley School of Law. Prior to assuming this position, from 2008 to 2017, he was the founding Dean and Distinguished Professor of Law, and Raymond Pryke Professor of First Amendment Law, at the University of California, Irvine School of Law, with a joint appointment in political science. Before that he was a professor of law at Duke University, the University of Southern California, and the DePaul College of Law.

He is the author of fourteen books, including leading casebooks and treatises about constitutional law, criminal procedure, and federal jurisdiction. He also is the author of more than 250 law review articles. He is a contributing writer for the opinion section of the *Los Angeles Times* and writes regular columns for the *Sacramento Bee*, the *ABA Journal*, and the *Daily Journal*. His op-eds appear frequently in newspapers across the country. As a practicing attorney, he frequently argues appellate cases, including in the U.S. Supreme Court.

In 2016 Dean Chemerinsky was named a fellow of the American Academy of Arts and Sciences. In 2017 *National Jurist* magazine named him the most influential person in legal education in the United States. In 2021, he was named president-elect of the Association of American Law Schools.